Collective Memory

After the Empire:
The Francophone World and
Postcolonial France

Series Editor
Valérie Orlando, University of Maryland

Advisory Board
Robert Bernasconi, Memphis University; Alec Hargreaves, Florida State University; Chima Korieh, Rowan University; Françoise Lionnet, UCLA; Obioma Nnaemeka, Indiana University; Kamal Salhi, University of Leeds; Tracy D. Sharpley-Whiting, Vanderbilt University; Nwachukwu Frank Ukadike, Tulane University

See www.lexingtonbooks.com/series for the series description and a complete list of published titles.

Recent and Forthcoming Titles

Collective Memory

France and the Algerian War (1954–1962)

Jo McCormack

LEXINGTON BOOKS

A division of
ROWMAN & LITTLEFIELD PUBLISHERS, INC.
Lanham • Boulder • New York • Toronto • Plymouth, UK

Published by Lexington Books
A division of Rowman & Littlefield Publishers, Inc.
A wholly owned subsidiary of The Rowman & Littlefield Publishing Group, Inc.
4501 Forbes Boulevard, Suite 200, Lanham, Maryland 20706
http://www.lexingtonbooks.com

Estover Road, Plymouth PL6 7PY, United Kingdom

British Library Cataloguing in Publication Information Available

Library of Congress Cataloging-in-Publication Data

The hardback edition of this book was previously published by the Library of Congress
as follows:

McCormack, Jo, 1973–
   Collective memory : France and the Algerian war, 1954–1962 / Jo McCormack.
      p. cm. — (After the empire : Francophone world and postcolonial France)
   Includes bibliographical references and index.
   ISBN-13: 978-0-7391-0921-2 (cloth : alk. paper)
   ISBN-10: 0-7391-0921-9 (cloth : alk. paper)
   1. Algeria—History—Revolution, 1954–1962—Influence. 2. Algeria—History—
Revolution, 1954–1962—Mass media and the revolution—Case studies. 3. France—
Social conditions—1945—Case studies. 4. Racism—France—Case studies. I. Title.
   DT295.M275 2007
965'.046—dc22   2007017488

ISBN: 978-0-7391-4562-3 (pbk. : alk. paper)
eISBN: 978-0-7391-5316-1

♾™ The paper used in this publication meets the minimum requirements of American
National Standard for Information Sciences—Permanence of Paper for Printed Library
Materials, ANSI/NISO Z39.48-1992.

Printed in the United States of America

Contents

Acknowledgments

I would like to thank my family, friends, and colleagues for all of their support over the years. I am indebted to my PhD director, supervisor, and panel members who helped to bring this project to fruition. Their regular comments have always been valuable. The University of Technology, Sydney enabled me to complete the book by providing a semester of sabbatical and funding in the form of an Early Career Research Grant, support that is gratefully acknowledged. The Institute for International Studies' regular symposia and workshops were an extremely helpful forum in which to present ideas developed in this book. The project would not have been possible without the help of all those—historians, teachers, and pupils—who agreed to an interview. I am extremely grateful for the time that they accorded me. Any remaining flaws are entirely my own and I am entirely responsible for this piece of work.

List of Abbreviations and Acronyms

ADATE	Association dauphinoise pour l'accueil des travailleurs étrangers (Dauphinois Association for Insertion of Foreign Workers)
AFAA	Association Française d'Action Artistique (French Association of Artistic Action)
APHG	Association de Professeurs d'Histoire et de Géographie (French Association of History and Geography Teachers)
ASMCF	Association for the Study of Modern and Contemporary France
CAPES	Certificat d'Aptitude Professionnel à l'Enseignement Secondaire (Postgraduate Certicate in Secondary Education Teaching)
CDI	Centre de Documentation et d'Information (School Documentary Centre)
CHRD	Centre d'Histoire de la Résistance et Déportation (Resistance and Deportation History Centre)
CNDP	Centre National de Documentation Pédagogique (National Centre for Pedagogical Documentation)
CNRS	Centre National de Recherche Scientifique (National Centre for Scientific Research)
DOM	Département d'Outre Mer (Overseas Department)
DOP	Détachement Opérationnel de Protection (Protective Operational Unit)
EHESS	Ecole de Hautes Etudes en Sciences Sociales (EHESS University)
ENA	Ecole Nationale d'Administration (ENA University)
FIDH	Fédération Internationale des Ligues des Droits de l'Homme (International Federation of the Rights of Man)
FLN	Front de Libération Nationale (National Liberation Front)
FN	Front National (National Front)
FNACA	Fédération Nationale des Anciens Combattants d'Algérie

	(FNACA Veterans' Association)
GAJE	Guerre d'Algérie Jeunesse et Enseignement (Algerian War, Youth, and Education)
GCSE	British General Certificate of Secondary Education
GTD	Groupe de Travail Disciplinaire (Disciplinary Working Group)
HSC	Australian High School Certificate
IEP	Institut d'Etudes Politiques (IEP University)
IHTP	Institut d'Histoire des Temps Présents (Institute for the Study of Contemporary History)
INSEE	Institut National de la Statistique et des Etudes Economiques (National Institute for Statistics and Economics)
MEDGA	Mémoire et Enseignement de la Guerre d'Algérie (Memory and Teaching of the Algerian War Conference)
MNA	Mouvement National Algérien (National Algerian Movement)
MRAP	Mouvement Républicain Pour l'Amitié Entre les Peuples (Republican Movement for Friendship between Peoples)
OAS	Organisation Armée Secrète (Secret Armed Organisation)
PACA	Provence-Alpes-Côte d'Azur (Provence and Riviera Region)
PCF	Parti Communiste Français (French Communist Party)
PGCE	Postgraduate Certificate in Education
RATP	Régie Autonome des Transports Parisiens (Parisian Subway Operator)
SHAT	Service Historique de l'Armée de Terre (Army Historical Service)
SNCF	Société National des Chemins de Fer (French Railway Operator)
TOM	Territoire d'Outre Mer (Overseas Territory)
UNC	Union Nationale des Combattants (UNC Veterans' Association)

Brief Chronology of
The Algerian War

1945

May 8   Nationalist demonstrations and insurrection in Sétif, Algeria. The police fire shots into the crowd. Algerian French massacre French Algerians (European Settlers). Colonial troops retaliate leading to thousands of deaths. Victory in Europe (VE) Day in Europe while de Gaulle is head of government.

1947

August   A reform creates two electoral colleges in Algeria.

1954

November 1   Beginning of the Algerian War. Series of attacks across Algeria organized by the Front de Libération Nationale (FLN) despite small number of people and weapons.

December   Messali Hadj creates the Mouvement National Algérien (MNA), which is a rival of the FLN, and replaces his Mouvement pour le Triomphe des Libertés Démocratiques (MTLD).

1955

May   Decision to recall people who had already done their military service (*rappelés*), who were sent to Algeria.

August 20-21   Uprising in Philippeville leads to savage repression.

1956

February 6   Guy Mollet, French Prime Minister at the head of the Republican Front, is bombarded with tomatoes in Algiers during an official visit.

March   "Pouvoirs spéciaux" (Special Powers) voted while Mollet head of government, which led to conscription and recall of reservists. Number of soldiers in Algeria to double to 400,000.

May 18   Nineteen French conscripts are killed and mutilated near Palestro.

September   FLN bombs coffee shops in Algiers frequented by young *pieds-noirs* (European Settlers).

October 22   Plane containing Ahmed Ben Bella, Mohammed Khider, Mo-
                 hammed Boudiaf, Hocine Aït Ahmed, and Mostefa Lacheraf
                 (leaders of the FLN) is forced to land in Algiers by the French
                 air force. The plane was flying from Rabat to Tunis so its pas-
                 sengers were hijacked.

1957
January-   Battle of Algiers during which General Massu, at the head of
September   the Tenth Division of Parachutists, fought against terrorist
                 attacks in the city. Widespread use of torture, which had been
                 used in Algeria since before the war and also took place in
                 France during the war.

May 29   FLN fighters massacre all the men in a village called Mélouza,
                 which was pro-MNA.

1958

February 8   Sakhiet-Sidi-Youssef, a village in Tunisia, is bombarded by
                 the French air force. Sixty-nine people killed, including many
                 children; over a hundred injured.

May 13   "Comité de salut public" (revolutionary committee) estab-
                 lished in Algiers. Army takes power. Call for the return of de
                 Gaulle from General Massu. Settlers also call for his return.

June 1   De Gaulle becomes Prime Minister.

June 4   De Gaulle speech "Je vous ai compris" (I have understood
                 you) in Algeria.

1959
September 16   De Gaulle in a speech declares Algerians' right to "autodéter-
                 mination" (self determination).

1960
January 24-31   "Semaine des barricades" (Week of Barricades) in Algiers.
                 Settlers rebel against de Gaulle.

September 5-   Trial in Paris of the "réseau Jeanson" (Jeanson network) who
October 1   were "porteurs de valise," that is, French people who resisted
                 the Algerian War by helping the FLN.

September 5   De Gaulle speaks of an "Algérie algérienne" (Algerian Algeria).

September 6   Publication of the "Manifeste des 121" (Manifesto signed by 121 people), which was a petition signed to state people's right to disobey and incite conscripts to desert.

1961
April 10   First attacks claimed by OAS, a group founded by defenders of French Algeria in the European community and the army. It used violence in this first period to oppose de Gaulle's Algerian policy.

April 21-22   "Putsch des généraux" (Putsch by Generals). Challe, Jouhaud, Zeller and Salan attempt to seize power in Algiers. Ultimately this is a failure.

October 17   Demonstration in Paris against curfew on "Français musulmans" (Muslim French). Severe repression by French police. Numerous deaths.

1962
February 8   Anti-OAS demonstration in Paris. Eight deaths at the subway station Charonne after violent charges by the police.

March 19   Accords d'Evian (Evian Peace Agreement) come into effect. Cease-fire.

March 26   Deaths at the Rue d'Isly in Algiers when a demonstration by *pieds-noirs* (European settlers) is fired upon by army. Over fifty people killed and more than one hundred injured.

March-
April   Numerous attacks by OAS. A second period of "politique de la terre brûlée" (scorched earth policy) in which this group destroyed what they had previously tried to defend. Massive exodus of *pieds-noirs*. Massacre of *harkis*.

July 1   Algerian Independence.

Introduction

The Algerian War: Between Memory and History

The Franco-Algerian War (1954-1962) was one of the hardest wars of decolonization ever fought. It pitted the mighty French State against Algerian nationalists in a battle over whether "l'Algérie française" (French Algeria) should continue or an independent Algerian nation should emerge. It lasted over seven years, brought down the French Fourth Republic and acted as a catalyst for the return to power of General de Gaulle in 1958, laying the foundations for the constitution that still defines the current political system in France. Algeria had actually been three French *départements*.[1] The French defeat in the war effectively signaled the end of the French Empire, a certain idea of "la France de Dunkerque à Tlemcen" (Greater France stretching from Dunkerque to Tlemcen; de Gaulle), after more than one hundred and thirty years of conquest, settlement, and colonial rule. Millions of French men were drafted to fight in Algeria, for up to twenty-seven months, alongside a professional army profoundly marked by the war and crushing defeat in Indo-China at Dien Bien Phu in 1954, in a "sale guerre" (dirty war) characterized by terrorism, massacres, and torture. Close to one million settlers fled from Algeria to France in dramatic conditions at the end of the war in an exodus, while some of those who remained were massacred and/or abducted. It is estimated that tens of thousands of *harkis* (Algerian soldiers who fought in the French army during the conflict) were massacred in 1962. While the war rendered Algeria independent, the cost to Algerians was huge—hundreds of thousands of deaths—and Algeria then endured decades of one-party rule and a very bloody civil war. Franco-Algerian relations are only just beginning to thaw, after decades of mutual suspicion. The Franco-Algerian War is similar in many ways to the American-led War in Iraq: urban warfare, terrorism, an insurgency with no clearly-identifiable enemy, in a "political" war where control of the populace is the key. This would explain why the Pentagon screened Gillo Pontecorvo's *La Bataille d'Algers* (The Battle of Algiers) in 2003.

Given that the war took place merely a few decades ago and that it involved so many people now living in France, the legacy of the conflict is still inescapably felt in contemporary France. However since it was such a painful and traumatic event, it is quite rare that the conflict is directly referred to or discussed dispassionately. The fortieth anniversary of the end of the war was commemorated throughout France in 2002 in a memorial landscape characterized by considerable tension and division. Memory battles have raged for the last few years after a long period of occlusion and repression of painful and divisive memories.[2] For decades the participants struggled to discuss the "war" (until 1999 the French government defended the myth that there had been no war, using euphemisms like "peacekeeping operations"), the French government amnestied the actors, and the war was a taboo subject. The divisive nature of the war itself, pitting various groups against one another in a "guerre civile larvée"[3] (latent civil war), as well as the unresolved nature of elements of the past and the stakes involved, explain why various groups are currently engaged in such fierce memory battles—including debates on when to commemorate, how to commemorate, the extent of the French army's use of torture, the treatment of *harkis*, recognition of massacres, and so on. There are millions of people now living in France who participated in the war: such as conscripts, settlers, professional soldiers, Algerians, *harkis*, and *porteurs de valise* (French who supported the Algerian nationalists). Indeed many commentators such as Benjamin Stora or Pierre Bourdieu point to a repetition of the Algerian War in contemporary France.[4]

The replaying of the conflict is particularly discernible in and highly relevant to debates surrounding immigration and ethnicity in France, undoubtedly one of the most important issues in contemporary French society, since many of France's immigrants have come from the ex-colonies. In 2004 Algerians were still the largest single nationality group amongst France's immigrant population.[5] Large numbers of Algerians came to France in the 1950s and 1960s to work and have subsequently settled. Jacques Chirac, President of France (1995-), himself a veteran of the Algerian War, fought his 1995 presidential campaign around the issue of a "fracture sociale" (social fracture), meaning an increasing problem of exclusion in society, that in reality operates largely along ethnic lines, and has in fact intensified and deepened over the last ten years. The riots that so dramatically engulfed many French towns and cities in late 2005 are tangible evidence, almost a decade later, of the persistence of the unresolved legacies of the colonial period. The *banlieues*—rundown suburbs on the outskirts of French cities—are home to mainly immigrants and their children or grandchildren. By their geographical location, sociological makeup and poor infrastructure they exist on the margins of French society as a very tangible example of the extent of (predominantly ethnic) exclusion in contemporary French society. As we will see throughout this book, the history of the Algerian War itself has not been integrated into French history. There has been insufficient "work of memory" in France on the Algerian War, a situation that contrasts starkly with the investment in working through memories of the Second World War that has gone hand in hand with Franco-German reconciliation and the drive toward European Union. Consequently, the resentment and the bitterness of defeat in the Algerian War continue to feed into racism in France and to a general ignorance of this period of French history that is inhibiting Algerian French being able to find a home in France. For far too long these issues have been swept under the carpet; there is a clear urgency for French society to address issues of ethnic exclusion and tension that have their origins in the colonial period more directly and systematically.

The legacy that is still palpable in contemporary France is inherently linked to collective memory—to the way the past is represented, managed, and understood by societies. Millions of people in contemporary France have memories of the Algerian War, but these memories have for the most part been repressed and occluded, leading to the perpetuation of the deep and numerous divisions that existed during the war in Algeria. Terminology is particularly important in this area, and as we will see throughout this book needs to be better employed and refined. The term collective memory itself is disputed.[6] Collective memory can be defined broadly as "the use and the instrumentalisation of the past."[7] Alternatively, for Henry Rousso "A nation's memory . . . is shaped by signals emanating from many sources,"[8] whereby vectors, carriers, or channels—that can, for example, be associative, official (commemorations), cultural, or scholarly—transmit or carry memories and historical representations between individuals, groups, and the Nation. Consequently individuals can "remember" events that they did not experience and relate to a wider "historical consciousness." "Collective memory" is a metaphor. We can begin to differentiate between these different levels of memory, with "collective memory" meaning (any) group memory—big (nation) or small (family). Konrad Jarausch adopts a similar position when discussing the ways that personal remembrances turn into public consciousness:

> as most incidents are forgotten, those that are retained are the result of repeated retelling, making individual recollection a social act. By being relived in communication rituals, such as family holidays, veterans' meetings or church socials, these personal experiences gradually blend into group recollections, coalescing into figures of remembrance for those who shared a similar fate. Such collective representations finally tend to interact with competing recollections in the public realm, vying to have their version accepted as binding for the national community in order to obtain material and political benefits. Interacting with scholarly research, intellectual critiques, or political guidance, these exchanges of individual accounts and group remembrances create a memory culture[9]

As David Thelen points out, the study of memory is resolutely interdisciplinary, with work being undertaken on the subject in anthropology, history, sociology, psychology, and other disciplines.[10] It is also an international phenomenon, as various countries struggle to deal with traumatic pasts—such as World Wars, civil wars, retreats from Empire, slavery, or colonialism amongst others. Re-

membering, representing and coming to terms with the Second World War and
the Holocaust have dominated much work on collective memory. Memory as a
subject of academic interest has shot to prominence in recent years, generating a
huge body of scholarly work. For some, history and memory are radically opposed. The approach adopted here is that history, while being a social science,
provides a historical memory that is one representation of the past amongst others. We will reflect more on the relationship between memory and history in the
following chapter.

French historians in the 1980s and 1990s have written numerous important
books on memory. This trend in itself reflects the trauma of twentieth century
French history, a very exceptional model of nation-building that draws considerably on historical memory, and historiographical changes. Rousso examined
representations of the Vichy period (1940-1944) since World War Two in France
in *The Vichy Syndrome*. Pierre Nora's magisterial three-volume *Les Lieux de
mémoire* (Realms of Memory) proposed a history of memory since the origins of
France, with particular focus on traces of memory in certain "sites." Benjamin
Stora in particular has studied French collective memory of the Algerian War,
firstly in his work *La Gangrène et l'oubli* (The Gangrene and the Forgetting)
published in the early 1990s. All of these works analyze the way history is represented in the present, the uses of selective aspects of the past in the present, and
the respective place of remembering and forgetting, individually or collectively,
with particular attention given to the role of memory and history in the construction of the Nation.

Such works draw on various theories or models of memory. The first of
these is a Halbwachsian model of collective memory. Maurice Halbwachs, a
French sociologist, is often credited with coining the term "collective memory"
and wrote two seminal works on the topic—*Les Cadres sociaux de la mémoire*
(The Social Frames of Memory) and *La Mémoire collective* (Collective Memory). He showed the importance to memory of the present, since memories are
reconstructed as a function of present needs. Memories are used in the present so
we can very usefully question what we remember, how, when, where, with
whom, and why. He also showed the social nature of memory, and the importance of groups and society to remembering. Sigmund Freud is often drawn upon
in memory studies due to his work on trauma, repression of memories, and the
subconscious. Historians working in a Freudian tradition include Rousso and
Stora—since they draw considerably on terms such as repression and mourning
and they argue that repression of memories is bad for French society.[11] Another
approach to memory consists of seeing collective memory as determined by
competition and pluralism. Jay Winter and Emmanuel Sivan's coedited book
War and Remembrance in the Twentieth Century outlines this understanding of
memory, with considerable focus on agency. Agency in collective memory can
consist of associative actions, writing, scholarship, and filmmaking, all of which
impacts upon the way the past is represented and remembered. In all instances,
memory is inherently linked to Identity—be it at an individual, group, or national level. The approach taken in this book will be to defend a *bricolage* of

theories. It is felt that drawing on as many theories as possible gives the richest understanding of collective memory.

Most commentators agree that the Algerian War was for a long time a taboo subject. It was an incredibly divisive war that polarized many into radically opposed groups—both drafted and professional veteran soldiers, settlers (*pieds noirs*), *harkis*, or French who opposed the war (*porteurs de valise*)—that now each have their own, often mutually hostile, memories. Significant divisions also exist within the groups so, for example, different veterans' associations have different stances on many issues, such as if, when, or how to commemorate the war. The actors repressed memories—memories were too traumatic and shameful to remember or express, and French society was unwilling to listen or engage in such conversations. The State facilitated forgetting by passing amnesties, keeping archives shut, and engaging in a policy of forgetting. Memories were therefore occluded. Periodically such repressed and occluded memories have reappeared suddenly and violently in the present, often around commemorations (twentieth, thirtieth) and in the form of "memory battles." An "opening" seemed to take place in the early 1990s, around the thirtieth anniversary of the end of the war, with the publication of important scholarship—particularly Jean-Pierre Rioux's edited volume *La Guerre d'Algérie et les Français* (The Algerian War and the French)—and the screening of films—such as Bertrand Tavernier and Patrick Rotman's *La Guerre sans nom* (The War Without a Name)—but this opening closed only for more progress to take place in the late 1990s, up to the fortieth anniversary of the end of the war. Such developments will be described in depth in the next chapter. We can note here that there are conflicting interpretations of these evolutions that leave numerous important questions unanswered. Where is France up to in coming to terms with its colonial history? Is the memory of the Algerian War an appeased memory? Has France turned the page on the Algerian episode? To some extent, these interpretative differences may be linked to a lack of theoretical understanding of collective memory. As we will see in our review of critical literature, many commentators tend to draw predominantly on one theoretical paradigm (e.g., Freud) or work in one discipline (e.g., history). In addition, a more long term or detached view can go along way to answering some of these questions.

This book aims to address some of these issues through an analysis of the way the Algerian War is remembered in contemporary France. Specifically, it examines transmission of memories in France through a detailed analysis of three key vectors—the education system, the family, and the media. These three vectors of memory are crucial to long term identity formation and, largely, public opinion. They allow us to consider individual memories, group memories, and the wider memory culture in France. They have not received a great deal of attention in previous work. All three of our chosen vectors are inherently social. The book adopts a resolutely interdisciplinary approach to the study of French collective memory of the Algerian War. Due to the age of participants in the two main recent periods of turbulent French history—Vichy and the Algerian War— transmission of memory is an important subject at present. Each vector will be the subject of a chapter of this book. For Rousso, author of the groundbreaking *Vichy Syndrome*, a vector (or carrier) is "any source that proposes a deliberate reconstruction of an event for a social purpose. The collective memory of an event is shaped by all representations of that event, whether conscious or unconscious, explicit or implicit."[12] Such vectors include films, literature, the media, and commemoration. They all transmit information on events and shape the way we conceive of the past. We aim to identify the extent that memories are transmitted and to account for such transmission. As Alfred Grosser points out "'collective memory' is less an actual memory than 'transmission via the family, school and the media,'" therefore we will focus on these three vectors of memory.[13] For Rousso, the educative vector is "the primary social means by which memory is transmitted from generation to generation."[14] The national school system continues to play an important role in the construction of French national identity, as will be shown in chapter two. The media are another way memories enter and are negotiated in the "public sphere." Given that Stora claims there are some six million people in France with "mémoires à vif" (still vivid memories) of the conflict, the family are also a potentially important source of information on the war, especially since the participants in the conflict are now predominantly of retirement age. It will be shown that there are inherent problems with each of these vectors of memory. Lack of transmission of memories contributes to the memory battles currently taking place. New models and new ways of "managing memories," defining national identity, and relating to history are needed.

The book studies the educative vector of memory in so far as it examines the place of the Algerian War in history classes. It focuses on the *terminale* year— the final year of high school—at the end of which pupils sit the *baccalauréat*, of crucial personal and communal significance in France. The annual examinations, in terms of their content and as a social event, are widely commented on in the media. Passing the *baccalauréat* allows pupils to go to university and crowns their time in secondary education. The examination itself is very symbolic, a central institution of the Republic, one that despite its practical disadvantages (e.g., cost and inefficiency) the French are not prepared yet to replace. Vincent Descombes, in his book *Le Même et l'autre* (The Same and the Other), describing the teaching of philosophy, refers to the *baccalauréat* as "cette incarnation de l'idéal égalitaire" (this incarnation of the egalitarian ideal).[15] The French education system can also be noted to be characterized by a highly centralized national organization, one that is very different from the British, Australian, or American systems.

This chapter includes analysis of all three links in what I call the "educational chain," that is, the whole continuum of policies and practices that link the highest offices of the State to the ordinary pupil in the classroom. It examines the "State link" through to the "end-users" in the educational process. Through interviews with two eminent French historians (Jean-Pierre Rioux and Serge Berstein) the point of view of the *inspection* (civil servants) and program designers or textbook authors is given. The chapter also examines written sources such as textbooks, examination questions, and the program. It shows that the Algerian War as such is present rather little in these areas. Crucially it also reflects on what the State is trying to achieve through the teaching of history. The interview with Rioux in particular draws out the way that the Algerian War is highly divisive so it is not studied in more detail. This chapter draws heavily on interviews conducted with eighteen teachers and twelve pupils in secondary schools around Lyon in France. In particular it shows that since the change in program in 1998 teachers now teach less in class. It is able to identify in depth what is taught and how the war is dealt with. We also learn how little pupils know about the Algerian War. I conclude by drawing on the work of scholars including Kristen Ross, Benedict Anderson, and Eric Hobsbawm. I show that the way the Algerian War is taught in France is an excellent example of a narrative that sees modernization and decolonization as separate, and where education can be seen to continue to be participating in very important ways to imagining the contemporary French nation.

In the following chapter, we analyze family transmission of memory. As Paul Thompson notes:

> Western oral historians have only recently begun to look at a process which needs much more attention, the process of historical transmission: of how we learn history, teach it, hand it down . . . We could do very much more worthwhile work of this kind, for not nearly enough is known about how history is handed down in Anglo-Saxon societies . . . Telling family history undoubtedly goes on, but we have scarcely studied how it happens.[16]

Information obtained in class is compared—where applicable—to information received from the family. By drawing on the interviews with pupils we can compare what is learnt in the classroom with what has been discovered through discussion in families concerned by the Algerian War. Fascinating differences emerge. By drawing on other varied sources—from film and literature to secondary research—the role of families in transmitting memories is analyzed. A detailed case study of the *harkis*—Algerian soldiers who fought for the French army and now live in France—is conducted since the "silence of the fathers" is particularly prevalent here. Previous work had been inconclusive on the role of transmission in families of Algerian origin, as will be shown in the critical literature reviews in the following chapter. My work shows the way in which family transmission of memories of the Algerian War is very incomplete and challenging for those concerned. I argue that in this domain it is not just the work of Freud on repression and occlusion of memories that is most useful and applicable to the study of collective memory, since we also need to consider the (Halbwachsian) social cohesion role of memory and pluralist theories of memories. I also demonstrate that we cannot argue that previously marginal memories are significantly challenging more dominant narratives of the Algerian War, in particular concerning ethnic minorities. Nonetheless, this process has begun, particularly in literature.

Through reference to an in-depth case study conducted in 2003 of articles from *Le Monde* a third chapter analyzes media transmission of memory, a subject that had previously received far too little attention. We focus on the media because discussion of the Algerian War in France (re)erupted into the public sphere through coverage of torture in 2000 with the publication in *Le Monde* of Louisette Ighilahriz's testimony that described how she had been tortured in 1957. Until this media event the subject of torture was very rarely evoked and its discussion was limited to periodic eruptions. This media "debate" lasted two years and has been described as a "very polemical and mediatized reactivation of the memory of the Algerian War."[17] Reference is also made to the data obtained in the interviews with pupils from the previous chapter. The study is diachronic and synchronic, qualitative and quantitative. I look at the number of articles on the Algerian War over the years and how their content has changed. I show how a pluralistic model of collective memory that highlights the role of "memory activists"—individuals and groups—largely explains how this "media event" came to be. Drawing on the work of Jürgen Habermas, I argue that the media do play an important role in constituting a "public sphere" for collective memory. However, the event needs to be seen more as a "return of repressed memories" rather than as a therapeutic working through of problematic memories in a Freudian perspective.

Memory changes over time, hence the interest of studying it. The following chapter will highlight a number of significant developments in French collective memory of the Algerian War. These include naming the war—that for decades was "the war without a name"—, discussing and recognizing the events of 17 October 1961, when dozens of Algerians were massacred by French police, a homage to *harkis*, the torture debate, and the creation of new sites of memory. In addition, a review of critical literature will be provided as well as a more in-depth discussion of memory theory. For Nora, France has entered an "era of commemoration." For Rousso, France is obsessed with Vichy and we would add that the Algerian War, for some, has become another "passé qui ne passe pas" (past that refuses to pass). For others, the increased interest in memory is a threat to very discipline of history. This book hopes to shed more light on these debates. Previous work in these three areas has been inconclusive or contradictory. These are important vectors of memory on a vital issue, with significant ramifications for many issues in contemporary French society—such as the place of ethnic minorities, politics, and national identity. French collective memory of the Algerian War also brings to light many issues that resonate well beyond France.

Notes

1. Metropolitan France is currently divided administratively into ninety-five departments. Morocco and Tunisia, the two other French colonial possessions in North Africa, were technically protectorates rather than departments, therefore not an integral part of France.

2. By "memory battle" we mean a polemical dispute over different representations of the past. One example would be the battles over the date on which to commemorate the end of the war. On this particular question see Frédéric Rouyard, "La bataille du 19 mars," in *La Guerre d'Algérie et les Français*, ed. Jean-Pierre Rioux (Paris: Fayard, 1990), 545-52. More recently, articles appearing in *L'Ancien d'Algérie*, the monthly bulletin of the Fédération nationale des anciens combattants d'Algérie (FNACA) veterans' association, show the current extent of hostility to plans to commemorate the end of the war annually on 5 December.

3. Bernard Droz, "Le cas très singulier de la guerre d'Algérie," *Vingtième Siècle. Revue d'histoire* no. 5, (January-March 1985): 81-90.

4. See Benjamin Stora, *Le Transfert d'une mémoire* (Paris: La Découverte, 1999); and Pierre Bourdieu, "Dévoiler et divulguer le refoulé," in *Algérie-France-Islam*, ed. Joseph Jurt (Paris: L'Harmattan, 1997), 21-27.

5. Catherine Borrel, "Près de cinq millions d'immigrés à la mi-2004," *Insee première* no. 1098, August 2006.

6. See for example Noa Gedi and Yigal Elam, "Collective Memory—What Is It?" *History and Memory* 8, no. 1 (1996): 30-50.

7. Didier Guyvar'h, "La Mémoire Collective, de la recherche à l'enseignement," *Cahiers d'Histoire Immédiate* no. 22 (Fall 2002): 101-19. Guyvac'h uses a definition defended by Marie-Claire Lavabre, "Usages du passé, usages de la mémoire," *Revue française de science politique* no. 3: 1994.

8. Henry Rousso, *The Vichy Syndrome. History and Memory in France since 1944* (Cambridge, MA and London, England: Harvard University Press, 1991): 219.

9. Konrad H. Jarausch, "Living with Broken Memories: Some Narratological Comments," in *The Divided Past: Reuniting Post-War Germany*, ed. Christoph Klessmann (Oxford: Berg, 2001), 172.

10. David Thelen, "Memory and American History," *The Journal of American History*, vol. 75, no. 4, (March 1989): 117.

11. See Stora's *Le Transfert d'une mémoire*.

12. Rousso, *The Vichy Syndrome*, 219.

13. Jane Freedman and Carrie Tarr, eds., *Women, Immigration and Identities in France* (Oxford and New York: Berg, 2000), 175.

14. Rousso, *The Vichy Syndrome*, 221.

15. Vincent Descombes, *Le Même et l'autre. 45 ans de philosophie française (1933-1978)* (Paris: Les Editions de Minuit, 1979), 16.

16. Paul Thompson, "Believe it or not: rethinking the historical interpretation of memory," www3.baylor.edu/Oral_History/Thompson.pdf.

17. Jack Lang, French Education Minister, in a speech given in August 2001, accessed at www.education.gouv.fr/discours/2001/algeriejl.htm.

Chapter One

Critical Literature and Recent Developments

Introduction

The Algerian War has been notoriously difficult to remember in France since 1962. The traumatic legacy of the Algerian conflict, in the shape of repressed and occluded memories, has persistently interfered in many aspects of contemporary French society, particularly with the rise of the National Front political party in the early 1980s and growing tensions surrounding ethnicity and exclusion in France through the 1980s and 1990s—consequently scholars have increasingly sought to examine French collective memory of the Algerian War. Works like Stora's *La Gangrène et l'oubli* (Gangrene and Forgetting; 1991) showed the occlusion of the war in French society and the "solitude des porteurs de mémoire" (solitude of carriers of memory). Tavernier and Rotman's documentary *La Guerre sans nom* (The War Without a Name; 1992) clearly demonstrated the extent that veterans had struggled to deal with the traumatic legacy of the conflict. In 1990 Robert Frank wrote of "les troubles de la mémoire" (the troubles of memory) in France, arguing that the war could not be commemorated, and in the same volume Rioux showed how an absence of social frames of memory (language, time, and space) was inhibiting memory. Elsewhere Rioux has argued that what is at stake in discussing the Algerian War in contemporary French society hinders remembering the conflict, and consequently there is no national memory, rather a set of mutually antagonistic group memories.[1] In this chapter we will review critical literature on French collective memory of the Algerian War, allowing us to assess the strengths and weaknesses of that work, to identify gaps that need researching, and to pinpoint questions that still need answering.

Yet this memory has evolved quite considerably in recent years—for Stora it "accelerated" in the period 1999-2003.[2] This has surprised a number of commentators who thought it would take longer before certain aspects of the Algerian War were discussed in France. Numerous developments have taken place, beginning with the State finally officially naming the "war without a name" by acknowledging it as a "war." "Developments" in collective memory since 1997 include new films, more television shows or coverage on the topic, media debate (particularly on the French army's use of torture during the war), burgeoning scholarship, commemorations, trials, construction of sites of memory, and official homages. In all of these developments there is a constant tension between discussion allowing healing (of the "troubled" or sick memory) or proving hugely divisive by reopening old wounds. In this chapter we will describe several of these developments. How are these developments to be interpreted and understood?

As French collective memory of the Algerian War has developed, so has historiography on the war. Indeed, new scholarship on the war is a development in itself—few commentators fail to mention the significance of the publication of PhDs in 2001 on torture during the Algerian War or the justice system in French Algeria.[3] Politicians—the then President Chirac and Prime Minister Jospin—faced with calls in 2001 for an Official Inquiry into the French army's use of torture during the Algerian War, have preferred to call on historians to write more history of the war. The (emerging and dynamic) relationship between memory and historiography is fascinating. Some question whether this period is memory or history and have argued that it is still impossible to write a scientific history of the Algerian War.[4] Many argue that it is history that needs to adjudicate in "memory battles."[5] Others argue that there has (already?) been a passage from memory to history.[6] A section of this chapter will chart historiography of the Algerian War and begin to examine these claims.

Ultimately, there are competing, varying analyses of all of these developments because our theoretical understanding of collective memory is quite weak. A section of this chapter summarizes theoretical reflections on memory. Three schools of thought will be retained as particularly useful to our case study. The first is a "social agency approach" to collective memory such as that eschewed by Jay Winter and Emmanuel Sivan in the book they coedited, *War and Remembrance in the Twentieth Century*. Such an approach highlights the behavior of groups and individuals involved in remembrance. It can be allied with what might be called a "pluralist" model, where various groups compete for a place in the collective memory. Another is a Halbwachsian model (after Maurice Halbwachs) of collective memory, that highlights the importance of groups (and belonging to groups) on individual memory and points to the significance of the present in recollections of the past. Thirdly, a Freudian model of collective memory emphasizes repression of memories and the therapeutic properties of "working through memories," including grieving, that may lead to closure and avoid a repetition of events and neurosis.

Lastly, this chapter will survey critical literature on the three vectors of memory that this book analyzes: education, the family, and the media. We will review work to date in each of these areas and outline some of the theoretical considerations in each area. A detailed review of this work will allow us to identify the gaps that exist in our knowledge on this topic and to shape our own approach to the study of these three vectors of memory. Let us now look at each of these points in more detail.

Critical Literature: French Collective Memory of the Algerian War

Scholars have increasingly sought to analyze French collective memory of the Algerian War throughout the 1980s and 1990s. There have been some key phases in that work, for example, the late 1980s and early 1990s. A constant central question—that has proved extremely difficult to answer—runs through all of this work: where is France up to in "working through" memories of this conflict? Has the work of grieving begun?[7] Has France turned the page on the Algerian episode yet?[8] Is the long period of amnesia finally over?[9] Historians have conducted the vast majority of this work. Due to the complexity of the topic, much of this work has taken the form of edited volumes. Most of these commentators draw predominantly on one model of collective memory (e.g., Halbwachsian or Freudian). The first major contribution to work on French collective memory of the Algerian War arose out of a conference organized by the CNRS/IHTP and held in 1988, whose proceedings were published as *La Guerre d'Algérie et les Français* (The Algerian War and the French).[10] Other scholars such as Stora have also contributed enormously to our understanding of this subject. Stora's work *La Gangrène et l'oubli* (Gangrene and Forgetting) was groundbreaking on this topic.[11] This work shows us that a first important step in understanding the memory of the Algerian War consists of differentiating between forgetting and occluding memories. Robert Frank has shown that for the Algerian War:

> Ce n'est pas de l'oubli, puisque oublier, c'est, sur un sujet donné, vider la mémoire de ses souvenirs; or la mémoire française est pleine de l'Algérie, mais de souvenirs qu'elle a longtemps enfouis, cachés, contenus. Il ne faut pas confondre oubli et occultation. Les souvenirs occultés peuvent resurgir violemment à la surface, lorsque l'actualité déchire un coin du voile. (It's not a question of forgetting, because to forget is, on a given subject, to empty one's memory of recollections; whereas French memory is full of Algeria, but of recollections the country has for a long time buried, hidden, and contained. We must not confuse forgetting and occlusion. Occluded memories can violently return to the surface, when current affairs tear a corner of the veil.)[12]

The Algerian War, at least at the end of the 1980s, was not therefore forgotten; its memory was repressed. Why are memories repressed and not truly forgotten? For Frank the present would seem to be crucial, hence his use of the image of a veil being torn or lifted by events in the present that bring back memories and render forgetting impossible. In other words, the present unveils elements of the past that one would rather forget. Rioux is also useful here. Writing in the same volume as Frank, he argued that because there were many sequels of the Algerian War to be found in contemporary French society, there could not be memory.[13] The present that was bringing back repressed memories (Frank), or hindering the creation of memory through the continuing existence of sequels and stakes of the war (Rioux), took the form of terrorism, events in Algeria, the independence of New Caledonia, the rise of the French National Front, and debates on immigration in general and on identity in particular. There would thus seem to be a two-way process. On the one hand the Algerian War historically speaking dictates parts of the present in terms of its sequels; on the other hand parts of the present affect the memory of the war by rendering it impossible to forget. In both cases, the Algerian conflict and its memory are of key importance in understanding contemporary French society. As an editorialist in *Le Monde* stated:

> Un tel passé ne peut que peser sur les rapports de l'ancienne puissance coloniale avec l'Algérie indépendante certes, mais aussi avec les Français d'origine algérienne qui, par choix ou par contrainte, ont décidé de vivre dans l'Hexagone. (Such a past can but weigh on the relationship between the ex-colonial power and the independent Algeria, but also on rapports with French people of Algerian origin who, whether by choice or not, have decided to live in mainland France.)[14]

Stora supports this view and argues that the Algerian War is being repeated in the present. When talking of the way that there was a contradiction between words and actions in colonial Algeria he states:

> (dans la France de nos jours) on proclame l'assimilation et l'intégration en droit, et dans les faits c'est le différentialisme qui est mis en œuvre, parce que les Arabes, les musulmans en général, sont trop différents pour pouvoir être intégrés. On assiste à un transfert de la problématique algérienne sur le territoire métropolitain. Ce qui existait sur le territoire algérien au temps des colonies se retrouve posé un siècle ou cinquante ans plus tard à l'intérieur de l'Hexagone, ici en France. ([in contemporary France] we proclaim assimilation and integration in law, whereas in reality it is differentialism that is put into practice, because Arabs, Muslims in general, are too different to be integrated. We are witnessing a transfer of the Algerian problematic onto mainland territory. What took place in Algeria during the colonial era is again relevant a century or fifty years later in the Hexagon, here in France.)[15]

He also agrees that "l'enjeu est énorme" (what is at stake is enormous) in the present concerning the memory of the Algerian War.[16] Memories of the conflict have therefore been repressed but are ultimately, for Frank, impossible to repress totally or definitively—there has been an "amnésie très partielle et non durable" (very partial and unsustainable amnesia).[17] The Algerian conflict's memory has been repressed whereas the war in Indo-China is truly forgotten as it almost never reappears in the present and is almost completely absent. Much of this work would therefore seem to be inspired by historians working within what might be called the Freudian tradition. The authors argue that repression is bad for French society as it leads to a repetition in the present of old divisions; it pre-

vents a serene memory from existing and perpetuates the injury caused by painful memories; and indeed the present will always bring back repressed memories
so it is futile to try and avoid facing such memories. The Algerian War is repressed because it was a very painful and divisive event in French history. It is
often referred to as "une plaie" (a wound) or "une cicatrice" (a scar) indicating
injury. A central question concerning the war in Algeria has been "le deuil"
(mourning) also indicating loss and death. Stora is perhaps the best person to
indicate why the nature of the war itself has shaped its memory. In *La Gangrène
et l'oubli* (The Gangrene and the Forgetting), published in 1991, he showed how
the occlusion since 1962 of what happened in Algeria stems directly from a denial to admit a state of war between 1954 and 1962. Rather than "guerre
d'Algérie" (Algerian War) one talked at the time of "opérations de maintien de
l'ordre" (peacekeeping operations) or "événements" (events in Algeria). Algeria
was claimed to be three French *départements* and therefore an internal question,
with "hors-la-loi" (outlaws) leading a "rébellion" (rebellion) rather than fighting
a war, all indicating why the Algerian War was often referred to as "une guerre
sans nom" (a war without a name). Rioux also insists on the importance of nomenclature by citing Halbwachs's three "social frames of memory," one of
which is language. The other two are space and time, also problematic, as Rioux
points out:

> Pas de mots pour le dire, pas d'images, ou si peu, pour le revivre, pas de dates
> pour le circonscrire et signaler son importance dans le cours des temps; pas de
> hauts lieux, pas de héros indiscutés, pas de batailles à localisation symbolique,
> pas d'ennemis clairement identifiés de bout en bout: on comprend que ce conflit
> n'ait pas été commémorable. (No words to relate it, no images, or so few, to re-
> live it, no dates to mark its beginning and end or signal its importance in the
> course of time, no important sites, no clear heroes, no symbolically place-
> specific battles, no clearly identifiable enemies from start to end, one can under-
> stand that this conflict has not been able to be commemorated.)[18]

Stora also insists on the elements of the Algerian War that people do not want to
remember or cannot bring themselves to remember because they are not proud of
what happened in Algeria. The history of the Algerian conflict is one of massacres, the use of internment camps, mass rounding up of populations, treason,
indifference, abandonment, executions, terrorism, torture, and so on. The Algerian conflict is quite rightly referred to as "une sale guerre" (a dirty war). A long
list of acts can be drawn up that people do not want to remember because they
are painful and shameful and therefore have immense difficulty accepting, talking about or facing up to. For Frank however the memory of the war in Algeria
was not a taboo subject at the end of the 1980s, although it had been so for a
long time.

     If the Algerian War was an incredibly divisive and violent conflict that has
made it difficult to remember, a parallel can be drawn between it and the French
memory of Vichy. This period of French history has also proved notoriously

difficulty for French society to face up to. Frank draws this parallel by showing how both wars contained defeat and "événements peu glorieux" (shameful events). However, for Frank there are positive aspects of the French experience of Vichy—essentially the Resistance and the Free French Forces—that can be remembered, whereas as concerns Algeria there is nothing positive to commemorate or remember. Furthermore, in the Algerian War there is a certain "replaying" of World War Two in so far as similar issues reoccur except that rather than it being the Germans who are "les bourreaux" (torturers/executioners) this time it is the French making the Algerian War far more difficult to remember than the Second World War. Crucial for an understanding of the French memory of the Algerian conflict is recognition that the war itself comprised "une guerre franco-algérienne" (Franco-Algerian War), "une guerre franco-française" (Franco-French War) and "une guerre algéro-algérienne" (Algero-Algerian War). This explains the immense division that the war created and that has shaped its memory. However, as Stora shows, difficult aspects to remember not only concern the war period but also the prewar colonial period. Ultimately perhaps the hardest points to remember are truths that shatter the dominant French discourse on Republican values. For Stora:

> Le problème algérien dans la société française est d'autant plus difficile à comprendre qu'il touche aux principes de la République (il s'agit de trois départements échappant à l'organisation républicaine de la société tout en étant partie prenante de cette organisation) et en même temps offre l'image d'une société du Sud sous domination . . . A partir de là, comment en France, l'Algérie peut-elle être intégrée dans un patrimoine de mémoire? (The Algerian problem in French society is all the more difficult to understand in that it concerns Republican principles [it is three departments that escape Republican organization of society while being part of that society] and at the same time embodies the image of a dominated Southern society . . . So, how can Algeria be integrated into a patrimony of memory in France?)[19]

The fact that the Algerian War has been occluded and was a "guerre franco-française" (Franco-French War) has led to the existence of group memories (plural) rather than a collective/national memory (singular). The various protagonists, forming groups, have different memories: conscripts, professional soldiers, OAS members ("Organisation Armée Secrète:" European activists who used violence to try to oppose de Gaulle and Algerian nationalists), the European settlers, metropolitan French people, *harkis*, immigrants, and so on. All commentators writing at the end of the 1980s or the beginning of the 1990s agreed on this point. For Stora this was what he called "la solitude des porteurs de mémoire" (the solitude of carriers of memory). Indeed, Stora produced a documentary at the beginning of the 1990s entitled *Les Années algériennes* (The Algerian Years) and, when explaining in an interview what he had hoped to accomplish by producing this documentary, Stora said he had wanted to "faire circuler la mémoire entre chacun des groupes qui ne se connaissent pas et qui ne veulent pas se parler" (circulate memories between each of the groups that do not know each other and do not want to speak to each other).[20]

However most of the above work was written at the end of the 1980s and the beginning of the 1990s, a key period in the memory of the Algerian War—eight to ten years after what Rioux called a "point d'orgue" (figuratively speaking a long interruption, therefore indicating a break with the previous twenty years) in the early 1980s, yet at the time of or at the beginning of what has been described by certain commentators as an "opening" in the memory of the war. The difficulty of writing at this moment can be seen in the work of the time. It was hard for authors to describe with certainty whether mourning had started, was taking place (and if so since when) or was finished (and if so what was beyond mourning—memory?). Rioux often understandably used the adverb "perhaps." For example Rioux stated "Si un travail de deuil est peut-être en cours" (if the work of grieving is perhaps underway) and "la mémoire a peut-être sa chance" (memory perhaps has a chance). However, later in the same essay he asks the question "Le travail de deuil aurait-il pris son cours?" (is the work of mourning finished?). Furthermore, he concluded his essay by stating "De petits signes s'accumulent, dont on pourra dire demain s'ils furent prémonitoires" (Small signs are appearing and in future we will know whether they were premonitory).[21]

The key question of where France had actually reached in the process of mourning the Algerian War was impossible to answer at that time. Authors also seemed to have great difficulty concluding their work. This reader at least detects differences between Charles-Robert Ageron's general conclusion to the book *La Guerre d'Algérie et les Français* (The Algerian War and the French) and the conclusions of each of the essays. I also find considerably different Ageron's fairly positive conclusion to that work (1991) and his relatively negative essay in *La Guerre d'Algérie dans l'enseignement en France et en Algérie* (The Algerian War in the Education Systems in France and Algeria; 1993)[22] where he highlighted the continuing difficulties (indeed impossibility) of writing a scientific history of the Algerian War. In Stora's work we can also detect hesitation in terms of what to conclude from his findings. For example, in *La Gangrène et l'oubli* (The Gangrene and the Forgetting; 1991) it is clear that Stora saw very few, if any, signs of lessening of tensions concerning the war in Algeria. However in an article in the French daily newspaper *Libération* published a year later he felt that a very long period of mourning was coming to an end due to a sudden rush of films on Indo-China and Algeria. He stated:

> Par le volume, le rythme et la fréquence rapprochée des productions d'images consacrées à ces deux pays, qui habitent fortement l'imaginaire français, le temps du travail de deuil, très long, semble aujourd'hui fini. (Judging by the volume, the rhythm and the close succession of the films about these two countries, that occupy a significant place in the French imaginary, the period of mourning, that lasted so long, seems now to have come to an end.)[23]

However, six years later Stora, writing in *La Guerre d'Algérie et les Algériens*

(The Algerian War and the Algerians; 1997), spoke of any easing of tensions being in fact a cruel illusion:

> La guerre d'Algérie, (comme la guerre du Viêt-nam), avec le temps qui passe, tente d'apparaître progressivement comme survivance anachronique et les séparations d'antan vécues comme autant d'anomalies. Le temps actuel, celui de l'immédiateté et de l'accélération, accentue cette impression/illusion. Cette vitesse semble tout effacer de la mémoire des vivants. Cruelle illusion. Les murs et les barrières, qui sont toujours là, peuvent vite se reformer. Les reproches reviennent. (The Algerian War, [like the Vietnam War], as time passes, tends little by little to appear like an anachronistic event and yesterday's divisions seem like anomalies. The current period—characterized by immediacy and the acceleration of history—accentuates this impression/illusion. This speed seems to erase everything from the memory of the living. This is a cruel illusion. The walls and the barriers, that are still there, can quickly reform. The reproaches resurface.)[24]

My interpretation of this statement is that at times commentators may think that the Algerian War is becoming less divisive and more consensual—notably by basing their conclusion on film production—yet old divisions that one may be led to believe belong to another era still in fact exist in the present. There is therefore an illusion in the present that the memory of the Algerian conflict is less problematic, fanned by the way that society now changes more rapidly than before.[25] This for Stora is only an illusion as there is still much division in the present concerning the Algerian War. At least for this reader this example would seem to confirm the difficulty that he and others have had drawing conclusions about the memory of the war in Algeria. This book is based on the belief that a longer-term view may help to draw conclusions concerning the memory of the Algerian War. Through writing in the year 2005, it aims to contribute to a greater understanding of this memory by adopting a longer-term view and trying to trace longer term trends in the memory of the Algerian conflict.

This approach is necessary because many things have changed since the beginning of the 1990s. Those recent developments are described in depth below. Collective memory does of course change over time. Rousso, in *The Vichy Syndrome*, commenting on the difference between memory and history, describes memory as being "a living phenomenon, something in perpetual evolution."[26] For Nora:

> Memory is life, borne by living societies founded in its name. It remains in permanent evolution, open to the dialectic of remembering and forgetting, unconscious of its successive deformations, vulnerable to manipulation and appropriation, susceptible to being long dormant and periodically revived.[27]

It would thus seem that the main work on the French memory of the Algerian War reveals that remembering this war has been highly problematic for French society. Extant critical literature gives us a solid analysis of individual and group memories of the Algerian War in France; however, that criticism was written for the most part in the late 1980s and early 1990s, hence the need to pay attention to developments in the 1990s. It is to be expected that the nature of the memory of the war is changing. It could also be argued that much, although not all, of this criticism would seem to be based on theoretical reflections based on Freudian concepts, that emphasize how what is repressed and occluded must be brought out into the open, thus perhaps neglecting other explanations that see collective memory as a necessary glue for society, something constructed by the interaction of different groups, or inherently (in France) linked to the Republic; and in all instances very much linked to the present and our identity. This book will try to reflect more on these issues through the detailed case study of transmission of memory in history classes, families and the media. These three vectors of memory, taken together, allow us to focus on individual memories, group memories, and the wider "memory culture" in France. They are three crucial ways that memories are transmitted in France.

Recent Developments: 1997-2005

Memory is constantly evolving. Vectors of memory also develop over time—new scholarship is published, films are made or "sites of memory" constructed, to take but a few examples. Recent years have undoubtedly seen a number of developments concerning memories of the Algerian War. For Stora there was an "acceleration" in this movement between 1999 and 2003. As we saw in the previous section, a key concern of work on this topic has been how to interpret such developments. This section provides a brief overview of a number of these developments. It argues that these developments need to be seen as stepping stones in a long and arduous, never complete, working through of memories of the Algerian War. Many of these developments are specifically related to one group (e.g., veterans). They often amount to increased "reconnaissance" (recognition), often by the French State, of that group's experiences. They all demonstrate how the "work of memory" is multifaceted, with many different actors, and how this process evolves with a constant tension between remembering and forgetting, reconciliation and division.

Nomenclature: Naming the *guerre sans nom*

One important change in French collective memory of the Algerian War consists of the emergence, since 1997, of a certain official recognition of a state of "war" in Algeria between 1954 and 1962. The Algerian War was for a very long time referred to as "the war without a name."[28] French authorities at the time referred to "pacification" or "opérations de maintien de l'ordre" (peace-keeping). On 28 February 1999 a plaque was laid on the Arc de Triomphe that reads "Aux morts pour la France lors de la guerre d'Algérie et des combats en

Tunisie et au Maroc, 1952-1962" (To those who died for France during the Algerian War and the Conflicts in Tunisia and Morocco, 1952-1962). On 16 October 1998 a similar plaque had been laid at Notre Dame de Lorette that reads "Ici repose un soldat inconnu mort pour la France lors de la guerre d'Algérie" (Here lies an unknown soldier who died for France during the Algerian War). In both cases the crucial point to note is the use of the term "guerre d'Algérie" (Algerian War) on key national public monuments.[29] Most important of all for this commentator is the aspect of recognition and acknowledgement of a certain state of events that is crucial for mourning and ultimately for, eventually, accepting the past.

Naming the war was hugely important for veterans. As a leading article noted in *La Voix du Combattant*, a publication of the French veterans' association the UNC (l'Union Nationale des Combattants: National Union of Veterans):

> Cette cérémonie marque la reconnaissance tangible et officielle de l'appellation de GUERRE à ce que précédemment, on qualifiait d'événements ou d'opérations . . . Ainsi l'intensité des combats est enfin reconnue, la fiction qu'une Nation ne peut se faire la guerre à elle-même parce que l'Algérie était départements français donc du ressort de la politique intérieure, tombe. (This ceremony represents the tangible and official recognition of the name WAR to what previously was referred to as "events" or "operations." Hence the intensity of the fighting is finally acknowledged, and the fiction that a Nation cannot fight a war against itself because Algeria was French departments and therefore was an interior matter, ends.)[30]

However, bitter divisions still remain. Veterans have felt aggrieved by debates about torture in the French media (2000-2001) described below, and that we will examine in detail in the fourth chapter of this book. One way that we can gauge this sentiment is in readers' letters. For veterans, relations have also deteriorated surrounding how/when to commemorate the war—it has still not yet been possible to agree upon a date to commemorate the end of the war, as the various veterans' associations continue to champion different dates.

Sites of Memory

Sites of memory have followed. Reading publications by veterans associations gives a good indication of the number of sites of memory that have emerged in recent years.[31] At the local level, thousands of "rues du 19 mars" (19 March Street) or steles have been created. At the departmental level, almost every department now has its memorial. At the national level, a national memorial was created quai Bondy. It takes the form of three pillars, each with a list of names of victims that continually scrolls. Elsewhere in Paris, in the nineteenth arrondissement, Jacques Chirac in 1996 inaugurated another memorial.[32] Rioux above noted the importance of "hauts lieux" (important sites) to memory and the work of Nora on what he calls "lieux de mémoire" (realms of memory) also indicates the significance of the creation of such sites.

17 October 1961: Remembering the Pogrom in Paris

Veterans are not the only group to have been officially "recognized."[33] There has also been greater recognition of the events of 17 October 1961, when significant numbers of Algerian French were killed by French police during a demonstration in Paris.[34] For nearly thirty years this was a taboo subject; the only significant time it was debated in public (at least in print) before 1991 perhaps being the publication of Didier Daeninckx's police novel *Meurtres pour Mémoire* (Murders for Memory) in 1984. The events of that night have certainly been one of the most occluded events of the Algerian War, with no recognition by the State of what happened leading Stora to describe this as a "massacre non-reconnu" (unacknowledged massacre). Elements that explain such a cover-up and subsequent suppression of truth include the way that perhaps over a hundred (estimations varying from certainly dozens to perhaps hundreds) "Français musulmans" (French Muslims) were killed that night by the French police, certainly including people being beaten to death or thrown in the Seine river. That the events took place in Paris, in 1961, while Maurice Papon was chief of police in the city and involved the French police have all also facilitated and encouraged a cover-up; as has the fact that General de Gaulle was in power at that time.

A key point in that process between 1984 and 1999 consisted of the early 1990s, as the French historian Guy Pervillé noted:

> Pour la première fois, à l'occasion de son trentième anniversaire, la commémoration de la manifestation et de la répression du 17 octobre 1961 à Paris a réussi à percer le mur d'ignorance et d'indifférence des medias. (For the first time, on its thirtieth anniversary, the commemoration of the demonstration of 17 October 1961 in Paris and its repression succeeded in breaking through the media's wall of ignorance and indifference.)[35]

Indeed, it was in 1991 that Jean-Luc Einaudi published his book *La Bataille de Paris* (The Battle of Paris) and that year also that Mehdi Lalaoui and Agnès Denis presented their film *Le Silence du fleuve* (The Silence of the River) at a film festival held at the "Institut du Monde arabe" (Institute of the Arab World) in October 1991. Both the book and the film examined what happened in Paris on 17 October 1961—a peaceful march at the time of negotiations between General de Gaulle and the FLN, organized by the French section of the FLN to protest against a curfew imposed on "Français musulmans" (French Muslims) in Paris, that was ferociously suppressed by the French authorities leading to it being described by certain historians as a "pogrom." The events were then publicized notably during Maurice Papon's trial in 1997 in Bordeaux for crimes against humanity committed during the Vichy regime (1940-1944) and his unsuccessful attempt to sue the journalist Jean-Luc Einaudi in 1999.[36] Papon was on trial for his activities as a functionary in the 1940s, however the trial also revealed to a wider public his activities as head of police in Paris in the 1960s. A journalist in *Le Point* noted that the Algerian War was like Pandora's box and said: "Trente-cinq ans après la signature des accords d'Evian, la guerre d'Algérie s'est invitée sans prévenir à la barre du procès Papon" (Thirty-five years after the Evian Peace Agreements were signed, the Algerian War has unexpectedly entered the Papon trial).[37]

Here too a site of memory has been created. It is a plaque on the Saint Michel bridge in central Paris. It was inaugurated by Bertrand Delanoë, Mayor of Paris, member of the French Socialist Party. It reads "A la mémoire des nombreux Algériens tués lors de la sanglante repression de la manifestation pacifique du 17 octobre 1961" (In memory of the numerous Algerians killed during the bloody repression of the pacific demonstration of 17 October 1961). It is discretely situated on the bridge. However, concerning the events of 17 October 1961, there is clearly still division, evident in reactions to the creation of that site of memory and also to the annual commemoration.

"Public Sphere" Discussion of Torture

A debate in the French media about the French army's use of torture during the Algerian War began in the French daily newspaper *Le Monde* with the publication of a series of testimony in June 2000 when the paper first published the experience on torture of an Algerian woman, Louisette Ighilahriz. She claimed to have been tortured in the presence of high ranking French officers. On 22 June the same paper published the conflicting viewpoints of General Jacques Massu and General Marcel Bigeard, in reaction to this testimony.[38] In Ighilahriz's testimony, she explicitly mentioned the role of Massu and Bigeard in her torture by saying they were present, insulted her, and gave orders. Massu commanded the Tenth division of French paratroopers during the crucial battle of Algiers. At that time Bigeard was a colonel. Broadly speaking Massu defended Ighilahriz's testimony whereas Bigeard denied all.

In November 2000 the paper again interviewed Massu and published the testimony of General Aussaresses, another key actor in the 1957 Battle of Algiers. *Le Monde* was not the only paper to publish extensively on this subject. *L'Humanité* in particular also published widely on the question. Nor was the written press the only medium used. Beyond the media, a petition was signed— the "Appel des douze intellectuels sur la reconnaissance et la condamnation de l'utilisation de la torture en Algérie" (Petition by twelve intellectuals for the recognition and condemnation of the use of torture in Algeria)—and Jacques Chirac and Lionel Jospin (then Prime Minister) were both called upon to comment and act. Lastly, in June 2001 Aussaresses published the book *Services Spéciaux: Algérie 1955-1957* (Special Services: Algeria 1955-1957) sparking more discussion. Whether or not this "debate" constitutes a working through of repressed memories or needs to be understood as simply an episode of memory battles perpetuating the division engendered by the Algerian War is a subject of disagreement amongst scholars, reflecting competing theories of collective memory—namely Freudian or pluralist.[39] We will examine this debate in more depth in a chapter of this book. Here we can note that the "media event" led to significant media coverage concerning the history of the Algerian War, and clearly proved highly divisive.

Harkis: Homages and Crimes Against Humanity

Similar tensions exist with the *harkis*—between an appeased memory, through greater recognition (in the form of a homage) and fierce memory battles, surrounding publications and attempts to try the French government for "crimes against humanity." The history of the *harkis* was for many years regarded as one of the most occluded aspects of the Algerian War.[40] They too now have received a site of memory, a plaque in the Invalides in Paris that reads: "La République française témoigne sa reconnaissance envers les rapatriés anciens membres des formations supplétives et assimilés ou victimes de la captivité en Algérie pour les sacrifices qu'ils ont consentis" (The French Republic acknowledges its gratitude to the repatriated members of additional and assimilated forces or victims of captivity in Algeria for the sacrifices that they made), that was inaugurated during the first "Journée d'hommage national aux harkis" (National Day of Homage to the *Harkis*) on 25 September 2001. Initially a one-off,[41] this is now an annual commemoration. Clearly both the commemoration and the site of memory are highly symbolic gestures from the French State toward the *harkis*. Conversely, *harkis* have recently attempted to try France for "crimes against humanity." According to the journalist Philippe Bernard they wanted to "saisir l'occasion de tenter de sortir de quarante ans d'oubli" (seize the chance to emerge from forty years of being forgotten). Similarly, polemical debates surrounded publications such as *Mon père ce harki* (My Father the *Harki*) or *Mohand le harki* (Mohand the *Harki*).

2003: El Djazair

In addition, 2003 was "El Djazair: The Year of Algeria in France"—a year long cultural event designed to foreground Algerian art and artists in France. In June 2000 the Algerian president, Abdelaziz Bouteflika, himself a veteran of the war (a member of the Algerian Liberation Movement) visited France: a historic visit since for nearly forty years the Heads of State of France and Algeria had not visited one another, reflecting the difficult international relations between the two countries prevalent since Algerian Independence in 1962. During the visit the two Heads of state agreed to initiate "El Djazaïr, Une année de l'Algérie en

France." France has quite a long history of "Cultural Years" (foreign cultural seasons), that are organized by the Ministry for Culture and the Ministry for Foreign Affairs. Very interestingly, Olivier Poivre d'Arvor, Director of AFAA (French Association of Artistic Action, an organization involved in the year) highlighted the specificity of this year by referring to it as "cette saison pas comme les autres" (this season unlike others) whereby he pointed to the importance of the Franco-Algerian relationship for both countries.[42]

As we can see, there continues to be a discernible tension, or dialectical relationship, between periodic or limited "openings"—in the form of symbolic gestures, commemorations, or publications—punctuating or punctuated by more polemical disputes that tend to lead to "closing down" concerning memory politics and management. In other words, the constant tension between remembering and forgetting continues. Having identified that the memory of the Algerian War is evolving over the years, as is to be expected, and is very much a concern in the present, let us now see how the writing of the history of the war has developed in France.

Historiography

There are several reasons for reflecting in this book on how the history of the Algerian War has been written. Above all, we need to reflect on the link between memory and history. Indeed, this book will argue that historiography is itself a memory of sorts. There is clearly a difference between memory and history as notably Nora and Rousso have examined.[43] Scholarship—beyond its direct link to providing the material to teach in schools—is in its own right a form of transmission of memory as Rousso mentions in his book *Le Syndrome de Vichy* (The Vichy Syndrome). He calls this "la mémoire savante" (scholarly memory). For Rousso:

> Les vecteurs savants reconstruisent et enseignent l'intelligiblité des faits, en proposant et en formalisant différentes lectures possibles: le livre d'histoire est, à ce titre, un vecteur du souvenir, tributaire des mêmes fluctuations que les autres, en tout cas fort peu détaché de son objet. Il influe par ailleurs sur les manuels et les programmes scolaires, le mode de transmission sociale par excellence. (Scholarly vectors reconstruct and teach understanding of facts, by proposing and formalizing different possible interpretations: the history book is, in this way, a vector of memory, susceptible to the same influences as the others, in any case extremely closely linked to its object. Furthermore they influence the textbooks and the programs, the foremost social mode of transmission.)[44]

Both Nora and Rousso claim memory is alive in society and continually evolving. There is a bond to the present whereby present needs and concerns determine what, when, and how we remember. Memory is affective, sometimes associated with the sacred or faith, and often associated with groups. It is varied and can be manipulated, occluded, or forgotten. Memory is said to be absolute. History however is a representation of the past that is critical and analytical, a scholarly reconstruction that tends to aim to be accepted beyond groups on a more universal level. History is said to be relative. *A priori*, nothing is taboo for an historian.

A very useful historiographical source on the Algerian War is *l'Annuaire de l'Afrique du Nord* (The Yearbook of North Africa).[45] Until 1993 the French historian Guy Pervillé each year listed in it the publications on the Algerian conflict, and provided his own commentaries. Since 1993 this work has been continued by other scholars. Reference will be made to this source. Beyond this source certain articles periodically make reference to the historiography of the war. Although these sources make it is possible to describe and comment on the historiography of the Algerian War, this section cannot study it exhaustively. We are more interested in the general trend over the last forty years.

The section is organized chronologically—tracing scholarly work on the war from 1962 to the present day—in order to bring out the key periods in the writing of the history of the war and to trace year by year the evolution of our knowledge about the conflict. We will see that historical knowledge about the Algerian War has increased tremendously over the last twenty years in particular. The writing of the history of the war only began in earnest in the early 1980s. It has been a challenging process. Although there is a general discernible trend from testimony and journalistic accounts of the war to scholarship, testimony continues to be published greatly. Lastly, the development of scholarship on the Algerian War itself introduces or accentuates another issue: how can this historical knowledge be more effectively transmitted?

1962 to the Late 1970s

1962-1968

In this initial period Pervillé qualifies most, or even all of the publications as "témoignages pour la politique" (testimony with a political motive) since the authors of such books are writing to score political points. For Pervillé:

> Jusqu'en 1968, la guerre d'Algérie n'est pas finie pour tout le monde, les derniers condamnés de l'OAS restent en prison ou en exil. D'ou l'écrasante prépondérance des plaidoyers pour l'Algérie française et des réquisitoires contre ses ennemis. Au contraire les gaullistes veulent tourner la page, et les partisans du FLN sont absorbés par les problèmes de l'Algérie indépendante. (Up to 1968 the Algerian War was not finished for everyone, the last condemned members of the OAS remain in prison or in exile. Hence the overwhelming weight of publications defending French Algeria and indicting its opponents. Gaullists, on the other hand, want to turn over a new leaf, and the supporters of the FLN are preoccupied with the problems facing the newly independent Algeria.)[46]

Such publications are therefore those written mainly by the losers in the war—

notably people who supported "l'Algérie française" (French Algeria) or the OAS
Such people often wrote in order to justify their actions and felt the need to write
out of perhaps frustration or anger. Of the three types of publication that are to
characterize the historiography of the Algerian War—"témoignages" (testimonies), "enquêtes journalistiques" (studies using journalistic methods) and "études
proprement scientifiques" (scholarship)—testimonies are the most numerous in
this first period. They are not books written by Algerian authors since it is not
until the end of the 1970s that such authors begin to write regularly on the Algerian War. Pervillé identifies three political leanings as characterizing the authors
who wrote on the Algerian War in the two decades after the conflict—those who
defended French colonial presence in Algeria, supporters of Algerian independence, and those in the middle who wrote to justify de Gaulle's politics. The first
group publish the most. Accounts and testimonies are to dominate the historiography of the Algerian conflict for many years. Bernard Droz and Evelyne Lever
in 1982 in their bibliography noted that:

> Les acteurs français du drame algérien se sont montrés d'une grande prolixité,
> mais rares sont ceux qui ont échappé au besoin de l'autojustification. (The
> French protagonists of the Algerian drama have been very vocal, but few have
> avoided feeling the need to justify their actions.)[47]

1968-1972

Pervillé argues that the publications in this period move away from "témoignages pour la politique" (testimony with a political motive) toward "témoignages pour l'histoire" (testimony for posterity) that are less polemical.
"Témoignages pour l'histoire" are essentially memoirs such as those published
by Vitalis Cros, General de Gaulle, Christian Fouchet, and Raoul Salan.[48] These
books are still often very partisan but are less controversial and more detached
than those published before 1968. They are accounts of the actors' experiences
during the war, and are essentially the material used when some of the later history of the Algerian War was written. This period is also important since it is at
this time that the first "récits journalistiques" (journalistic accounts) and also
"tentatives d'explication historique" (attempts at historical explanation) are published. Pervillé accounts for such developments by pointing to the changing political climate: May 1968, OAS amnesties, de Gaulle's retirement from the political scene, the publication of de Gaulle's *Mémoires d'espoir* (Memoirs of
Hope), and de Gaulle's death. In this way the Algerian War begins to cease to be
an item of current affairs and to enter into the realm of history.

Here we can see very clearly the way changes in society have influenced the
history that is written on the Algerian War. A parallel can be drawn with the way
factors in society dictate in different ways how the Algerian War is taught or
discussed, as will be seen throughout this book. The "récits journalistiques" include Yves Courrière's *La Guerre d'Algérie* (The Algerian War)—that
Droz/Lever described as: "Une somme qui tient plus du journalisme que de
l'histoire, mais qui repose sur une information orale de grande valeur"[49] (A book

that is more journalism than history, but that draws on very rich oral testimony). Nonetheless, testimonies continue to dominate French historiography of the Algerian War in this period. Despite the changing political climate, the memory of the Algerian War is far from consensual as can be seen from the events surrounding the publication of Massu's *La vraie bataille d'Alger* (The Real Battle of Algiers; 1971) and the screening of Pontecorvo's film *La bataille d'Alger* (The Battle of Algiers). This film was first shown in 1970 in France in Coutances and then regularly shown in Paris in 1971, in a cinema whose windows were broken several times during this period.

1972-Late 1970s

This third period in the historiography of the Algerian War, as described by Pervillé, is similar to the previous period in so far as the three genres continue to be published ("testimony for history," "studies using journalistic methods" and "scientific work") although the respective place of each becomes more balanced. But one change does occur in this period: Algerian authors also regularly publish work. For example, Commandant Azzedine's *On nous appelait fellaghas* (They Called Us *fellaghas*; 1976). This is especially true for the year 1980: Commandant Azzedine's *Et Alger ne brûla pas* (And Algiers Did Not Burn); Ferhat Abbas's *Autopsie d'une guerre—L'Aurore* (Autopsy of a War—The Aurore) and Mohammed Harbi's *Le FLN Mirage et Réalité* (The FLN Mirage and Reality).

A last point to note is the publication in English of work on the Algerian War: Alistair Horne's *A Savage War of Peace* in 1977 (published in French in 1980) and Tony Smith's *The French Stake in Algeria* in 1978. These were not the first pieces of work in English on the Algerian War but taken together were a significant step in the general move away from testimonies to actual history writing.

The Early 1980s

The early 1980s are a key moment in the historiography of the Algerian War. Not only are books by Algerian authors published but crucially the first historical study of the war in Algeria was published in French by French historians: Droz and Lever's *Histoire de la guerre d'Algérie* (History of the Algerian War) in 1982. Of the Algerian authors Mohammed Harbi perhaps contributes the most to the historiography of the Algerian War due to his two books *Le FLN, mirages et réalités* (The FLN, Mirages and Reality; 1980) and *Les Archives de la Révolution algérienne* (The Archives of the Algerian Revolution; 1981). Droz and Lever described Harbi (1980) as "fondamental" (essential reading).

It is interesting to note that Droz and Lever's book was published in 1982 while the history of the Algerian War began to be taught in *terminale* classes in 1983. It broke dramatically with the publications of the previous twenty years.

As they noted:

> pour beaucoup les passions restent vives et les protagonistes du drame
> s'emploient inlassablement depuis vingt ans à justifier leur choix. Si la sincérité
> de leur témoignage n'est pas en cause, il manque évidemment à l'objectivité né-
> cessaire. (for a lot of people the passions have not subsided and the protagonists
> of the drama have spent twenty years untiringly defending their choices. Al-
> though their testimony is clearly sincere, it obviously lacks the necessary objec-
> tivity.)[50]

Despite the significance of these books it is important to note that the historiography of the Algerian War was still, at this point, very poor. Pervillé, speaking in
1983 at "les Agoras Méditerranéennes" conference in Marseilles,[51] pointed to the
absence of scientific debate on the war. More generally it was the early 1980s
when the French government decided to include post-1939 history in the *terminale* history program, leaving many with the feeling that a subject was being
taught that had not yet been sufficiently researched. For the Algerian War, this
situation was to continue until the end of the 1980s—the period when it was examined and discussed by scholars at international conferences. One book that
certainly was groundbreaking in terms of research on the Algerian War was
Haroun's *La 7e wilaya, la guerre du FLN en France 1954-1962* (The Seventh
Wilaya, the FLN's War in France) published in 1986. It was described by Pervillé as the most important book on the Algerian War published that year since it
was of a considerable size and it examined an area that had only previously been
glimpsed at indirectly through work, for example, on the "porteurs de valise"
(French people who in France helped the FLN).

The Late 1980s/Early 1990s

The late 1980s and early 1990s are the second key period concerning significant advances in the historiography of the Algerian War. At the end of the
1980s a large international conference was held on the Algerian conflict, as were
certain "round table" discussion groups. The "Institut d'histoire du temps
présent" (IHTP: Institute of Contemporary History), part of the CNRS, created in
the early 1980s to specialize in contemporary history, in December 1988 organized a conference entitled "La Guerre d'Algérie et les Français" (The Algerian
War and the French), the findings of which were published by Fayard in 1990.
This was the first time that such a conference had been held. The book included
contributions by fifty-four authors and totaled about seven hundred pages on the
war in Algeria. It examined metropolitan public opinion and the war; the Republic and the war; the impact of the war on the French economy; the war and
France's international standing, and lastly the memory of the Algerian War. It
did not examine the Algerian War itself—in terms of battles or events, etc.—due
to the lack of access to the necessary archives.

The proceedings of the two round tables also organized by the IHTP that preceded this conference were published under the titles of *La Guerre d'Algérie et les intellectuels français* (The Algerian War and French Intellectuals) and *La Guerre d'Algérie et les chrétiens* (The Algerian War and Christians) both published in *les Cahiers de l'IHTP* in 1988 and later by other publishers. For Perville "Il a prouvé qu'une histoire de la guerre d'Algérie était possible"[52] (It proved that a history of the Algerian War was possible) and he rejoiced "il y a enfin du nouveau dans l'historiographie française de la guerre d'Algérie" (at last there is new work in French historiography of the Algerian War).[53] Why was it in 1988 that such a sudden progression in scholarly writing took place? Obviously the role of the IHTP was central, as were certain historians.

At the end of 1989 Alain-Gérard Slama wrote an article in *Le Point* that also gives us an idea of publications at this time on the Algerian War. In this article he pointed to the fact that "En quelques années, le Sud a brutalement réinvesti les consciences" (In a matter of a few years, the South has brutally reentered people's consciousness)[54] and identified twenty-five books published in the year 1989 on the war, that he qualified as a record. Why was there a new "opening of the old war wounds" that the title of his article makes reference to? Events in Algeria are often cited in explaining this "retour du refoulé" (return of the repressed) that other commentators such as Frank have identified. When explaining what in the present was bringing back such memories since the late 1980s (whereas before it had perhaps been easier to repress such memories), Stora argues that:

C'est un double basculement qui explique ce changement de situation. D'une part l'apparition des beurs, des Franco-Algériens et des enfants de pieds noirs sur les bancs des universités, en pleine réalité bien visible. Depuis 1985-1986, en gros. Et puis le tournant algérien de 1988. Voilà l'Algérie revenue doublement en force en France, dans la mémoire française. (Two major shifts explain this change in situation. On the one hand, more or less since 1985-1986, the entry on the scene of the *beurs*, Franco-Algerians and children of *pieds noirs* in lecture halls in universities; a visible and very real presence. And then the Algerian turning point in 1988. So Algeria reaffirmed its presence in France, in French memory.)[55]

The fallout from the late-1980s' conferences continued in the early 1990s, especially as 1992 was the thirtieth anniversary of the end of the war. This period saw the film by Tavernier and Rotman *La Guerre sans nom* (The War Without a Name) in cinemas; on French television Stora's *Les Années algériennes* (The Algerian Years); in bookstores Stora's *La Gangrène et l'oubli* (Gangrene and the Forgetting), *Histoire de l'Algérie coloniale* (History of Colonial Algeria), *Ils venaient d'Algérie* (They Came From Algeria) and *Histoire de la guerre d'Algérie* (History of the Algerian War). Two conferences were held in Paris, one entitled "Mémoire et Enseignement de la Guerre d'Algérie" (Memory and Teaching the Algerian War) and the other "Les accords d'Evian" (The Evian Peace Agreements). There were also the anniversaries of the end of the war and

the events of 17 October 1961; as well as the beginning of the opening of archives. There was such an "opening" around 1992 that Benjamin Stora wrote
that the work of grieving seemed to be finished due to the amount of film production on the colonial period.[56] Stora in his article in *Libération* (30 April-1
May 1992) also talked of "l'homme du Sud" (the man from the South) who it
would seem has allowed this opening to take place in two ways: firstly in his
country of origin by letting film makers actually work in Algeria and secondly in
France by the research, filmmaking or book-writing of people whose parents
came from Algeria and who have provided a lot of the impetus for studying this
period of French history (by doing it themselves).

As concerns the 1992 opening, the granting of access to archives after the
legal thirty year delay is particularly interesting. If we think about the writing of
the history of the Algerian War, and more generally what is called contemporary
history then it is important to reflect on the sources for this history. Since 1992
certain archives have been opened, previously inaccessible due to the legal requirement in France that public archives remain closed for thirty years. For example, on 1 July 1992 most of the military archives held in Vincennes were
opened. In this way it is quite common after 1992 to read in *l'Annuaire de
l'Afrique du Nord* comments such as "L'auteur retrace l'histoire de la guerre
d'Algérie grâce à l'accès récent aux archives militaires françaises" (The author
retraces the history of the Algerian War thanks to recent access to French military archives) or "Le travail de documentation, qui s'appuie sur des sources
variées, a été facilité par l'ouverture progressive des archives au public" (The
documentary work, that draws on a variety of sources, has been made easier by
the gradual opening of public archives).[57] However, we can note that archives
are not yet completely (or even perhaps significantly) open. As an article in *Le
Monde* in 1999 shows,[58] what has been published by the "Service historique de
l'armée de terre" (SHAT: Historical Service of the Army) stops in 1954, since
two volumes have been published: in 1990 the period 1943-1946, and in 1999
the period 1946-1954. The latter volume is entitled *La Guerre d'Algérie par les
documents* and includes a little over one thousand pages. The article therefore
announced that: "L'armée de terre ouvre ses archives militaires secrètes jusqu'en
décembre 1954" (The Army opens its military archives up to December 1954).[59]
Nothing has therefore yet been published by the SHAT on the crucial period of
the war itself.

Anniversaries of the end of the Algerian War have always led to a sharp
increase in the number of publications. For example Pervillé identifies ten works
on the war in Algeria in 1970, ten in 1971, seven in 1973 yet twenty-eight in
1972 for the tenth anniversary of the end of the war.[60] 1982 was also a rich year
in terms of publications and the Thirtieth anniversary of the end of the war was
no different. The Thirtieth anniversary of the events of 17 October 1961 was the
first time that this "massacre non-reconnu" (non-acknowledged massacre), in the
words of Stora, was examined in the media. This was perhaps in large part
achieved by the publication of Einaudi's book *La Bataille de Paris* (The Battle
of Paris) and the film *Le Silence du fleuve* (The Silence of the River). The role of

certain scholars is also important—at the beginning of the 1990s Stora stands out by the number of books he published and the television program he produced. He was perhaps one of the more visible historians of the Algerian War but was not the only person to be working on it around then as *La Guerre d'Algérie et les Français* (The Algerian War and the French; 1990) and numerous other publications show.

1992-2004

In my opinion, progress is still taking place but is back to the rather slow pace that characterizes the historiography of the Algerian War (except for the acceleration seen at the end of the 1980s/early 1990s). Claire Mauss-Copeaux, in her book on *Les Appelés en Algérie* (Conscripts in Algeria), remarks that:

> La mémoire de la guerre d'Algérie semblait définitivement libérée de la chape du silence qui le recouvrait. Cependant, ces initiatives provoquées en grande partie par la commémoration de l'anniversaire, n'ont pas fait disparaître le "syndrome algérien" (The memory of the Algerian War seemed definitively liberated from the stifling silence that had surrounded it. However, these initiatives that to a large extent emerged through the commemoration of the anniversary (of the end of the conflict), did not overcome the "Algerian syndrome.")[61]

The question of the amount of original research on the war in recent years is a very important one. It would seem that in 1993 there were twenty-five publications on the Algerian War, eighteen in 1994, thirteen in 1995, twenty in 1996, and eight in 1997.

There were therefore numerous publications on the Algerian War; more importantly the vast majority were what Pervillé would have called "études historiques proprement scientifiques" (scholarly historical works). It would appear therefore that the trend away from testimonies/memoirs toward scholarly research has continued since 1992. Nonetheless, Philip Dine has shown that throughout the 1990s testimony did continue to be published, particularly by *pieds noirs*.[62] Also, reading *L'Ancien d'Algérie* (a publication of the FNACA veterans association) shows the extent of testimony still being published by conscripts. Thus one may say that publications continue unabated and that the trend is slowly continuing toward the writing of history. Certain publications in recent years have been fascinating and progress is being made albeit slowly. Raphaëlle Branche and Sylvie Thénault's PhD theses stand out in this respect, that were both quickly published as books: Branche's *La torture et l'armée pendant la guerre d'Algérie* (Torture and the Army during the Algerian War; 2001) and Thénault's *Une drôle de justice, les magistrats dans la guerre d'Algérie* (Strange Justice: Magistrates during the Algerian War; 2001).

Perhaps more problematic is the argument that it is impossible at present to actually write the history of the war. This is a stance repeatedly taken by

Charles-Robert Ageron. In 1992, in the proceedings of the MEDGA Conference,[63] he published a contribution entitled "Une histoire de la guerre d'Algérie
est-elle possible en 1992?" (Is it possible to write the history of the Algerian War
in 1992?) and stated that "il n'est pas encore possible de rédiger cette histoire"
(It is not yet possible to write this history).[64] Ageron justified this view by pointing to the fact that the Algerian War is still a sore point that generates a lot of
passion despite the passing of time. He also shows the importance of written
sources in history and thought that in 1992 the amount of written documents that
had been made accessible to the public was insufficient. For him it is imperative
to study written documents that are dated rather than to base history on oral
sources that give *a posteriori* justifications. Thirdly, he shows that on the Algerian side there are and have been too many obstacles to writing history. Only a
part of the story had been discovered by 1992 with the publication of work by
Harbi and Haroun. To highlight the difficulty of writing a history of the Algerian
War Ageron chose to give the example of figures for deaths during the war—that
is an area that has proved notoriously difficult to evaluate.

Also of concern, in my opinion, is that certain other areas of the history of
the war have still not been written in many senses. Areas of discord, to take just
a few examples, include what happened in Paris on 17 October 1961. Although
historians tend to universally refute the "official version" given by the French
authorities at the time, it is more difficult to say exactly what happened. The
question of the extent of the use of torture is also an area of the war that is difficult to describe with precision, although Branche's magistral *La Torture et
l'armée pedant la guerre d'Algérie* (Torture and the Army during the Algerian
War), published in 2001, largely filled that gap. Many examples could be given,
often concerning the less glorious, most occluded events in the war. It is obvious
that in any war it is never easy to examine such questions and that the Algerian
War is no different. Clearly, the memory of such parts of the war is still extremely difficult to face for different parts of French society that has made writing the history of elements of the war extremely difficult until now.

In 1996 a "round table" was organized in Paris entitled "La Guerre
d'Algérie et les Algériens 1954-1962" (The Algerian War and Algerians 1954-
1962) at which sixteen scholars spoke—eight French and eight Algerian. The
proceedings of this meeting were published a year later.[65] In the preface Ageron
again addressed the subject of the difficulties of writing a history of the Algerian
War. He was still arguing in favor of the need for a "scientific history" of the
war. He was somewhat more positive in terms of the possibilities of writing a
definitive history of the war due principally to the opening of archives that had
already led to progress being made in the historiography of the war. However he
finished on what was still a fairly negative note:

> Parce que nous historiens français avons l'expérience des longs efforts qui fu-
> rent nécessaires avant d'aboutir à un traitement impartial des guerres franco-
> allemandes, nous savons que l'heure n'est pas venue où l'on pourrait écrire une
> histoire de la guerre d'Algérie qui serait acceptée par tous les Algériens et par
> tous les Français. (We know that the time has not yet come when it is possible to

write a history of the Algerian War that would be accepted by all Algerians and all French people, because we, as French historians, know how long and hard it was before we were able to achieve an impartial treatment of the Franco-German wars.)[66]

It is also possible to compare what Stora wrote in 1992 and in 1996. As was mentioned above, Stora writing in 1992 talked of a significant opening (in terms of images of the war) and spoke of a possible end to the long period of grieving since the war. However in 1996, he wrote that this was merely a cruel illusion.[67]

To conclude this section, there has been a trend to gradually move away from testimonies and memoirs toward scholarly writing on the Algerian conflict. However this has been a long and difficult process which is to date far from finished. There are still considerable areas of the war that we know little about and where it is impossible to identify what exactly happened. It is clear that the memory of the war still tends, in certain areas, to overshadow the history of the war. In terms of my book on transmission of memories of the Algerian War in the education system, the media and the family it is important to note the limited state of knowledge on the war when it began to be taught in *terminale* classes in 1983. Furthermore we can note the advances in our state of knowledge since then and see whether such advances have been translated into changes in the type of knowledge which is transmitted in schools. The findings of this book would tend very much to show the opposite. Rather than advances in knowledge about the war leading to more aspects of the war being able to be taught, it would seem that less and less is being taught in history lessons in schools on this subject. Moreover, as shown here, the difficulty of writing the history of the Algerian War is accompanied by difficulty in teaching its history. Nor is it evident that work published by historians has yet been able to play a role of adjudicating, as one might expect, in the polemical "memory battles"—frequently played out in the media—that if anything seem to have worsened in recent years. We will see that during the media debate a number of aspects of the history of the Algerian War were reviewed and contested, including in readers' letters, without a great deal of reference to scholarship on this topic. Advances in historiography do not seem either to have provided stronger "social frames of memory" for family memory, as we will see in this book.

Theoretical Reflections on Memory

This section provides a theoretical framework for my empirical research on the transmission of the memory of the Algerian War carried out in France. The following chapters will include a detailed case study of three crucial vectors of memory, with a focus on primarily assessing the extent of transmission of memories in these areas. A theoretical framework is needed to interpret and analyze these findings. The empirical findings will also be used to try and extend memory theory. It presents the broad schools of thought that exist as concerns memory and it also provides an idea of the ways that focuses of enquiry have developed over time. Three schools of thought are retained as particularly useful and against which the empirical findings will be tested: a Halbwachsian school that sees collective memory as a necessary glue for society, a pluralist school that focuses on various groups vying for a place in the collective memory and a Freudian school emphasizing repression and occlusion of memories as a way of dealing with past trauma. The approach taken in this book will be to defend a *bricolage* of theories. It is felt that drawing on as many theories as possible gives the richest understanding of collective memory. In addition, the approach will be resolutely social. In terms of the organization of this section, we can begin by identifying the main disciplines that are linked to the study of memory; then we will examine each of the schools of thought in turn.

The first point to be made is that the study of memory is interdisciplinary, providing the opportunity to form quite a rich theoretical understanding of this concept. The challenge then is more to draw on so many diverse insights and to try and weave them together. The interdisciplinary nature of the work conducted on memory is well expressed in the following quotation by David Thelen in *The Journal of American History*:

> At one end of the spectrum are psychological issues of individual motivation and perception in the creation of memories. At the other end are linguistic and anthropological issues of how cultures establish traditions and myths from the past to guide the conduct of their members in the present. While history touches both ends of the spectrum, its concerns fall most comfortably on points between those ends.[68]

The sources consulted for this book reflect this "spectrum" that Thelen identifies. They could be divided into the following broad categories: Psychology/Psychoanalysis; History; Philosophy; and Cultural Studies/Literature. This division is designed solely to show the variety of research conducted, since it is difficult to divide the authors into such categories given that some of their work falls into more than one of the groups. It would therefore be fair to say that the sources are not only interdisciplinary but also multidisciplinary.

Having identified the variety of disciplines that are involved in the study of memory, let us now turn to the findings and the conclusions of these books and articles. The logical starting point is the work of Maurice Halbwachs that, as will become clearer below, can be linked to much contemporary research. Halbwachs invented the term "collective memory" and founded the discipline of the sociology of memory, so his work is central to much of the research that has followed. His work is of interest since he examines both individual memory and collective memory in *La Mémoire collective* (Collective Memory) and *Les Cadres sociaux de la mémoire* (The Social Frames of Memory). The title of this latter work is a good starting point to examine his findings. The two key words are "cadres" (frames) and "sociaux" (social). "Cadres" are described for man as "les clous avec lesquels il fixe ses souvenirs"[69] (the nails with which he fixes his memories) and as the organizers of our memory. They "enframe" our memory. They are language, time, and space. These three "cadres" are quoted by Rioux in his essay in *La Guerre d'Algérie et les Français* (The Algerian War and the French) with regard to the memory of the Algerian War in the late 1980s. Language in this respect consisted of euphemisms like "une guerre sans nom" (a war without a name), "opérations de maintien de l'ordre" (peacekeeping) and "rébellion" (rebellion) that denied the existence of a war and therefore hindered its remembrance. Time was problematic for memory since there were problems dating events in the war. Space was equally lacking due to the absence of *hauts lieux* and since "L'Algérie demeure lointaine, peu ou mal montrée" (Algeria remains far-off, shown little or badly).[70]

These three "cadres" (although Halbwachs indicates the possibility of others) are very important in order to understand the factors that enable us to remember, but I feel that the insistence on "sociaux" is ultimately the most important of Halbwachs's findings, since this is a belief that now divides the psychology community into two schools of thought. Halbwachs maintained that there is a social dimension to memory in part since people rely on the memory of others to provide confirmation of their own memories. It is also social since our individual memory is influenced by the group we belong to: "se souvenir pour un individu c'est reconstruire son passé en partant des cadres sociaux présents de son groupe" (remembering for an individual consists of reconstructing her/his past using the current social frames of her/his group).[71] It is in society that we find the ways to remember. Those who effectively follow Halbwachs constitute the "social constructionist" school—members of which include Michael Billig, David Edwards, and Derek Middleton. The other school of thought is the "cognitive" school (that was for a long time, and perhaps still is, the main focus of enquiry), that examines memory strictly in terms of the individual. It seems to me that the "social constructionist" school is becoming more and more influential and that this type of social approach is of fundamental importance to my research since this project is focused on transmission of memory from generation to generation via education, the family, and the media. This kind of memory is therefore very social in nature. Indeed, a Halbwachsian theory of memory, when taken at the collective level, can be seen to be one in which memory contributes to provide necessary unity in society. This view originally comes from Emile Durkheim. We will see examples of this role of memory in this book.

The basic premise of the "social constructionist" school is that it is necessary to view "remembering and forgetting as inherently social activities,"[72] since remembering is seen as "une activité sociale, qui passe par le discours et qui se construit en relation avec d'autres individus" (a social activity, that is dependent on speech and is constructed in relation with other people).[73] Memory is constructed, not reproduced. The reason that "social constructionist" psychologists are grouped here with Halbwachs is the insistence on the "social" aspect of memory, but also due to the focus on speech that reminds us of the "cadre" of language identified by Halbwachs. Billig, Middleton, and Edwards explain in depth their interest in language by pointing to the fact that the difference between the memories of animals and humans is that the latter can remember events that they did not experience personally—via language. As will be seen later, this fact is very important as concerns memory and the wider "frames" of education, the family, or the media. They argue that remembering is an "epistemological enterprise,"[74] and they examine the interaction between people as a determining factor in memory. Their methodology therefore includes conversational and discourse analyses, and their corpus includes observing members of a family recall the Royal wedding of Prince Charles and Lady Diana. They conclude that: "Les souvenirs sont donc *produits* d'une manière déterminée par l'interaction actuelle au sein de la famille" (Memories are *produced* in a way that is determined by the current interaction within the family).[75] For this reason their view of memory can loosely be associated with a kind of pluralist model of collective memory in which different groups, at the collective level, compete to influence memory in the same way members of a family interact and produce memories. We will see concrete examples of the influence of groups on memory in this book.

The last point for the moment concerning Halbwachs and the "social constructionist" school of psychology is their view of the present in the determination of memory. As Gérard Namer points out:

> Le fil rouge qui parcourt son livre est que le souvenir est une reconstruction du passé à partir de la représentation qu'un groupe a de ses intérêts actuels. (The central thread running throughout his book is that memories are a reconstruction of the past from the stand point of the group's representation of its own current interests.)[76]

In this way, adopting a social approach consists of refusing to view memory as "stocking" and "encoding" in an individual's head—as Halbwachs argued against Henri Bergson's description of a "une mémoire pure, individuelle, en images"[77] (a pure, individual memory, made up of images)—by pointing to the present production and construction of memory. David Thelen resumes these views as follows:

> The starting place for the construction of an individual recollection is a present need or circumstance . . . Since an individual's starting points change as the person grows and changes, people reshape their recollections of the past to fit their present needs . . . and select from the present material that supports deeply held interpretations from the past.[78]

Hence "the present" must be examined in terms of "a person's motives or biases or mood or audience"[79] rather than simply in terms of its distance from the event to be remembered. This also applies to groups. Halbwachs argued, for example, that religious collective memory was a reconstruction of the past to satisfy present needs. Halbwachs also shows class collective memory to be a response to present needs in so far as it acts as an ideology that justifies conflict with other groups. Having discussed Halbwachs and the social constructionist view of memory, let us know turn to a second school of thought—that which draws on the work of Sigmund Freud.

As a glance at my bibliography shows, there has been considerable academic interest in "l'oubli" (forgetting): for example, the collection of essays *Usages de l'oubli* (Uses of Forgetting), the special issue of the review *Communications* dedicated to "La mémoire et l'oubli" (Memory and Forgetting) and that of *Le Genre Humain* on "Politiques de l'oubli" (The Politics of Forgetting). The reason that "memory" and "forgetting" can be treated in different parts of this section is mentioned by Paul-Laurent Assoun in his essay on Freud:

> le "souvenir" et l'"oublier" doivent être pensés dans leur cohérence (*Zusammenhang*), comme deux faces d'un même "phénomène." Il s'agit de s'arracher à la conception de l'oubli comme simple privation de souvenir: il faut parvenir à une pensée complète de ce phénomène composite. ("memory" and "forgetting" have to be thought of together (*Zusammenhang*), as two sides of the same "phenomenon." We need to move away from conceiving of forgetting as simply not having memory: we need to develop a complete theory of this composite phenomenon.)[80]

Freud's theories are also very useful for reflections on forgetting and the "subconscious," albeit focused on the individual. He introduces the idea of *refoulement* that becomes of central importance to work on the memory of the Algerian War. Robert Frank insists on the question of *refoulement* (repression) and *occultation* (occlusion) by stating that the memory of the war is a "selective memory" and that the Algerian War is not a forgotten war, unlike the war in Indo-China.[81] Reading Frank's contribution in *La Guerre d'Algérie et les Français* (The Algerian War and the French), perhaps we can identify a difference between *occultation*, that seems to be an act (maybe by government authorities) to hide something, and *refoulement*, that is possibly more a question of individual difficulty or refusal to remember. Freud speaks of forgetting as a "sort of security" and a "narrative failure" and, as Assoun states, concludes that:

> L'oubli s'instaure ainsi dans l'après-coup d'un récit impossible: c'est en effet faute de pouvoir (se) raconter que le sujet choisit l'oubli. L'oubli n'est donc pas exactement le contraire du souvenir: c'est le destin d'un récit impossible du souvenir. (Forgetting therefore takes place as a result of the impossibility of voicing: it is effectively due to an inability to recount that the subject chooses to forget. Forgetting is therefore not exactly the opposite of remembering: it is the result of an impossible telling of a memory.)[82]

Freud also introduces the idea of the "work of grieving," showing us how difficult remembering can be. This idea also implies that what is repressed should be brought out into the open. We will see in this book examples of repression of the memory of the Algerian War in so far as there is no dialogue on the subject, and since it is repressed one can argue it is problematic for French society. Freud argued that if what is repressed is not brought out into the open it is unconsciously repeated. Grieving can be seen to be a process of dialogue and not silence on a subject. This is a difficult process that involves suffering. It involves accepting death or loss of a person or a thing. If there is no "work of grieving" then there is repression. In this way after the "work of grieving" there can be memory. As the authors of *Deuils. Vivre c'est perdre* (Mourning: To Live is to Lose) state:

> Lorsque le deuil est fait—s'il est jamais fait—, il reste des êtres un peu moins neufs, un peu plus fêtés, mais vivants. Et s'il n'y a pas de honte à vivre après, tout rêve de remplacer, combler ou effacer est illusoire. Prendre en compte cette réalité de la blessure et ses traces indélébiles, c'est la condition du deuil accompli qui permet d'avancer sans trop trébucher, riche d'un mémoire. (When mourning takes place—if ever it is completed—, people become less fresh, a bit more fêted, but alive. Although there is no shame in living again, any dream of replacing, making up, or erasing is pointless. Understanding this fact of injuries and their indelible traces is a condition for a successful mourning period that allows one to go forward without too much stumbling, armed with memories.)[83]

A different approach to forgetting is given by Gianni Vattimo in his essay on Friedrich Nietzsche, some of the ideas of which are supported by the lecture of Ernest Renan "Qu'est-ce qu'une nation?" (What is a Nation?) that is published in Homi Bhabha's *Nation and Narration*. Vattimo examines Nietzsche's *Second Untimely Meditation* (1874) that reflects on historiography and on the historicist movement that developed rapidly during the nineteenth century—thereby examining "l'utilité et le dommage de l'histoire pour la vie" (the use of history for life).[84] Nietzsche concludes that there is too much focus on history, leading to forgetting becoming very difficult or impossible, a situation that in turn rules out what he calls an "oubli créateur" (creative forgetting). In effect "l'homme du XIXe siècle souffre d'une maladie historique" (nineteenth century man is suffering from the illness of history).[85] The relationship between life or society and forgetting is of fundamental importance to my research as is the link between historiography and memory. Ernest Renan can also be of use in understanding these relationships. Writing at the same epoch as Nietzsche, his view concurs that forgetting is necessary:

> Forgetting, I would even go so far as to say historical error, is a crucial factor in the creation of a nation, which is why progress in historical studies often constitutes a danger for (the principle of) nationality.[86]

Renan's argument reinforces the views of Nietzsche and also introduces the central idea of "nationality" and memory/forgetting that is examined in more depth below. Again we can see the way collective memory can be seen to be a sort of necessary glue for society. This can involve forgetting certain memories to create cohesion in the present. People develop a shared identity through shared memories. In this way collective memory can be argued to be essential to the integrity of a community. What may perhaps be called a "philosophical" school of thought presents the argument of forgetting being necessary to a nation.

Nietzsche and Renan were instrumental in the development of this idea, that has been examined more recently by Yosef Yerushalmi in *Usages de l'oubli*. He focuses on the necessity of forgetting and summarizes the problem by introducing the following questions, that he feels remain unanswerable at present:

> si nous avons besoin et de nous souvenir et d'oublier, où devons-nous tracer la frontière? Nietzsche nous est ici de quelque utilité. Dans quelle *mesure* avons-nous besoin de l'histoire? Et quelle *sorte* d'histoire? De quoi devrions-nous nous souvenir, que pouvons-nous nous autoriser à oublier? (if we need both to forget and to remember, where do we draw the line? Nietzsche is useful here. To what *extent* do we need history? And what *sort* of history? What should we remember, what can we allow ourselves to forget?)[87]

Let us now examine in more depth the link between memory and the nation. Having just examined the arguments of Nietzsche and Renan, the sources for this topic consist essentially of Benedict Anderson, Homi Bhabha, Eric Hobsbawm, and David Lowenthal. This is a vast area of study, but it would perhaps be logical to begin by outlining the historical perspective of the nation and the way in which relationships to the past have developed—topics that both Benedict Anderson and David Lowenthal examine in depth. To summarize Lowenthal's findings, he traces what he calls the "modern impulse to preserve" back to the Renaissance, by underlining "the Renaissance perception of a classical antiquity sharply distinguishable from, and superior to, the recent past" that led to the appreciation and the emulation of classical times.[88] Throughout the sixteenth and seventeenth centuries the rise of modern science brought with it rationalism that culminated in the Enlightenment and the removal of superstition through appeals to abstract reason, considerably changing relationships to the past: destruction replaced appreciation. However, the nineteenth century saw the rise of historicism, that again had important consequences in terms of attitudes to the past. Lowenthal concludes that:

> Not until the early nineteenth century did Europeans and Americans strongly identify themselves with their material heritage, and only within the past half-century have most countries come to promote preservation as a positive public programme.[89]

Anderson adopts a similar approach, albeit based on nationalism and not on preservation, in terms of identifying a time frame and factors that explain relatively new conceptions—these new concepts now refer to "the possibility of imagining the nation" rather than to historical preservation. As he states:

> nationalism has to be understood by aligning it not with self-consciously held political ideologies, but with the large cultural systems that preceded it, out of which—as well as against which—it came into being.[90]

Anderson's *Imagined Communities* provides a fascinating account of how it became possible to "imagine the nation." His work is important to memory studies in so far as it draws attention to the fundamental changes of recent centuries that have modified human relationships to the past and to the nation. More importantly, he introduces the concept of an "imagined community" and explains what "belonging to a nation" consists of, that provides the link to memory/forgetting. Lastly, his work elucidates the complex question of the age of nations—as does research by Homi Bhabha and Eric Hobsbawm. Anderson expresses this idea as follows:

> If nation states are widely considered to be "new" and "historical," the nations to which they give political expression always loom out of an immemorial past and . . . glide into a limitless future.[91]

Bhabha supports Anderson's argument by stating that "nations lose their origins in the myths of time"[92] and Hobsbawm bases his work on the link between tradition and the nation by formulating the concept of "invented traditions." "Traditions" are seen to be practices "which seek to inculcate certain values and norms of behavior by repetition" that use the past to "structure" life, and they are "invented" since "continuity with the past is largely factitious."[93] The book *The Invention of Tradition* includes several contributions that examine different uses of "invented traditions," but the section that is the most relevant to this project is that by Eric Hobsbawm (Mass-Producing Traditions: Europe, 1870-1914) and especially the example of the French Third Republic. This is a fascinating account of how the Third Republic was "maintained" and "safeguarded" by reference to the past, and more precisely to the French Revolution. Hobsbawm cites three major uses of invented traditions: primary education, public ceremonies, and public monuments. We will deal with his argument as concerns primary education below, since it clearly links memory and education. Public ceremonies were used to foster invariance by reference to the past and included Bastille Day (as of 1880):

> It combined official and unofficial demonstrations and popular festivities— fireworks, dancing in the streets—in an annual assertion of France as the nation of 1789, in which every French man, woman and child could take part.[94]

In this way, a public ceremony was invented in 1880, nearly a hundred years after the Revolution, that strengthened the Third Republic and the nation against its adversaries (anarcho-syndicalists and the Right) by celebrating its origins. Other public ceremonies that performed the same role were world expositions, highlighting technical progress and the French Empire (perhaps the colonial exposition of 1931, albeit much later, would be the apogee of such exhibitions). However, public ceremonies were not the only "invented tradition," since they were accompanied by the mass production of public monuments:

> The major characteristic of French "statuomania" was its democracy, anticipating that of the war memorials after 1914-18. It spread two kinds of monuments

throughout the cities and rural communes of the country: the image of the Republic itself (in the form of Marianne which now became universally familiar), and the bearded civilian figures of whoever local patriotism chose to regard as its notable, past and present.[95]

To these two main "inventions of tradition" (and the third, in the form of primary education, that will be examined later) of the early Third Republic can be added other forms of reference to the Revolution: the tricolor, the Republican monogram (RF), the Marseillaise, and the Republican motto (liberty, equality, fraternity). All of these phenomena, when examined in depth, provide a striking example of how history can be used to strengthen a nation.

At present, we can turn to the last part of this section that introduces a third broad school of thought: agency and collective memory. The "social agency approach" to collective memory, eschewed by Jay Winter and Emmanuel Sivan in the book they coedited entitled *War and Remembrance in the Twentieth Century*, highlights the behavior of groups and individuals involved in remembrance. It can be allied with what might be called a "pluralist" model, where various groups compete for a place in the collective memory. Winter describes the book's purpose as "to examine collective remembrance as the outcome of agency, as the product of individuals and groups who come together, not at the behest of the state or any of its subsidiary organizations, but because they have to speak out."[96] For the authors "Agency in the constitution of social learning about the past is crucial, but it operates from below, not only from above" so the thrust of their analysis "is towards highlighting the role of second and third-order elites within civil society. The social organization of remembrance tends to be decentralized. This claim shifts the emphasis in this field away from central organizations of the state, both from top downward and sideways. That is to say, away from the state central institutions, and towards civil society groupings, their leaders and activists."[97] They criticize Halbwachsian models of collective memory since "Durkheimians held tenaciously that individual memory was entirely socially constructed."[98]

Winter focuses on civil society—defined as the arena between the family and the State. Yerushalmi also examines civil society when he explains that memory effectively consists of the transmission of the past from generation to generation. In his fascinating essay on the Jewish people and memory, by selecting texts from the Torah, he states that Jewish people were "des recepteurs attentifs et de superbes transmetteurs"[99] (attentive receivers and superb transmitters) of memory. This is of crucial importance since:

quand nous disons qu'un peuple "se souvient," disons-nous en réalité d'abord qu'un passé a été activement transmis aux générations contemporaines . . . qu'ensuite ce passé transmis a été reçu comme étant chargé d'un sens propre. En conséquence, un peuple "oublie" quand la génération détentrice du passé ne le transmet pas à la suivante, ou quand celle-ci rejette ce qu'elle a reçu ou cesse de le transmettre à son tour. (when we say that a people "remembers," we are really saying firstly that a past has been actively transmitted to contemporary genera-

tions . . . and then that this transmitted past has been received and acknowledged
as meaningful. Consequently a people "forgets" when a generation that controls
a past does not transmit it to the next generation, or when the latter rejects what
it has received or does not transmit it itself in due course.)[100]

One of the ways that this transmission takes place is education. The collective
memory of the Algerian War depends to some extent on the active transmission
by teachers of the curriculum and whether the past is received by younger generations. Indeed Yerushalmi describes Jewish transmission of memory as the
transmission of the Torah, that as he reminds us itself means "teaching," "education" or "lesson" (in French he uses the word "enseignement") taken in their
widest meaning. Furthermore, the Torah was taught at Yabneh, an academy in
Israel, and we can note that: "L'enseignement inclut une bonne partie d'histoire"
(The teaching included a large place for history). This however was not all history, only history that could be integrated into the value system of the *halakhah*,
the Law/the Way ("Loi" in French); the rest was forgotten. As Yerushalmi
states:

> *halakhah*, c'est donc le chemin sur lequel on marche, la Route, la Voie, le Tao,
> cet ensemble de rites et de croyances qui donne à un peuple le sens de son iden-
> tité et de sa destination. Du passé ne sont transmis que les épisodes que l'on juge
> exemplaires ou édifiants pour la *halakhah* d'un peuple telle qu'elle est vécue au
> présent. Le reste de "l'histoire"—risquons l'image—bascule dans le fosse. (*ha-
> lakhah*, is therefore the path we walk, the Route, the Way, the Tao, that sum of
> rites and beliefs that give a people the meaning of its identity and its destination.
> Only episodes from the past that are judged exemplary or edifying for the *ha-
> lakhah* of a people's lived reality in the present are transmitted. The rest of "his-
> tory"—let us risk the image—ends up in the ditch.)[101]

Michael Billig and Derek Edwards also insist on the importance of education
and the family to memory and explain the importance of the teacher or parents in
this process:

> De même que les parents, les enseignants orientent la rhétorique de la mémoire
> des enfants, qui ne porte pas seulement sur l'utilisation d'un langage descriptif
> adapté mais aussi sur la manière de passer au crible et de distinguer ce qui est
> pertinent et possède une valeur explicative ou non. Les enfants apprennent des
> manières de décrire, de relater et d'oublier; ils apprennent à ignorer ce qui est
> considéré comme trivial. (Like parents, teachers orientate the rhetoric of the
> memory of children, which is determined not only by the use of a suitable de-
> scriptive language but also by decisions about what is pertinent and genuinely
> has a value in explaining things. Children learn ways to describe, to relate and to
> forget; they learn to ignore what is considered trivial.)[102]

In terms of research on the teaching of the Algerian War in Lyon's schools (as
well as family transmission of memory and reporting on the Algerian War in the
media), this approach to the role of the teacher (or the journalist or the family

member) means that it is necessary to examine the dynamics of history lessons (media coverage or family life) on the Algerian War, and more importantly, to identify what exactly is viewed as "important" and "pertinent." The importance of the content of what is taught is also highlighted by Hobsbawm as one of the three major innovations of the French Third Republic in terms of the invention of tradition (the other two have already been examined). He discusses the Ferry laws that instituted free, secular, and compulsory primary education. We can note that Jules Ferry not only pursued an ambitious policy of State schooling, but also one of French colonial expansion. Hobsbawm argues that education was used to strengthen the Republic by its reference to the past, since primary education was:

> imbued with revolutionary and republican principles and content, and conducted by the secular equivalent of the priesthood—or perhaps given their poverty, the friars—the *instituteurs*. There is no doubt that this was a deliberate construction of the early Third Republic, and, given the proverbial centralization of French government, that the content of the manuals which were to turn not only peasants into Frenchmen but all Frenchmen into good Republicans, was not left to chance.[103]

There is therefore a clear link between memory, education and the nation/the Republic. Examining the same period, Nora makes reference to the book the *Tour de la France par deux enfants* (Tour of France by Two Children) and describes it as a *lieu de mémoire* (site of memory). As he explains, it "trained the memory of millions of French boys and girls" as it was "an inventory of what one ought to know about France, an exercise in identification and a voyage of initiation."[104]

In conclusion, this section has attempted to identify the main disciplines that can be studied in order to provide a theoretical framework to my research on the memory of the Algerian War. The sources give a comprehensive theoretical framework since they enable us to identify different schools of thought that all provide valuable insights into memory—the three "cadres" described by Halbwachs, the importance of the present in the determination of memory, a social approach to memory as opposed to that defended by "cognitive" psychologists, Freud's theory of forgetting as a form of "security," the difference between *oubli* and *occultation* or *refoulement*, historicist views versus Nietzsche's concept of an "historical illness," the role of agency in collective memory, and lastly the key concepts of "invented traditions" and "imagined communities." Indeed three particular schools of thought can be identified as highly important concerning social memory: a Halbwachsian view of memory that sees the construction of collective memory as linked to cohesion in society; a Freudian view of memory in which what is repressed should be brought out into the open to avoid its repetition in the present; and lastly a pluralistic view of collective memory in which groups compete to influence memory. Reference will be made throughout the book to these three schools as the case study con-

ducted in France will give concrete examples of these theories, and the book will
rely on such theories to try to explain why the Algerian War is taught, discussed,
and reported the way it is. The approach taken in this book will be to defend a
bricolage of theories. We will attempt to draw together insights from various
schools of thought. Although at the outset we identified three schools of thought,
they can already be seen to be reconcilable rather than mutually exclusive. For
example, we can reconcile Freud's views on repression with more social constructionist views in the way Billig does in his work *Freudian Repression*, since
he sees "repression as something that is socially, rather than biologically, constituted."[105] Indeed one of Halbwach's case studies is family collective memory,
and we have already argued that social constructionist/Halbwachsian views of
memory can loosely be associated with a pluralist model of collective memory in
which different groups, at the collective level, compete to influence memory in
the same way members of a family interact and produce memories. We will see
how this can be achieved in each of the domains to be studied—education, family, and the media—throughout this book.

Critical Literature: Transmission of Memory in Education, the Family, and the Media

As Alfred Grosser points out "'collective memory' is less an actual memory than
'transmission via the family, school and the media.'"[106] For Yerushalmi, collective memory is a metaphor and essentially amounts to transmission and reception
of memories. These three vectors of memory are resolutely social. They allow us
to focus on individuals (transmitters and receptors), groups, and the wider society or "memory culture." Let us review critical literature in these three areas
concerning French collective memory of the Algerian War.

Education

The main research on the place of the Algerian War in the French education
system to date comes from the conference "Mémoire et enseignement de la
guerre d'Algérie" (MEDGA: Memory and Teaching of the Algerian War) held
in Paris on 13-14 March 1992 (close to the thirtieth anniversary of the end of the
Algerian War), organized by the "Institut du monde arabe" (Institute of the Arab
World) and the "Ligue de l'enseignement" (Education League) and published in
the book *Mémoire et enseignement de la guerre d'Algérie: actes du colloque* in
1993. The Conference was aimed at furthering a "réflexion commune" (shared
reflection) in Algeria and in France on the way the Algerian War is portrayed in
the media and in the education system in order to "faire progresser la connaissance objective des faits parmi les jeunes générations" (advance objective
knowledge of the facts amongst younger generations).[107]

Of particular relevance to my research in this book were four papers given at the conference, all of which are linked to the *terminale* year. They were given by Danièle Djamila Amrane-Minne, Alexis Berchadsky, Madeleine Guyon et al., and Geneviève Pastor. Amrane-Minne examined "La guerre d'Algérie à travers les manuels français et algériens de classes terminales" (The Algerian War in French and Algerian *Terminale* Textbooks). The paper examined French textbooks in terms of the presentation of the massacres of 20 August 1955, that she described as a "vision réductrice de l'histoire" (reductive vision of history).[108] Her paper examined both French *and* Algerian textbooks, and was therefore interesting to a large extent because it was comparative. Berchadsky discussed "La question de la torture à travers les manuels français de classes terminales" (The Question of Torture in French Textbooks in *Terminale*). He examined five out of twelve of the 1989 textbooks' coverage of torture, and argued that torture had a double presence in textbooks: in terms of the battle of Algiers and in terms of metropolitan protests.

Guyon et al.'s short paper, "Trente ans après: la guerre d'Algérie à travers les manuels d'histoire des classes terminales" (Thirty Years On: The Algerian War in *Terminale* Textbooks), was based on a study of how five events from the war were presented in textbooks, showing that the less glorious aspects of the war were often ignored or at best only partially treated. Guyon et al. conducted a study of seven of the twelve textbooks published in 1989. Their study only examined textbooks. This project, although it will examine textbooks, will attempt as far as possible to situate textbooks in relation to the rest of the educational chain (rather than simply criticizing them in isolation). Guyon et al.'s paper lacked reflection on what textbooks are and what can be done in a textbook; therefore there was not enough thought given to wider questions of the place of textbooks in the educational chain, the place of the educational chain in the transmission of memory, the wider memory of the Algerian War, and ultimately what the role of social memory is or may be.

Lastly, Pastor examined "L'enseignement de la guerre d'Algérie en classe de terminale. Instructions officielles et sujets au baccalauréat en France" (The Teaching of the Algerian War in *Terminale*. Official Instructions and Examination Questions in France). The paper studied examination questions in the period from June 1984 to 1991, through a predominantly quantitative study in which she qualifies the period as one of a "disappointment." The rest of the papers examined the way the Algerian War is taught in Algeria, an area that this book does not address. They also examined different points in the education system where the Algerian War may be taught—for example, at university level. This book only examines the *terminale* year, for the *baccalauréat général*, in order to keep the project within manageable proportions.

Also of interest is the opinion poll conducted by Alain Coulon and his team at Paris VIII University entitled "Connaissances et opinions des jeunes Français" (Knowledge and Opinions of French Young People) on 1,234 French people aged 17-30 in December 1991.[109] I found this survey fascinating because lack of resources prevented my doing this type of survey for my project. My project includes interviews of *terminale* pupils that are designed to be qualitative, since only a few pupils were interviewed, but this was done in depth i.e. a lot of questions in relatively long interviews. Beyond the MEDGA Conference we can also note work by Guy Pervillé and Paul Fournier on the place of the Algerian War in textbooks. They studied 1983 editions of textbooks that this book has not been able to do (except for one textbook published by Hatier). They were speaking at the "Agoras Mediterranéennes" and their findings were published in the French periodical *Historiens et Géographes*.[110] In this way, the main source of research on the way the Algerian War is taught is the MEDGA Conference and we can say that most of the research previously conducted on this question focused on textbook content.

My book necessarily refers to this previous work. However, the fact that my project examines the teaching of the Algerian War until the year 2000 has allowed me to build on and move away from previous research in important ways. Firstly, this book adds another eight years to the research already conducted. I have concentrated mainly on the 1990s and relied on this source for the 1980s, for example, essentially for examination questions and studies of the 1989 editions of textbooks. Secondly, this book takes a long-term view over seventeen years and therefore is able to conduct a diachronic study which has helped me to identify and compare different reforms, periods, and trends.   My research in the same area has allowed me to go beyond the previous work by taking into account and avoiding some of the shortcomings that can be seen concerning the 1992 Conference. The first of these is the way the education section of the conference was not based solely on the *terminale* year and was therefore less detailed than my research project is. My project is based exclusively on the *terminale* year. Secondly, in my opinion, there was a lack of reflection on the general memory of the Algerian War and other aspects of the question. The three main focuses of enquiry that were present at the conference concerned history programs/examination questions, textbooks, and young people's knowledge of the Algerian War. There are certain aspects of the teaching of the conflict that have not been examined. The first of these areas is the process of reform of history programs in the 1980s and the 1990s and the motivation for such reforms. Another is the relationship between the different actors in the field of education involved in the teaching of the Algerian War. The book also aims to provide a more detailed analysis of the impact of education on young people's knowledge of the war in Algeria, especially in relation to other vectors of memory. To do so it will focus more on the classroom level and the educational chain. The whole study will also tie the way the Algerian War is taught to the general memory of this colonial war.

What the Conference lacked especially was any attempt at an explanation of why the Algerian War is taught the way it is. Furthermore, we can note criticism of individual papers, for example, Rioux mentioned in his preface that he found that certain of the paper's content to be unfairly critical. Indeed he went as far as to speak of "une véhémence qui semble parfois bien peu fondée" (sometimes completely ungrounded vehemence).[111] In addition, as can be seen from the press at the time of the conference, it was criticized as not being neutral. Pervillé in the *Annuaire de l'Afrique du Nord* said that the Conference was interesting mainly for its comparative angle. Often, papers at the conference were given by partisan commentators—such as secondary school teachers and people marked by the Algerian War.

Lastly, we can note that the conference was not a study of the educational chain. My choice of Lyon as an example of the way that the Algerian War is taught in France is an attempt to conduct more detailed research in this area than can currently be found, since it has allowed me to go further than simply examining textbooks, history programs, and examination questions. In particular, I have interviewed teachers, pupils, and two historians, and thus placed more emphasis on what is actually taught (and how and with what results) in schools as well as studying what is supposed to be taught. In this way the book has tried to examine what can be called the educational chain from the Department of Education's decisions to the classroom. This commentator felt that what is actually taught is dependant on local factors such as individual personalities or experiences and the end result of the complex interaction between governments, school principals, teachers, associations, and pupils. Furthermore we will see the way in which what takes place in the classroom—notably through teacher and pupil (sociological) identity—in itself helps us to explain how the war is taught. What is meant here by this term is that teachers and pupils will be shown in some cases to have important links to the Algerian War. Examples of this are those of *pied-noir* or Maghrebian origin. These links constitute a part of their identity in terms of their personal history, family history, community belonging, knowledge, or interest.

The Family

A chapter of this book will focus on the extent that memories of the Algerian War are being transmitted in families, with a particular focus on the extent that young people of Algerian origin can be said to be challenging dominant narratives of the Algerian War. Again, this is an area where scholars disagree. Benjamin Stora has argued that young people of Algerian origin are key players in developments in French collective memory of the war in Algeria, whereas Claude Liauzu has argued that only a tiny minority of such people are engaged in this kind of memory work. For Stora:

> Sur les circonstances du retour de la guerre d'Algérie dans la société française d'aujourd'hui, un élément domine, le passage des générations. Celui qui a vécu un événement décisif éprouve le désir de laisser une trace. Au soir d'une vie apparaît la nécessité de se délivrer davantage d'un poids, d'un secret ou d'un remords. De leur côté, les jeunes générations éprouvent le besoin de s'inscrire dans une généalogie, dans une filiation, de savoir quelle a été l'attitude de père ou du grand-père dans cette guerre. Cette situation-là s'observe dans la jeunesse

française, mais aussi dans la jeunesse d'origine algérienne. (One element in particular is the most important in explaining the return of the Algerian War in French society: generations. Generations that live through a decisive event feel the need to leave a trace. In the twilight of a life one feels more acutely the need to rid oneself of a burden, a secret or remorse. Younger generations want to find their origins, to know what the attitude of their father or grandfather was in this war. This situation is discernible in French youth, but also in youth of Algerian origin.)[112]

Stora goes on to say that he feels that a new group is important: children and grandchildren of Algerian immigrants. For him: "Ils veulent, au contraire, comprendre le présent qu'ils vivent au quotidien comme exclus, ou stigmatisés. Dans cette recherche, ils butent sur la question coloniale. A partir de là, ce nouveau groupe bouscule le récit traditionnel de l'Algérie coloniale" (They want to understand a present that everyday excludes or stigmatizes them. In this quest, they are faced with the colonial question. From this position, this new group challenges and overturns the traditional narrative of colonial Algeria).[113] Stora has defended this view several times. My literature review has revealed that this is an area where scholars disagree. Claude Liauzu in an article in 1999 has argued:

> La "Marche des Beurs" de 1983 a ouvert une nouvelle phase. Au delà de l'action directement politique, un travail culturel, une quête identitaire ont été engagés. Ils sont à l'origine de la création de l'association "Au nom de la mémoire", du livre et du film de Yamina Benguigui, *Mémoires d'immigrés*, de publications, etc. Mais cela concerne-t-il la majorité? Dans les situations d'anomie, dans les banlieues en déréliction, dans les familles désagrégées, ce qui l'emporte c'est sans doute l'impossibilité d'accéder à une mémoire, de se reconnaître et d'être reconnu dans l'histoire enseignée. (The "Marche des Beurs" in 1983 inaugurated a new phase. Beyond the directly political action, a cultural project, a search for identity have been begun. They have given rise to the creation of the association "Au nom de la mémoire" (In the name of memory), to the book and the film by Yamina Benguigui entitled *Mémoires d'immigrés* (Memories of Immigrants), to publications, etc. But does this involve the majority? In situations of anomy, in run down housing estates, in broken up families, what certainly occurs is the impossibility of reaching or obtaining a memory, of recognising and being recognised in the history which is taught.)[114]

A chapter of this book will therefore discuss to what extent previously marginalized groups can be said to have challenged dominant narratives of the Algerian War. Can one identify in contemporary France any such challenges? If so, how are these challenges expressed and channeled? Or do these memories continue to be repressed and occluded? It draws mainly on secondary sources on collective memory, ethnicity, *beurs* and *harkis*. It also draws on interviews conducted with pupils of Algerian origin. Do these pupils learn much from their families relating to the Algerian War? How does what is taught compare to what is discussed in families? Is the Algerian War discussed in families? If not, what are the implications for the families? The central thrust of my readings has been the concept of

Identity, with particular reference to the role that historical representations and memory (may) play in constructions of "group" identity.[115]

The Media

The Algerian War has dramatically resurfaced in contemporary France—principally through media coverage (predominantly in *Le Monde*) which has discussed the French army's use of torture during the Algerian conflict. This process began with the publication of Louisette Ighilahriz's testimony in June 2000, intensified with the publication of *Services Spéciaux* by Paul Ausseresses and tailed off after he was tried for "apologie de crimes de guerre" (justifying war crimes). Discussion of the Algerian war in France (re)erupted into the public sphere through coverage of torture in 2000 with the publication in *Le Monde* of Ighilahriz's testimony which described how she had been tortured in 1957. Until this mediatic event the subject of torture was very rarely evoked and its discussion was limited to periodic eruptions such as the publication (in the early 1970s) of General Massu's *La Vraie bataille d'Alger* (The Real Battle of Algiers) or discussion (in the early 1980s) of Jean-Marie Le Pen's activity in Algeria. Ighilahriz's testimony was swiftly followed by interviews with Generals Massu and Bigeard, whom Ighilahriz claimed were present during her torture. Later, General Aussaresses was also interviewed and he admitted using torture and executing prisoners, which led to widespread condemnation. He then published in May 2001 *Services Spéciaux: Algérie 1955-1957*, which caused much furore. Jacques Chirac and Lionel Jospin condemned it, and various groups have since attempted to sue Aussaresses for "apology for war crimes." Beyond *Le Monde* other newspapers have devoted much space to torture and French radio and television have also discussed the question. This media "debate" has lasted two years and has been described as a "very polemical and mediatised reactivation of the memory of the Algerian war."[116] Debate tailed off after Ausssresses and his editors were tried for "apologie de crimes de guerre."

Scholars disagree in their interpretation of these developments. For some the media "debate" in 2000-2001 constituted a move toward a new history of the Algerian War and served to enable individuals who had repressed memories to work through these difficult recollections.[117] They claim that the "passions and tensions which have, in the past, bitterly divided the participants in the war and prevented an objective historical investigation or dialogue, are now receding." The Algerian War is no longer a taboo subject, for "a relative serenity allowed for an objective reflection, ideological tensions had declined, while a certain maturity indicated a willingness to 'regarder la vérité en face et l'assumer' (face up to the truth and assume it)."[118] For others, it was more an example of memory battles taking place in contemporary France and one group (predominantly anti-colonial activists) gaining ascendancy in the collective memory. As Paul Thibauld has noted: "On voit qu'il ne s'agit pas de comprendre ce qu'a été la guerre et d'en tirer les leçons, mais d'y revenir . . . Dans l'esprit des pétitionnaires, la guerre d'Algérie n'est pas terminée" (It clearly was not an attempt to understand the nature of the war and to draw lessons from it, but to relive it . . . In the minds of the signatories of the petition, the Algerian War is not over).[119]

Previous work on the role of the media in creating a collective memory is virtually nonexistent. My literature search has uncovered only one such piece on the print media: Isabelle Lambert's "Vingt ans après" (Twenty Years Later) contribution to *La Guerre d'Algérie et les Français* (The Algerian War and the French), edited by Jean-Pierre Rioux. However, this research was undertaken over ten years ago and had a very specific corpus: media coverage of the Algerian War around its anniversary in 1982. The very recent media coverage has not been the subject of any in depth study to date. Another relevant work is Béatrice Fleury-Vilatte's *La Mémoire télévisuelle de la guerre d'Algérie* (Televisual Memory of the Algerian War). Her book-length work is a study of the televisual memory of the Algerian War since 1962.

My work aims to address the following questions. What did the media coverage portray, and thus remember? Why did it occur when it did? What impact has it had? Furthermore, it is problematic since it was not the first time such issues had been addressed—although the last occasion was a long time ago. Is this then just another example of "repressed memories" violently reappearing in the present soon once more to take back stage; or should it be seen as a new turn toward more sustained public sphere discussion of the Algerian conflict?

This chapter has reviewed literature linked to French collective memory of the Algerian War, and provided a theoretical framework for and general background to the topic. Let us now turn to our detailed case study of three vectors of memory.

Notes

1. See Jean-Pierre Rioux, "Trous de mémoire," *Télérama* (1995), 90-92.

2. See Benjamin Stora, "1999-2003, guerre d'Algérie, les accélérations de la mémoire," in *La Guerre d'Algérie: 1954-2004, la fin de l'amnésie*, ed. Mohammed Harbi and Benjamin Stora (Paris: Robert Laffont, 2004).

3. See Raphaëlle Branche and Sylvie Thénault's theses, that were both quickly published as books: Raphaëlle Branche, *La torture et l'armée pendant la guerre d'Algérie* (Paris: Gallimard, 2001); Sylvie Thénault, *Une drôle de justice, les magistrats dans la guerre d'Algérie* (Paris: La Découverte, 2001).

4. This is the position of Charles-Robert Ageron. On the question of the *harkis*, one can understand his position given that he was criticized and accused of revisionism, hence the title of one of his articles "'Drame des harkis' mémoire ou histoire?" *Vingtième Siècle*, no. 68 (October-December 2000): 3-15.

5. Claude Liauzu, "Mémoires souffrantes de la guerre d'Algérie," *L'Histoire*, no. 260 (December 2001): 32.

6. Pierre Vidal-Naquet, "Algérie, du témoignage à l'histoire," *Le Monde*, 14 September 2001.

7. Jean-Pierre Rioux, "La flamme et les bûchers," in *La Guerre d'Algérie et les*

Français, ed. Jean-Pierre Rioux (Paris: Fayard, 1990), 497-508.

8. Alec G. Hargreaves, "France and Algeria 1962-2002: turning the page?" *Modern and Contemporary France* 10, no. 4 (2002): 445-47.

9. Benjamin Stora and Mohammed Harbi, eds., *La Guerre d'Algérie 1954-2004: la fin de l'amnésie* (Paris: Robert Laffont, 2004).

10. Jean-Pierre Rioux, ed., *La Guerre d'Algérie et les Français* (Paris: Fayard, 1990).

11. Benjamin Stora, *La Gangrène et l'oubli: la mémoire de la guerre d'Algérie* (Paris: La Découverte, 1992).

12. Robert Frank, "Les troubles de la mémoire française," in *La Guerre d'Algérie et les Français*, ed. Jean-Pierre Rioux (Paris: Fayard, 1990), 604.

13. Rioux, "La flamme et les bûchers."

14. Editorial, "Notre mémoire algérienne", *Le Monde*, 5 February 1999, 14.

15. Benjamin Stora, interview, "Cicatriser l'Algérie," in *Oublier nos crimes: l'amnésie nationale, une spécificité française?* ed. Dimitri Nicolaidis (Paris: Editions Autrement, Série Mutations, 1994, no. 144), 229. "(Dans la France de nos jours)" added by me to clarify the context of the quotation.

16. Stora, "Cicatriser l'Algérie," 240.

17. Frank, "Les troubles de la mémoire française,"603.

18. Rioux, "La flamme et les bûchers," 502.

19. Stora, "Cicatriser l'Algérie," 228.

20. Stora, "Cicatriser l'Algérie," 233.

21. Rioux, "La flamme et les bûchers," respectively 497, 498, 507, and 508.

22. Charles-Robert Ageron, "Une histoire de la guerre d'Algérie est-elle possible en 1992?" in *La Guerre d'Algérie dans l'enseignement en France et en Algérie* (Paris: CNDP, 1993), 155-58.

23. Benjamin Stora, "Indochine, Algérie, autorisations de retour," *Libération*, 30 April -1 May 1992, 5.

24. Benjamin Stora, "Quelques réflexions sur les images de la guerre d'Algérie," in *La Guerre d'Algérie et les Algériens 1954-1962*, ed. Charles-Robert Ageron (Paris: Armand Colin, 1997), 339.

25. Pierre Nora's work has introduced the concept of the acceleration of history which he describes as: "An increasingly rapid slippage of the present into a historical past that is gone for good, a general perception that anything and everything may disappear." See Pierre Nora, "Between Memory and History: Les Lieux de Mémoire," *Representations*, no. 26 (Spring 1989): 7.

26. Rousso, *The Vichy Syndrome*, 2.

27. Nora, "Between Memory and History," 8.

28. John Talbott, *The War Without a Name: France in Algeria, 1954-1962* (London: Faber and Faber, 1981). Bertrand Tavernier and Patrick Rotman, *La Guerre sans nom*, 1991 (film).

29. Also important is the way in which this has been a process, started in September 1997 when Jean-Pierre Masseret, Secretary of State for Veterans, first gave a speech in which he in public verbally used the term "the Algerian War." This process ran through to 10 June 1999 when the French Parliament passed a law making official the use of the term "guerre d'Algérie" in legal texts.

30. Leading article in *La Voix du Combattant*, no. 1644 (April 1999), 6-7.

31. For example *L'Ancien d'Algérie*, published monthly by the FNACA.

32. "La Mémoire de la guerre d'Algérie," editorial in *Le Monde*, 12 November 1996,

18.

33. Nor are they the only group to have sites of memory. Indeed, many sites of memory associated with *pieds noirs* date from the colonial period/1960s. See Alain Amato, *Monuments en Exil* (Paris: Editions de l'Atlanthrope, 1979).

34. Nomenclature remains problematic here. Technically there were no Algerians before 1962. But only a relatively small percentage of people in Algeria had French citizenship. Therefore in many domains a whole host of names may and have applied: Français de souche nord-africaine (French of North African descent), Français musulmans d'Algérie (Muslim French of Algeria) . . .

35. Guy Pervillé, "Bibliographie critique sur la guerre d'Algérie," *l'Annuaire de l'Afrique du Nord*, 1992, 1179.

36. Claude Liauzu, "Voyage à travers la mémoire et l'amnésie: le 17 octobre 1961," *Hommes et Migrations*, no. 1219 (May-June 1999): 56-61.
Abdallah, Mogniss, H. 2000, "Le 17 octobre et les médias. De la couverture de l'Histoire immédiate au 'travail de mémoire,'" *Hommes et Migrations*, no. 1228, (November-December 2000): 125-33.

37. Dufay, François, "L'Octobre noir de Maurice Papon" in an edition entitled "La France malade, de sa mémoire," *Le Point*, no. 1311 (November 1, 1997): 54.

38. Florence Beaugé, "Le général Massu exprime ses regrets pour la torture en Algérie," *Le Monde*, 22 June 2000, 6.

39. We can contrast MacMaster 2002, Thibault 2000.

40. See Jean-Jacques Jordi and Mohand Hamoumou, *Les harkis, une mémoire enfouie* (Autrement, 1999).

41. "Jacques Chirac demande une journée d'hommage aux harkis," *Le Monde hébdomadaire*, 17 February 2001, 10.

42. *Djazairinfos* no. 3, February-March 2003.

43. Pierre Nora, "Between Memory and History: Les Lieux de Mémoire," *Representations*, no. 26 (spring 1989): 7-25; on the difference between memory and history see pp. 8-9 or the introduction to Pierre Nora, ed., *Les Lieux de mémoire* (Paris: Gallimard, 1984-1992). Henry Rousso, *Le Syndrome de Vichy* (Paris: Le Seuil, Second Edition, 1990); see 10-13.

44. Rousso, *Le Syndrome*, 253.

45. Published annually by the CNRS ("Centre National de Recherche Scientifique:" French National Centre for Scientific Research).

46. Guy Pervillé, "Le point sur la guerre d'Algérie," *Historiens et Géographes*, no. 293 (February 1983): 636.

47. Bernard Droz and Evelyne Lever, *Histoire de la guerre d'Algérie 1954-1962* (Paris: Le Seuil, 1982), 363.

48. Vitalis Cros, *Le temps de la violence* (Paris: Ed. Presses de la Cité, 1971); Charles de Gaulle, *Mémoires d'espoir : Le renouveau* (Paris: Plon, 1970); Christian Fouchet, *Au service du général de Gaulle* (Paris: Plon, 1971); Raoul Salan, *Mémoires : fin d'un empire* (Paris: Presses de la Cité, 1972-1974).

49. Droz and Lever, *Histoire*, 358.

50. Droz and Lever, *Histoire*, foreward.

51. Guy Pervillé, speaking at "Les Agoras Méditerranéennes" held in Marseilles 26-29 October, 1983, published in *Historiens et Géographes*, no. 308 (March 1986).

52. Guy Pervillé, "Bibliographie critique sur la guerre d'Algérie," *l'Annuaire de l'Afrique du Nord* (1992), 961.

53. Pervillé, "Bibliographie," 962.

54. Alain-Gérard Slama, "La cicatrice ouverte," *Le Point*, no. 899, (11 December

1989), 18.
55. Benjamin Stora, quoted in Kajman, "L'Algérie de la deuxième mémoire," 15.
56. Stora, "Indochine, Algérie, autorisations de retour," 5.
57. Respectively in *l'Annuaire de l'Afrique du Nord* 1993, 865; and 1995, 1096.
58. "La mémoire enfouie de la guerre d'Algérie," *Le Monde*, 5 February 1999, 1 and 9.
59. "La mémoire enfouie," 1.
60. Guy Pervillé, "Bibliographie critique sur la guerre d'Algérie," *l'Annuaire de l'Afrique du Nord*, 1976.
61. Claire Mauss-Copeaux, *Les Appelés en Algérie: la parole confisquée* (Paris: Hachette, 1999), 7.
62. Philip Dine, "(Still) *A la recherche de l'Algérie perdue*: French Fiction and Film, 1992-2001," *Historical Reflections* vol. 28, no. 2, (summer 2002): 255-75.
63. *La Guerre d'Algérie dans l'enseignement en France et en Algérie* (Paris: CNDP, 1993).
64. *La Guerre d'Algérie dans l'enseignement*, 155.
65. Charles-Robert Ageron, ed., *La Guerre d'Algérie et les Algériens 1954-1962* (Paris: Armand Colin, 1997).
66. Ageron, *La Guerre d'Algérie*, 4.
67. Benjamin Stora, "Quelques réflexions sur les images de la guerre d'Algérie," in *La Guerre d'Algérie et les Algériens 1954-1962*, ed. Charles-Robert Ageron (Paris: Armand Colin, 1997), 339.
68. David Thelen, "Memory and American History," *The Journal of American History*, vol. 75, no. 4 (March 1989): 117.
69. Halbwachs, *Les Cadres sociaux*, xxiii. The use of the pronoun "il" (he) refers to a man in the original text.
70. Rioux, *La Guerre d'Algérie et les Français*, 501.
71. Gérard Namer, in the postface to Maurice Halbwachs, *Les Cadres sociaux de la mémoire* (Paris: Albin Michel, 1994), 321.
72. Derek Middleton and David Edwards, *Collective Remembering* (London: Sage, 1990), 1.
73. Michael Billig and David Edwards, "La construction sociale de la mémoire," *La Recherche* vol. 25, no. 267 (July-August 1994): 742.
74. Middleton and Edwards, *Collective Remembering*, 9.
75. Billig and Edwards, "La construction sociale de la mémoire," 744. My use of italics.
76. Gérard Namer, "Quand la société batît son passé," *Sciences Humaines* no. 43 (October 1994): 29. My use of italics.
77. Namer in Halbwachs, *Les Cadres sociaux*, 321.
78. Thelen, "Memory and American History," 1121.
79. Thelen, "Memory and American History," 1121.
80. Paul-Laurent Assoun, "Le sujet de l'oubli selon Freud," *Communications*, no. 49 (1989): 98.
81. Frank, "Les troubles de la mémoire française," 603-8.
82. Assoun, "Le sujet de l'oubli selon Freud," 102.
83. Nicole Czechowski and Claudie Danzinger (eds.), *Deuils. Vivre c'est perdre* (Paris: Editions Autrement, 1992).
84. Gianni Vattimo, "L'impossible oubli," in *Usages de l'oubli*, Yosef H. Yerushalmi, Nicole Loraux et al. (Paris: Le Seuil, 1988), 77.

85. Vattimo, "L'impossible oubli," 77.

86. Ernest Renan, "What is a Nation?" in *Nation and Narration*, ed. Homi Bhabha (London: Routledge, 1990), 11.

87. Yosef H. Yerushalmi, "Réflexions sur l'oubli", in *Usages de l'oubli*, Contributions from Yosef H. Yerushalmi, Nicole Loraux at the conference held in Royaumont (Paris, Le Seuil, 1988), 9.

88. David Lowenthal, *Our past before us: Why do we save it?*, (London: Temple Smith, 1981), 11 and 10 respectively.

89. Lowenthal, *Our past before us*, 17.

90. Benedict Anderson, *Imagined Communities* (London, New York: Verso, 1991), 12.

91. Anderson, *Imagined Communities*, 11.

92. Homi Bhabha, *Nation and Narration* (London: Routledge, 1990), 1.

93. Eric Hobsbawm and Terence Ranger, eds., *The Invention of Tradition* (Cambridge: Cambridge University Press, 1992), 1 and 2.

94. Hobsbawm and Ranger, *The Invention of Tradition*, 271.

95. Hobsbawm and Ranger, *The Invention of Tradition*, 272.

96. Jay Winter and Emmanuel Sivan, eds., *War and Remembrance in the Twentieth Century* (Cambridge: Cambridge University Press, 1999), 9.

97. Winter and Sivan, *War and Remembrance*, 17 and 38.

98. Winter and Sivan, *War and Remembrance*, 23.

99. Yerushalmi, "Réflexions sur l'oubli," 13.

100. Yerushalmi, "Réflexions sur l'oubli," 11.

101. Yerushalmi, "Réflexions sur l'oubli," 16.

102. Billig and Edwards, "La construction sociale de la mémoire," 745.

103. Hobsbawm and Ranger, *The Invention of Tradition*, 271.

104. Pierre Nora, "Between Memory and History," 20.

105. Michael Billig, *Freudian Repression* (Cambridge: Cambridge University Press, 1999), 10.

106. Quoted in Jane Freedman and Carrie Tarr, eds., *Women, Immigration and Identities in France* (Oxford & New York: Berg, 2000), 175.

107. *Mémoire et enseignement de la guerre d'Algérie*, 5.

108. Danièle Djamila Amrane-Minne, "La guerre d'Algérie à travers les manuels français et algériens de classes terminales," in *Mémoire et enseignement de la guerre d'Algérie: actes du colloque, 13-14 mars 1992, Paris*, vol. 2 (Paris: Institut du Monde arabe/Ligue de l'enseignement, 1993), 375.

109. Alain Coulon, *Connaissance de la guerre d'Algérie. Trente ans après : enquête auprès des jeunes Français de 17 à 30 ans* (Paris: Université de Paris VIII, 1993).

110. Paul Fournier, "La guerre d'Algérie dans les manuels scolaires de Terminale," *Historiens et Géographes*, no. 308 (March 1986): 897-98; and Guy Pervillé, "La guerre d'Algérie dans les manuels scolaires de Terminale," *Historiens et Géographes*, no. 308 (March 1986): 893-97.

111. Jean-Pierre Rioux, preface to *La Guerre d'Algérie dans l'enseignement en France et en Algérie* (Paris: CNDP, 1993), 6.

112. Benjamin Stora, "La mémoire retrouvée de la guerre d'Algérie?" *Le Monde*, 19 March 2002.

113. Stora, "La mémoire retrouvée?"

114. Liauzu, "Voyage à travers la mémoire et l'amnésie," 61.

115. I use the term "group" aware of its problems and limitations, hence the inverted commas. Ethnicity is a complex concept, which is difficult to define and even more so to

use in practice. In particular, one must remember that there is a different ascribed ethnicity" and "prescribed ethnicity." In France matters are fur by the Republican principle of assimilation that makes any reference to ethnicity all the more difficult. Hence, Maghrebis may feel closer to the culture of the French population than to that of their parents whereas majority French respondents may see them as Arab rather than French. See Alec G. Hargreaves and Mark McKinney, eds., *Post-colonial cultures in France* (London and New York: Routledge, 1997), 19 for a discussion of opinion polls that demonstrate this phenomenon.

116. Jack Lang, French Education Minister, in a speech given in August 2001, accessed at www.education.gouv.fr/discours/2001/algeriejl.htm.

117. For example see Neil MacMaster, "The Torture Controversy (1998-2002): Towards a 'New History' of the Algerian War?" *Modern and Contemporary France* 10, no. 4 (2002): 449-59.

118. MacMaster, "The Torture controversy," 449 and 457.

119. See Paul Thibault, "La torture en Algérie. L'avenir en panne," *Le Monde*, 14 December 2000, 17.

Chapter Two

Pedagogy: Imagining the French Nation

Introduction

The French State education system is a crucial way that collective memory is transmitted in France across generations. Individual and group collective memories are here transformed into common national memories. Whereas the family is a small important group in the socialization of young people, and one that, as Halbwachs has shown us, moulds its own collective memory and provides the social frames of memory to individuals, the education system operates at the national "public sphere" level. The media also operate at the national "public sphere" level, but education is run by the State, whereas the media are no longer controlled by the State and, as we will see in a subsequent chapter, the media are also an important site of contestation for private "memory activists." As Rousso reminds us, the educative vector is the "the mode of social transmission of memory par excellence."[1] Hobsbawm's work has shown the crucial role of the *école de la République* (Republican school) in constructing the French nation during the Third Republic, the period when the Republican model of society managed to impose itself and turn "peasants into Frenchmen."[2] During that time the school subjects of history and philosophy were particularly important due to their civic content. Commenting on the teaching of philosophy in France, Vincent Descombes remarks: "Que le professeur de philosophie, en France, soit un fonctionnaire de l'Etat explique que cet enseignement ait inévitablement des incidences politiques" (In France the philosophy teacher is a civil servant, therefore the teaching of this subject inevitably has political ramifications).[3] The 1980s and 1990s have demonstrated that public education is still a site of considerable importance in France—evident in particular in the *affaires du foulard* (Islamic headscarf affairs) and the role of education in Jacques Chirac's "sursaut laïque" (secular renewal).[4]

This chapter examines the way the Algerian War is taught in history classes in French secondary schools in *terminale* (the final year of high school). The war has been taught here since 1983, but how is it taught? Is the Algerian War taught in significant detail in France? To answer these questions, it draws on interviews with Serge Berstein and Jean-Pierre Rioux that were conducted in Paris in February 2000. Berstein is a historian, co-chairman of the history GTD (Groupe de Travail Disciplinaire: group that designs the program) between 1993 and 1998 and longtime editor of a *terminale* history textbook published by Hatier. Rioux is a historian and "Inspecteur général de l'éducation nationale" (Inspector of Schools).[5] Both are eminent historians and have key positions in the French education system at the national level. The teacher link section draws on eighteen interviews conducted with history teachers in secondary schools in the Lyon area in the period from February 1998 to June 1999. Eight interviews were also conducted with twelve pupils in *terminale* history classes in Lyon. The chapter also examines textbooks and examination questions.[6]

In this way we are able to examine the "educational chain" from the State to the pupil. Unlike previous work on the question, we are able to go beyond representations in textbooks and examination questions to obtain a better idea of what is actually taught, to what effect, and why. We can compare what is supposed to be taught with what is actually taught and learnt and reflect on why this is the case. The chapter is therefore organized into different sections—the State-prescribed link, where we examine the program, textbooks, examination questions; the teacher link drawing predominantly on interviews with teachers; and the pupil link examining what pupils say about history classes. As we examine each link in the chain we will see that less and less is being taught on the Algerian War as a shift has taken place from factual history to more global history. The amount of time spent on the war in class and the number of pages in textbooks are two of the ways that we can determine how much is taught on the war. Furthermore, the Algerian War is not studied in itself in the program—rather the program covers the French Fourth and Fifth Republics, Charles de Gaulle's presidency and Decolonization. The context for the study of the Algerian War has important consequences for what is discussed on this topic. Examination questions follow this model and teachers emphasized in interviews the importance of the chapter to the content they give on the Algerian War. Pupils are therefore quite weak on the details of the Algerian War. Qualitatively the classes involve above all note-taking, limiting the possibility of testimony or film on the war in Algeria. This situation contrasts very strongly with that of the teaching of World War Two and Vichy. While teachers are constrained by the program, fascinating differences emerged between how much time was spent on the Algerian War in class. Let us now turn to look at each of these points in more depth.

The State-Prescribed Link in Teaching

The Program

Throughout France all school subjects have a national program that is approved by the Ministry for Education and that teachers follow in the classroom. The program is a very powerful determining force in actual lesson content. Teachers can devote more or less time to the Algerian War in their actual class if they want, but there are significant constraints (the examination, time) that limit their margin for maneuver. What takes place in the classroom generally corresponds closely to what is supposed to be taught. The educational authorities (program designers, *Inspections*, government) therefore significantly influence and control what is actually taught. The program especially dictates the context in which the Algerian War is studied and therefore what the war is used to show. That said, the program on its own is not very informative and it is important to reflect on the relationship between the program, the questions set at the *baccalauréat*, the textbooks, and the actual lessons given.

The program that is published only gives the broad topics to be studied and no details of what elements within these topics are to be covered. The *Instructions officielles* (Official Instructions) and other accompanying documents give more indications but still not a clear idea of what will be taught. Textbooks are one way of having a much clearer idea of the actual content of the program. They are effectively an interpretation of the program and also take into consideration the examination questions set on the program in order to offer a textbook that prepares the pupil for the *baccalauréat* examination. The examination questions set are a very powerful determining factor in textbook content and actual lesson content as both editors and teachers attempt to prepare the pupils for the examination.

Until September 1983 *terminale* history programs in France studied the period from 1914 to 1945 (and a broad study of postwar civilizations that was taught very little). Since then the program has studied "Le monde de 1939 à nos jours" (The World from 1939 to the Present Day), therefore including events such as the Algerian War, May 1968, and the Cold War. Two reforms to this program have taken place since 1983, one implemented in September 1989 and the other coming into effect in September 1998. The 1983 and 1989 programs were developed by the *Inspection générale* whereas the later reform was designed by the *Groupe de Travail Disciplinaire* (GTD) chaired by Serge Berstein and Dominique Borne. The program that came into effect in 1998 has three parts: "La Seconde Guerre mondiale" (The Second World War), "Le monde de 1945 à nos jours" (The World from 1945 to the Present Day) and "La France depuis 1945" (France since 1945). The Second World War was not studied in *terminale* in the 1989 program and has therefore been reintroduced in *terminale*. However the main change between 1983 and 1989/1998 is the nature of the program—the type of history taught—as can be seen clearly in the wording of the *Instructions officielles* that accompany the programs. Concerning the 1983 program, the *Instructions officielles* stated that: "Il faudra donner une place importante à la décolonisation, en mettant l'accent sur ses facteurs historiques, ses caractères, ses étapes" (Decolonization should occupy an important place, with the accent put on its historical factors, its characteristics and its stages).[7] By 1989 however the *Instructions officielles* also stated: "Le récit des différents conflits n'est pas exigible. Il suffit de les localiser, d'en proposer un typologie et surtout de les situer dans le système international" (The history of the different conflicts is not necessary. It suffices to localize them, propose a typology and above all situate them in the international system).[8]

This trend has continued and indeed accelerated since the 1998 program as, according to Berstein, the aim of the program was for teachers to "modifier en profondeur les pratiques de l'enseignement de l'histoire pour faire que ce qui est enseigné soit, non plus une accumulation indigeste de faits, mais une vision problématique de l'évolution historique" (profoundly modify the way the teaching of history is practiced so that what is taught is, rather than a vain accumulation of facts, a problematic vision of historical evolution)[9] and thus to avoid the study of short periods in detail as: "Cela exclut, par exemple, qu'on étudie la crise de Cuba" (That rules out, for example, studying the Cuban missile crisis).[10]

These moves have significantly changed how the Algerian War is taught as we will see below in numerous comments in interviews with teachers 1998-1999. The trend began in 1989 so, in terms of information transmitted on the Algerian War through history classes in *terminale*, we can say that since this time not much information has been transmitted; indeed less and less. Berstein in the interview conducted by the author said that what was important in the program was to focus on "grandes évolutions" (broad developments) and "qu'on ne se perde pas dans le détail événementiel" (get lost in factual detail). However he accepted that to describe these "grandes évolutions" (broad developments) to teenagers in *terminale* details would be necessary, but these should be "faits significatifs, événements importants qui veulent dire quelque chose pour l'évolution globale des sociétés" (significant facts, important events that are relevant to global evolutions in societies). In this way the Algerian War is not studied in itself, including a study of the events of the war. Rather than being studied for its own sake, the conflict is itself an event in wider phenomena. It is the wider phenomena that are studied through reference, in part, to the Algerian War. So, while studying "Decolonization" or the "French Fourth and Fifth Republics" teachers mention aspects of the Algerian War. For Berstein:

> La guerre d'Algérie ne se suffisant pas à mon avis elle-même mais prenant sens ou dans le courant général de la décolonisation qui est prévu dans les programmes, ou dans l'histoire de la France qui est également prévue dans les programmes. (The Algerian War in my opinion does not suffice in itself rather it becomes meaningful either in the general current of decolonization that is included in the program, or in the history of France that is also a part of the program; Berstein 2000.)

While this commentator can accept how important it is for pupils to understand the significance of an event and to situate the event in wider movements, he is sure that this focus considerably reduces the information that is transmitted on the Algerian War and that consequently the program somewhat fails to meet other objectives that it has set itself or been set. These include the "objectif civique" (civic objective) and transmission of memory functions generally accepted as inherent in the teaching of history. In other words what is taught does not include memories of the Algerian War in what is transmitted across generations through this vector of memory. The focus also somewhat contradicts what the program designers have said elsewhere:

> Pour chaque niveau, un sort particulier est réservé à l'histoire nationale. Celle-ci fait l'objet de sujets d'études propres qui supposent un degré de précision plus grand que celui réservé aux autres sujets . . . Il semble non moins légitime de procurer aux jeunes Français ces éléments d'une mémoire nationale qui forge leur identité et de leur permettre d'apprécier la manière dont l'histoire de la France s'intègre dans celle de l'Europe et du monde et en quoi elle s'en différentie. (At each stage, a particular place is reserved for national history. This involves subjects that require a greater degree of precision than for the other subjects . . . It seems no less legitimate to provide French youth with those elements of a national memory that forge their identity and allow them to appreciate how the history of France is integrated in that of Europe and of the world and the ways in which it is different.)[11]

While in this quotation French history is itself firmly anchored in European and world history, explicit mention is nonetheless made of the importance of national history and the way that French history is primordial for memory and pupils' identity. Rioux also said in my interview with him that the way the Algerian War is taught is heavily influenced by the type of history that is to be taught when he stated that in mainland France in future there will be (and already have been for some years) far fewer questions on the Algerian War since the aim is to set questions on "grands ensembles" (broad ensembles) not "questions ponctuelles" (punctual questions). That means questions on "Décolonisation" (Decolonization) and "Evolution de la France depuis 1945" (Evolution of France since 1945) but not on Algeria or the "guerre d'Algérie proprement dite" (the Algerian War itself).

For Rioux the whole program now is set up to give a "vision mondiale, très générale" (very general, world vision) and to study "grandes questions" (broad questions), so it is not possible to do that for all questions bar the Algerian War, and there is no objective reason to do so. He thinks this poses a problem for certain teachers and those (e.g., some historians) who want to talk more of the Algerian conflict in France and think the conflict is occluded. Yet for him this place of the war in the program is not an example of dissimulation where one denies what happened in Algeria and tries to forget this period, rather results from the desire to put the Algerian War in perspective in decolonization as a whole. In his view it is not possible to isolate the Algerian conflict like that. This approach for him is not necessarily the best solution, he does not know what is, but it partly explains the place of the Algerian War. Rioux in the interview also mentioned how teachers and pupils can work outside of class on this subject. This book however argues that the Algerian War's place in the program, and therefore in history classes, does not reflect its historical or memorial importance.

Unlike the Algerian War, the study of World War Two contrasts with other parts of the program and can be referred to as an "exception." Rioux for example mentioned that it was really only World War Two veterans who were invited into class. Indeed while the study of World War Two is also designed to be a "global study" it is fairly detailed given the way one year is studied for certain themes. This is not a factual military history or a history of all the events during the war, but it is detailed and rich unlike the study of the Algerian War. Its treatment reflects choices and priorities, the memorability of the event, distance from the event, pressure groups, scholarly research, identity, other vectors of memory, and so on. The study of the Second World War clearly overshadows the study of the Algerian War. Pupils in interviews emphasized how long they had spent on the study of the Second World War. The importance of this aspect of the program also emerges in textbooks: one hundred pages, in four chapters, in textbooks that have four hundred pages. It is a very detailed study in both the program and the textbooks. The *Instructions officielles* for teachers for the second section of three that compose the study of World War Two entitled "L'Europe et la France dans la guerre" (Europe and France at War) state:

> À partir d'une carte de l'Europe en 1942, on analysera les formes de l'occupation, les collaborations, les résistances. On insistera sur l'univers concentrationnaire et l'extermination systématique des Juifs et des Tziganes. L'étude de la France ("drôle de guerre," défaite, régime de Vichy, Libération) permettra d'analyser la nature et le rôle du régime de Vichy, les différentes formes de collaboration, le rôle de la Résistance intérieure et de la France libre. (Working from a map of Europe in 1942, we will analyze the forms of occupation, the types of collaboration, and resistance movements. We will put particular emphasis on the concentration camp system and the systematic extermination of the Jews and the Tsiganes. The study of France ["Phoney War," defeat, Vichy regime, Liberation] will allow a study of the nature and the role of the Vichy regime, the different forms of collaboration, the role of the Resistance within France and in Free France.)[12]

Clearly when there is sufficient pressure to study a subject, even within a program described as being "global history," it is possible to study chosen aspects in detail in order to ensure that they are not forgotten but are transmitted to younger generations. The study of World War Two is an exception and has a unique place in the program as both Berstein and Rioux stated in their respective interviews. The wording of the *Bulletin officiel* (Official Government Bulletin) quoted above has not been left to chance and is probably something that has been negotiated at length.

One of the three questions proposed to candidates (from which they would choose one) at the June 1999 *baccalauréat* in France was on the Second World War: "Comment caractériser le régime de Vichy?" (What were the characteristics of the Vichy regime?). What is more, at the June 2000 sitting of the *bacca-*

lauréat, another question was set on Vichy, one of only two questions proposed to pupils. Clearly this is an extremely high proportion of questions on Vichy set in this key national examination, demonstrating the importance of the *baccalauréat*, and more importantly of history classes as a vector of memory. We will also see below the relatively high number of pupils who had attended a testimony given on an aspect of World War Two. It appears that concepts such as deportation or resistance allow the transmission of values in a way that would seem to be judged impossible concerning the Algerian War. Compared to the Algerian War, the Second World War is more memorable *and* its memory is deemed necessary to transmit, in particular through history classes in French secondary schools. While it can be admitted that the Second World War is more important than the Algerian War and that the memory of the Second World War should be transmitted, we need to recognize that the Algerian conflict is more important than two or three pages in four-hundred-page textbooks. However it seems clear that the Algerian War is not an event that can be used to transmit values deemed important by society in the present (especially Resistance). What is required is more of an effort to examine the Algerian War. If this "work of memory" were carried out, values and lessons could be drawn from a greater study of the war in Algeria—the position of conscripts (and their choices) faced with torture occurring around them, the role of the conscripts in not following the *putsch*, the cost and ineffectiveness of war, and the position of soldiers in relation to the State are but a few elements of the Algerian War that are rich in lessons for young people and that could make for a fascinating historical study in classrooms around France.

Berstein and Borne in the 1998 program tried to move away from *histoire événementielle* (detailed factual history) to a more *histoire globale* (global history). This shift has reduced the place of the Algerian War in textbooks and the time spent on this aspect of French history in class. If the Algerian conflict were to be studied autonomously, then other more varied aspects of the war would be covered. This is due to its place in the program and to the nature of any pedagogical discourse. It is not however only the program that dictates what kind of information will be taught but also the examination questions.

The *Baccalauréat*

Reflecting the small place of the Algerian War in the program, few questions are set on this topic at the *baccalauréat*. Geneviève Pastor has qualified the period from June 1984 to 1991 in terms of examination questions on the Algerian War as one of an "espoir deçu" (dashed hopes) since in 1984, the first year that questions were set on contemporary history, a question was set on the Algerian War in Rouen yet for the rest of the 1980s this was never repeated. The question was an essay entitled "La guerre d'Algérie" (the Algerian War) with instructions to discuss the war's development, to examine its origins, its implications in France, and to locate it in the international context. The historian Michel

Winock wrote a possible model answer to the question in the French daily news-paper *Libération*.[13] In it he stated that for people of his generation the Algerian War was more memory than history. He mentioned many of the memories the name brought back and hinted at the boldness of setting such a question in 1984, before describing the place of the Algerian War in decolonization, French his-tory, Algerian history, and other contexts. Clearly, one needs more knowledge of the Algerian War to answer this question than to answer other more general questions (e.g., "French Decolonization") that need knowledge of other subjects (i.e., other decolonizations). The Algerian War is central to the question rather than being an event in wider movements.

Pastor, for the period 1984 to 1989, counts five questions directly on "la guerre d'Algérie" (the Algerian War), seven on "décolonisation" (Decoloniza-tion) and three on "nationalismes et indépendances" (Nationalisms and Inde-pendence Movements) out of a total of roughly three hundred and fifty ques-tions—that is, in all of the *académies* including those abroad such as Morocco, Tunisia, Pondichéry, South America, and North America.[14] She concludes that four fifths of the questions on the Algerian War were set outside of France. In the two years after 1989, one more question on Algeria was set in France—in Poitiers in 1990. It was a textual commentary entitled "Le problème algérien" (The Algerian Problem) based on de Gaulle's speech on September 16, 1959.

This trend continued in the 1990s since, from 1991 to 1997 for the June ses-sions, one question was set in France on the Algerian War out of a total of sev-enty-eight questions on all subjects. In 1993 a textual commentary question was set entitled "De Gaulle face au problème algérien" (De Gaulle and the Algerian Problem) with four documents (radio speeches and press conferences from 1958 to 1961). Four questions were set in France on decolonization in this same pe-riod (nine abroad). Six questions on the French Fourth and Fifth Republics in which the Algerian War can be partially studied were set in France between 1991 and 1997, most of which were "bilan" (appraisal) type questions, that is, analyzing the positive and negative aspects of the Fourth Republic. In 1998 and 1999 no questions were set on the Algerian War. One question was set in 1998 on the Fourth Republic and three questions were set on decolonization that year. In 1999 one question was set on decolonization.

In June 2000 a question was set at the *baccalauréat* on the Algerian War—a textual commentary based on de Gaulle's reaction to the April 1961 putsch by French army generals. This is rare due to the total number of questions we have noted on the Algerian War over the years. Also in 2000 there were only two na-tional questions, whereas before there had been different questions in different *académies*, in itself reducing the statistical likelihood of a question on the Alge-rian War. We will also see below how the change in program has led textbook editors to cut a lot of information on the Algerian War, and teachers to do far less in class on the conflict. It is therefore rather paradoxical that a question on the Algerian conflict be set. The fact that Rioux explicitly mentioned in the in-terview how there would be even fewer questions on the Algerian War in future in examinations, while a question was set in June 2000, shows the importance of the setting of this question. However as the question was a textual commentary on de Gaulle it is the kind of question that had been set before. For the rest of the 1980s and 1990s therefore it is possible to say that the Algerian War has rarely been set on its own as an examination question, and the broad essay subject set in 1984 has not been repeated as the three questions set since then on the war focused on de Gaulle (again reflecting the drive of the program, as will be developed concerning teacher content below) and were all textual commentaries. It is far more common for the Algerian War to be examined in wider subjects such as decolonization, the Fourth Republic, or the Fifth Republic than on its own. As will be seen throughout this chapter, such placing of the Algerian War determines what information on the conflict is used to explain wider phenomena and leads to an incomplete and small study of the war. The fact that the war in Algeria is studied in these wider chapters is therefore extremely important. During one interview, after remarking that the study of the Algerian War could not be a detailed one, a teacher stated:

> On essaie de faire un ensemble pour voir à la fois en quoi c'est un problème de décolonisation—ce qui est l'ensemble du chapitre concerné—et en même temps en quoi ça concerne la vie politique française aussi bien intérieure que internationale. (We try to look at the whole picture to see both how it is a problem of decolonization—the principal relevant chapter—and at the same time how it impacts on French political life both domestically and internationally; Teacher 5.)

Another teacher stated: "La guerre d'Algérie n'est pas vraiment étudiée en elle-même, elle est étudiée plutôt dans les incidences sur la vie politique française" (The Algerian War isn't really studied in itself, rather it is studied in terms of its impact on French political life; Teacher 1). To my mind, in France, the absence of questions that are directly about the Algerian War is very important since it is taught in *terminale* in history at the end of which is the *baccalauréat*; therefore the main aim of teachers is to prepare the pupils for this key examination. As Borne, co-chairman of the history GTD and the head of the *Inspection*, puts it:

> Les sujets posés au baccalauréat dans les différentes académies trahissent la pratique réelle d'un programme dans les classes. Ces sujets établissent, en effet, une sorte de jurisprudence et orientent l'enseignement dispensé par les professeurs. (The questions set at the *baccalauréat* in the different school areas indicate the real practice of a program in the classroom. These topics create, effectively, a sort of hierarchy and orientate the classes given by teachers.)[15]

Furthermore, for commercial reasons, the content of textbooks is heavily influenced by the desire to offer a book that helps pupils to prepare for this examination. Consequently, the method sections in textbooks have certainly improved over the years. These are designed to help students prepare for the *baccalauréat*. They always include plans and proposed models on questions on decolonization, the Fourth or Fifth Republics and never directly on the Algerian War. This is a key way that the Algerian War's importance is minimized in class. One interesting way that the importance of the placement of the Algerian War can be seen is in a survey published in 1985 of the teaching of the *terminale* program. Teachers were asked questions via a written questionnaire. We must note the very important difference between reactions to the study of the Algerian War on its own and those to (its study somewhere in) decolonization. This point could also be made for the reactions to the Occupation (Vichy: top of the list) and the more general topic of World War Two. We can read:

> Quels sont, pour les élèves, les sujets chauds? D'abord, et ce n'est pas une surprise, la France, citée par près de la moitié des enseignants (l'Occupation à elle seule fait réagir près d'une classe sur cinq contre 8 pour cent seulement pour mai 68). La guerre d'Algérie, traitée de façon autonome, arrive en deuxième rang (dans près d'une classe sur trois) . . . Assez loin derrière, la seconde guerre mondiale (13 pour cent), la décolonisation et le Viêt-Nam (11 pour cent) (What, for the pupils, are the hot topics? Firstly, and it's not a surprise, France, cited by almost half the teachers [the Occupation alone leads to reactions in one class out of five compared to only 8 percent for May 1968]. The Algerian War, treated autonomously, is in second place [in nearly one class in three] . . . Quite far behind, the Second World War [13 percent], Decolonization and the Vietnam War [11 percent])[16]

The term "les sujets chauds" (hot topics), while being a somewhat vague term, means the type of subjects that gave rise to pupil reactions, for example, pupil indignation at an event. This survey also showed that what motivated the reactions of pupils was above all family history, a point we will examine in far more detail in a subsequent chapter.

Textbook Content

In addition to the program and examination questions we need to analyze textbooks. Textbooks have received a lot of scholarly attention.[17] The years 1983, 1989 and 1998 all witnessed new programs and therefore new textbook editions. As Henri Gibelin has stated:

> les manuels sont le reflet des programmes définis par le ministère de l'Education nationale. En cela, ils jouent un rôle central. En effet, qui lit les programmes publiés dans le Bulletin Officiel? Les manuels comportent donc tous un exposé des connaissances à acquérir. (textbooks are a reflection of the programs as defined by the Minister for National Education. As such, they play a key role. In effect, who reads the programs published in the *Bulletin Officiel*? The textbooks all contain a synthesis of the knowledge that needs to be acquired.)[18]

Less and less is being included on the Algerian War in textbooks. There was a very pronounced decrease in the number of words (text) on the Algerian conflict between 1995 and 1998. For example, the textbook published by Nathan had 1,600 words on the war in Algeria in 1995 and 1,000 in 1998. The textbook published by Hatier had 2,800 words in 1995 and 600 in 1998; the one published by Belin 1,050 words in 1995 and 500 words in 1998 and the Bordas 1,860 words in 1989 and 1,200 words in 1998. Only two textbooks, those published by Hachette and Bréal, stay the same length on the Algerian War. Very importantly these two textbooks also have the same total number of pages in these years.

For the 1998 editions the average amount of words is 950, amounting to about one and a half pages of text to which can be added on average eleven documents (roughly two pages of documents). In 1995, the average was 1,500 words or about two and a half pages of text to which were added on average sixteen documents. There is therefore significantly less coverage, all the more so if we also take into consideration the findings of Pervillé and Fournier who in 1983 identified an average of about nine or ten pages on the Algerian War, ranging from two to twenty pages. The textbook published by Hatier, edited by Serge Berstein and Pierre Milza (highly instructive given the place of Berstein in the GTD), has experienced the most pronounced changes between 1983 and 1998 as in 1983 there were 3,500 words on the Algerian War and in 1998 only 600 words.

The decrease in the number of words on the Algerian War in textbooks was a point discussed in the author's interview with Berstein. He claimed that "c'est le cas de toutes les questions sans exception" (without exception it is the case of all questions) and said that this was due to "allègements" (cuts) wanted by teachers. For him, it also reflects a change in the role of textbooks: in the past a textbook contained a lot of information, more recently they only contain a summary of information and pupils need the teacher to understand the textbook. Yet we can note that in 1983 the textbook published by Hatier had four hundred and forty-seven pages whereas in 1998 it had three hundred and twenty; so roughly a third less. However in 1983 there were 3,500 words on the Algerian War and in 1998 only 600 words—a reduction of over 80 per cent. The textbook published by Nathan is the same length in 1995 and 1998 in total number of pages but also devotes less space to the Algerian War; and the same can be said of the textbook published by Belin. The textbook published by Bordas however is different on the Algerian War and on the total number of pages. In 1995 it had four hundred and fifty pages and in 1998 three hundred and fifty pages. We can therefore conclude that in some instances the reduction in total number of pages (resulting from a desire to simplify the *terminale* program) is probably to blame for less information on the Algerian War, but that this is not always the case. It is clear that every time there is less space for the war then there is inevitably a lack of explanation, only mention made of points, and fewer points mentioned.

Diachronically there are fewer details, as we can remark in an excerpt of the same section of the Hatier textbook that has changed over time and that contains less detail. In this textbook, while the same aspects of the war are studied in the 1983 and 1993 editions, the text provided is significantly less informative. For example, in the section present in both editions entitled "Les origines de la guerre d'Algérie" (the origins of the Algerian War), that in part examines the problems present in Algeria in 1954, we can read:

1983/1984 edition:

> On trouve en Algérie une agriculture moderne aux mains des Européens, dispo-
> sant de crédits, de machines et tournée vers l'exportation du vin, des céréales,
> des agrumes, des primeurs. L'industrie commence à s'implanter du fait des in-
> vestissements des groupes financiers français.

> Face à ce secteur moderne, l'économie musulmane apparaît archaïque: une agri-
> culture routinière et peu productive; une absence d'emplois industriels condam-
> nant au chômage ou à des emplois précaires la plus grande partie des citadins.
> La majorité des musulmans connaît la sujétion économique.

> (In Algeria there is a modern agricultural sector controlled by the Europeans,
> benefiting from funding, machines and orientated towards exporting wine, cere-
> als, citrus fruit, and early fruit and vegetables. Industry is beginning to develop
> because of investments from French financial groups.

> Compared to this modern sector, the Muslim economy appears archaic: a routine
> and unproductive type of farming; an absence of industrial jobs that leaves the
> vast majority of city dwellers unemployed or employed in insecure positions.
> Most Muslims experience economic subjection.)[19]

1993 edition:

> il existe une agriculture moderne, qui exporte ses produits, et une industrie nais-
> sante, mais elles sont aux mains des Européens, alors que les musulmans prati-
> quent une agriculture archaïque et routinière et connaissent le chômage ou les
> emplois précaires.

> (there is a modern agriculture sector, that exports its products, and a burgeoning
> industry, but they are controlled by Europeans, while Muslims engage in archaic
> and routine farming methods and experience unemployment or jobs lacking se-
> curity.)[20]

In this way the textbooks in 1993/1995 provide less information than previous
editions, a point that was confirmed in interviews with teachers. When asked
whether they have noticed an improvement in textbooks some teachers spoke of
an "allègement" (cutting) or an "appauvrissement" (dumbing down) in terms of
textbook content. Making cuts is not necessarily only the case for the Algerian
War, but the Algerian conflict probably suffers more than certain other subjects
since it has ceased to be a topic in its own right studied in terms of its events, and
has become itself an event in much wider processes.

Other examples can be found to show that from 1995 to 1998 there is generally less information in the textbooks, and more importantly to show what is cut.
In the textbook published by Nathan, comparing the 1995 and the 1998 editions,
the period of the war 1958-1962 is cut and its word length is condensed from
600 words in 1995 to only 130 words in 1998. Details of the violence of the war,
the battle of Algiers, mention of Sakhiet-Sidi-Youssef and the lengthening of

military service to twenty-seven months are also cut. The period of the war after de Gaulle's return to power in the 1998 edition is therefore reduced to a brief mention of public opinion; the putsch; 17 October 1961; Charonne and the Evian peace accords that amounts to 130 words to replace what was previously one page of text. The textbook published by Bordas (1989 and 1995 editions) provides another example of the cutting of the last four years of the war, as well as less on the origins of the war.

Therefore in general less information is available in the 1998 textbooks on the Algerian War. There is less text through the use of an (even) more synthesized wording devoid of explanations and details or development. It is not only a summary of what was in the previous edition but also omits events—the last four years of the war suffering in particular. A poignant example of the way that issues or events are mentioned yet not developed is that of torture. On average torture is described in one or two phrases, that is, perhaps thirty words, and five of the textbooks also provide a document. The question of detail is not only applicable to textbooks' coverage of the war but was also brought up during several interviews as teachers often emphasized the lack of detail on the Algerian War (in actual lessons) by pointing to the spirit or nature of the program. The question of detail will therefore be developed further below as will the way torture is dealt with. An illustration of the general lack of detail in the program was given by one interviewee who, when asked about the content of the lessons on the Algerian War, stated that:

> L'esprit du programme c'est plutôt d'expliquer l'enchaînement des événements sans rentrer dans les détails eux-mêmes . . . Comment on passe d'un simple conflit local à la décolonisation/volonté d'indépendance. (The spirit of the program is more geared towards explaining the sequence of events without really going into the details themselves . . . How a simple local conflict transforms into decolonization/an independence movement; Teacher 4.)

In another interview, a teacher explained how the Algerian War could not be done in detail because of its place in the program (in wider chapters) and the fact that examination questions were not set on this subject. We can also note the concept of the "utility" of what is done in class which will be developed further below:

> La guerre d'Algérie ne tombe pas à l'examen en tant que telle, donc il est déconseillé de s'y arrêter trop longtemps parce que c'est peu utile pour les élèves, donc ils me rapprocheraient de ne pas avoir assez traité les parties qui tombent plus souvent, comme par exemple les relations internationales ou bien l'histoire intérieure de la France. (The Algerian War is not a question set as such in exams, so spending too long on the subject is not recommended because it's not very useful for the pupils, so they would criticize me for not having spent more time on the parts of the program that questions are set on more often, like for example international relations or the domestic history of France; Teacher 5.)

Also, in the 1998 editions of textbooks, in general, fewer documents are presented. Dossiers on the Algerian War are one principal way that the conflict is examined as six of the eight textbooks contain dossiers consisting of two pages of documents. In 1983 Paul Fournier criticized an extensive use of documents that he qualified as "un paravent ou camouflage documentaire" (a documentary screen or camouflage):

> les auteurs s'abritent derrière des documents ou commentaires contradictoires souvent intéressants, mais toujours très nombreux, et livrés à peu près bruts. (the authors hide behind often interesting but contradictory documents and commentary pieces, that are always numerous and presented pretty much as they are.)[21]

The documents provided are very often the same: the "Manifeste/programme du FLN" (Manifesto of the FLN); a quotation of François Mitterrand's or Pierre Mendès France's reactions to the 1 November 1954 uprising; an extract from Mitterrand's book *Le Coup d'Etat permanent* concerning de Gaulle's return to power; a "bilan" of the war; quotations from de Gaulle; Effel's caricature of 13 May 1958, published in the weekly news magazine *L'Express*; a photo of soldiers; OAS tracts, and a photograph of the putsch members all appear in at least three or four of the textbooks.

In terms of the content of the text, the placing of the Algerian War in the much broader contexts and chapters of the French Fourth/Fifth Republic and Decolonization has very important implications for textbook content. Often in the text the origins of the war are given. For example the textbook published by Magnard mentions the different populations and inequality in Algeria, the 1947 reform, the creation of the FLN; but does not present the nationalist movements before 1954. The Algerian War can be presented within decolonization as an "indépendance arrachée" (violent movement towards independence). Some detail of the initial insurrection is given (for example the textbook published by Nathan presents documents on the reaction of the French government and the "proclamation du FLN") as is the increased war effort after 1956 under Guy Mollet. The events of May 1958 are examined in detail, in on average 200 words plus two or three documents (representing an average of twenty per cent of the coverage of the Algerian War) after which there is often very little. Usually the last half of the war is seen through de Gaulle's changes in policy and mention is made of the putsch, the OAS, the exodus or such events are only present in documents. For example in the textbook published by Hatier there is only one paragraph of text on de Gaulle, the "semaine des barricades," the putsch, the OAS and three documents; and in the textbook published by Belin there is only one paragraph of text on de Gaulle's policy change and documents on the OAS.

As will be seen in the following sections, teachers' lessons also follow this model and examine the second and longest half of the war principally via de Gaulle and reactions to de Gaulle's Algerian policy, reflecting the place of the Algerian conflict in wider chapters (the French Fourth and Fifth Republics) in the program and in *baccalauréat* questions. The textbook published by Belin is a good example of the focus in the textbooks on de Gaulle. This textbook provides two supplementary "Plans de composition" (essay plans)—one to answer the question "Le bilan politique de la IVe République est-il seulement négatif?" (Would a political assessment of the Fourth Republic be only negative?) and the other "La présidence de de Gaulle, 1958-69" (The Presidency of de Gaulle, 1958-69). In both the place of the Algerian War is small in the answer, yet these are the questions that teachers and textbooks prepare pupils to answer. In the textbook published by Belin the Algerian War is studied in three separate chapters: Decolonization, Fourth Republic and Fifth Republic. The text from the Decolonization and Fifth Republic chapters essentially concerns de Gaulle and reactions to his policy (less than two hundred words in each chapter). The textbooks published by Bordas, Bréal, Hachette and Magnard are similar. In the latter interest in the Algerian War post-1958 is only in de Gaulle and the "règlement du conflit" (settlement of the conflict) and the oppositions to him (in the putsch, the "semaine des barricades" and the OAS) then the exodus.

Textbooks' treatment of the origins of the Algerian conflict is inherently linked to the fact that the war is not studied in its own right but in the wider chapters in the program of Decolonization and the Fourth (and sometimes Fifth) Republic(s). If we take the example of the textbook published by Belin (1998 edition), it is chapter 15 that examines decolonization. It is fifteen pages long in a textbook that has a little over three hundred and fifty pages. In the chapter there are two hundred words on the Algerian War and nine documents. However those two hundred words do not concern the origins of the war, rather they give a two-hundred-word summary of the war after 1 November 1954, two thirds of which insists on de Gaulle's role in the conflict. The chapter compares different decolonizations (e.g., French versus British and pacific versus violent). This is obviously a vast topic that leaves little place for the Algerian War.

The content of the chapter examines the origins of decolonization in general by examining "La Crise du colonialisme" (The Crisis of the Colonial System), "L'Éveil des nationalismes" (The Awakening of Nationalist Movements) and "L'Épreuve de la Seconde Guerre mondiale" (The Ordeal of the Second World War). The only specific points on the Algerian War are mention on page two hundred and thirty-six of the events of Sétif on 8 May 1945 in a one-page discussion of the general causes of all decolonizations; the fact that France was more reticent to let go of her colonies than other countries on page two hundred and thirty-eight; and the (non-commented) document the "Proclamation du Front de Libération Nationale" (Manifesto of the FLN) on page two hundred and forty-four. While there are limited exceptions, this model seems to be very typical of all textbooks' treatment of decolonization, and of the origins of this movement and of the Algerian War. In the textbook published by Hachette (1998 edition) five lines of text and one document help the pupil to understand the specificity of Algeria. The textbook published by Magnard is not bad on the origins of the war, either. As will be seen below, this textbook content is very much reflected in teacher lessons and pupil knowledge.

There is a universal lack of any detail or explanation. Furthermore, there is almost never a description of the nature of the war or its military aspects, for example battles, *quadrillage* (division of Algeria into zones) and *regroupement* (population regrouping), the role of terrorism, the violence, or the role of the army. Nor is there any reflection on the Algerian side, for example on Algerian nationalism or the war between the FLN and the MNA ("Mouvement National Algérien:" a rival Algerian nationalist movement to the FLN). The *contingent* (conscripts) are never examined (except in the textbook published by Bréal); nor is censorship or literature.

The "Stakes" of the Program

Having identified that the Algerian War is marginalized in the State-prescribed link in teaching, let us now reflect more on why this might be the case.

In addition to factors already considered such as the wider aims of the program, the problem of time, or the preponderant place of World War Two in the program, a crucial point to consider is the role of State education in the French Republic. The Third Republic provides a historical model in which education was used to strengthen the nation notably through the use of history, but also through the teaching of philosophy. The Third Republic's use of education to strengthen the nation cannot be found to the same extent in the Fifth Republic, yet this role is still considered to be present as we can see in numerous comments by observers of or participants in education. For example, Dominique Borne[22] has written that: "même si la fonction de l'enseignement de l'histoire n'est plus tout à fait celle que lui assignaient les fondateurs de la République, la dimension civique, sous une autre forme, reste essentielle" (even if the function of the teaching of history is no longer exactly that given to it by the founders of the Republic, the civic dimension, in another form, remains essential).[23] Indeed, one of the four broad aims of the history program is an "objectif civique" (civic objective). As the authors of the 1998 history program state: "le rôle d'un programme d'histoire est capital pour l'insertion dans la cité, à travers la découverte de ce qui fonde une communauté humaine" (the role of a history program is crucial for insertion into the City, through the discovery of what a human community is built upon).[24]

Such comments are mirrored in those of the former president of the influential French "Association des Professeurs d'Histoire et de Géographie" (French Association of History and Geography Teachers: APHG), Jean Peyrot, for whom: "L'enseignement de l'histoire est fondamentalement un enseignement pour insérer l'individu dans une Cité" (The teaching of history is fundamentally aimed at inserting the individual into a City).[25] For him one of the functions of history is to "transmettre une mémoire collective revue et corrigée à chaque génération" (transmit a collective memory that is reviewed and corrected each generation); and he has stated that: "L'histoire et la géographie sont aussi instruments de cohésion sociale, mémoire d'un groupe qui prend conscience d'un destin commun sur un territoire commun" (History and Geography are also instruments of social cohesion, the memory of a group that becomes conscious of a common destiny on a common territory).[26] In 1996, Rioux, emphasizing the importance of history classes in contemporary France, wrote:

> Jamais, surtout, le pari sur le rôle et la place de l'histoire dans la formation des jeunes n'a été si clairement exprimé . . . *"Donner aux élèves une mémoire, . . . aider à constituer le patrimoine qui permet à chacun de trouver son identité:"* Lavisse ne désavouerait pas. *"Former* à *l'intelligence active:"* il y aura toujours des "hussards noirs" de l'histoire, tant qu'il y aura des enfants qu'il faut aider à grandir en leur apprenant à ne pas oublier. (Never before, above all, has so much emphasis been explicitly placed on the role and place of history in young people's education . . . "Provide pupils with a memory, . . . help to construct a patrimony that allows each pupil to find his or her identity:" Lavisse would approve. "Educate active intelligence:" there will always be "defenders of the Republic" as long as there are children who we need to help grow up and not to forget.)[27]

Peyrot also wrote that: "L'enseignement de l'histoire a pour but de transformer les mémoires individuelles et collectives en une mémoire commune" (The aim of the teaching of history is to transform individual and collective memories into a common memory).[28] The above aims of the program are not reconcilable with a detailed study of the Algerian War since its memory is not a "collective national memory" rather still a series of "group memories." The study in *terminale* of the Algerian War is not a detailed study. If there is no "collective national memory," as Rioux et al. argued in *La Guerre d'Algérie et les Français* (The Algerian War and the French) then Peyrot's "mémoire commune" is highly limited. As Rioux states below the school authorities do not (yet) want to significantly engage with "mémoires individuelles et collectives" of the Algerian War. This position is fairly similar to Ernest Renan's points in "What is a Nation?" Common memories are an integral part of national identity. The stakes are still high in terms of the memory of the Algerian War due to the way various communities still very much exist in French society—communities formed by drafted soldiers, *pieds-noirs*, *harkis*, OAS members, and immigrants who lived through the war (including members or supporters of the FLN, MNA) that still have memories that they do not share with other groups, indeed that separate them from other groups.

Rioux in the interview with the author also mentioned the Republic. This book argues that if we accept Peyrot's definition of school history as the "memory of a group that becomes conscious of a common destiny on a common territory" this involves, as Renan argued, minimizing community memories in the interests of forging national identity. As concerns ethnic minorities, it is also linked to *intégration* (but beyond this group it concerns all groups, here concerned by the Algerian War). The idea of "saying the same thing to all French children" is inherently linked to notions of the Republic. Given the importance of "l'école" in "la République"—indeed they are but one in what is referred to as *l'école de la République*—surely a detailed study of the Algerian War is impossible even forty years after the end of the war. It may be impossible for a long time concerning a subject such as the Algerian conflict (that was so divisive and engendered groups and communities) in the French Republic, and those who look to the education system as a catalyst for changes in the wider memory of the war in Algeria may be wrong to do so since, concerning immigration:

> l'école est parfois tentée par des politiques de reconnaissance, jusqu'au moment où elle se rétracte, incapable de trouver un moyen terme entre un républicanisme négateur des différences, et un droit à la différence qui ouvre la voie au communautarisme. (the school system is sometimes tempted by policies of recognition, until it pulls back, incapable of finding a balance between Republican principles negating differences, and a right to be different that opens the way to communitiarism.)[29]

Michel Wieviorka is talking here of the school and ethnic minorities in general but his comments are applicable to the teaching of the Algerian War in particular. The idea of isolating the Algerian War in *terminale* could be likened to "politiques de reconnaissance" (policies of recognition) in schools concerning immigration whereas a view that favored a "républicanisme négateur des différences" (Republicanism that negates difference) strikes me as analogous with not isolating the Algerian War and avoiding voluntarily attempting to influence and change the memory of the conflict through history classes. One can argue that the principle of "laïcité" (secularism) is used to defend the way the Algerian War is not taught in significantly more detail. A significant effort will need to be made to overcome this particular view of secularism.

History is still an essential component of identity—national and of groups and individuals—and what makes people want to live together in the present is to some extent the past. We partly judge the present community (and consequently act in that community) that we belong to in terms of what we know about its past. For Borne: "Le professeur, conservateur d'un patrimoine culturel, doit entretenir l'histoire de France comme on entretient les monuments du passé" (The teacher, curator of a cultural patrimony, has to maintain the history of France as one would look after past monuments) and he has likened history to "'l'album de photos national' qui soude une communauté comme l'album familial donne l'épaisseur aux familles" ("the national photo album" that binds a community like the family album supports families).[30] However, as we will see below, in the classroom these comments translate as a very small, incomplete and selective study of the Algerian War and on this question we encounter very similar positions to those held by Renan on "historical error" and "forgetting" being necessary. Rioux in the interview with the author mentioned the way the education system did not want to inflame or aggravate memories:

> En l'état c'est cela, pour ne pas non plus je dirais, en isolant la guerre d'Algérie, pour ne pas envenimer je dirais des conflits de mémoire ou des conflits d'appartenance qui peuvent exister à son propos, qui peuvent exister sur la guerre d'Algérie bien sûr . . . Nous ne pensons pas qu'il soit sage d'entretenir ces mémoires à l'école parce qu'il faut donner à tous les jeunes Français un mi-

nimum et une vision d'ensemble. (That broadly explains it, also, I would say, to avoid, by isolating the Algerian War, worsening what I would call memory battles or battles surrounding belonging that can exist concerning this topic, on the Algerian War of course . . . We think it would be unwise to foster these memories at school because we have to provide all young French children with a minimum amount of knowledge and a global view; Rioux 2000.)

These aims of the teaching of history translate for the Algerian War into a minimizing of the division and violence of the war because that is not what provides social cohesion or a desire to live together, principally because the Algerian War still tangibly effects present day France.

Also, we need to acknowledge the importance of negotiating and discussing program content, and wider societal pressures. There are surely many influences on the program designers. We can contrast World War Two and the Algerian War. The Algerian conflict is perhaps currently unlike World War Two/Vichy in so far as its memory still significantly hinders its study. Developments in collective memory in French society can impact upon the teaching of conflicts in the classroom. What is at stake in French society in terms of discussing the Algerian War is still undoubtedly considerable. Clearly there is a significant difference between the memory of Vichy and the memory of the Algerian War, largely emanating from wider society and reflected in the *terminale* program. For Vichy there have been trials, wide coverage in the media, films, and publications, that all arguably lead to pressures on what should be taught in *terminale* favoring a study of World War Two/Vichy. French school authorities would seem to be in the camp of those who think that it is better to forget division rather than bring what has been "repressed" out into the open. Indeed that is not really the role of schools, the program, or textbooks. Berstein in the interview with the author stated:

Faire un manuel scolaire c'est . . . dire d'abord ce qui est historiquement admis par l'ensemble de la communauté scientifique . . . Et il y a ensuite un phénomène . . . de respect de la société. Je veux dire qu'un certain nombre de choses qu'on ne peut inscrire au fond que si la société les accepte, et que il est absolument impossible dans un manuel scolaire de faire valoir un point de vue minoritaire, . . . parce qu'un manuel scolaire doit au fond délivrer une connaissance historique, je dirais même en ce qui concerne l'histoire un contenu civique, mais n'a pas pour objet de choquer une partie de la société. (When one writes a textbook . . . one states what has been historically accepted by the whole scientific community . . . And then there is a phenomenon . . . of respecting society. I mean there are a certain number of things that one can publish only if society accepts them, and it is absolutely impossible in a textbook to defend a minority point of view . . . because a textbook must above all provide historical knowledge, I would say even concerning history a civic content, but is not meant to shock a part of society; Berstein 2000.)

While World War Two and Vichy may still be problematic for French society, much progress has been made, notably since the early 1970s, a fact discernible in its study in *terminale*. The history program (in *terminale*) is a difficult compromise between different interest groups and a fought-over commodity. As Vincent Descombes argued for philosophy:

> Selon la doctrine officielle, le Programme, chef-d'œuvre de cohérence et de rigueur, ferait l'objet d'un consensus unanime. En réalité, il est plutôt le résultat d'un compromis entre les différentes tendances existantes, et c'est pourquoi le Chef-d'œuvre si souvent célébré fait périodiquement l'objet de remaniements importants. (According to official doctrine, the Program, a masterpiece of coherence and rigour, would be supported by a unanimous consensus. In reality, it is more the result of a compromise between different existing factions, so the often celebrated Masterpiece is periodically considerably reworked.)[31]

When Berstein talked in the interview about presenting the Algerian War in textbooks he often used the word "equitable." He talked of respecting the historical reality and respecting different points of view: he explicitly mentioned those of the Algerian nationalists who started and subsequently fought the war, and that of the French government of the time. He then talked of the way one can "distribuer très équitablement les éléments qui sont de nature à deplaire aux uns et à deplaire aux autres plus qu'à plaire aux uns et aux autres" (distribute very equitably the elements that will displease some or others rather than pleasing some and others). Examples were given: saying that the French army tortured and that the FLN used terror to secure the Algerian population's support. He concluded that: "Le tout c'est un équilibre" (It's all a question of balance). The impression he left on me was one of a very fine balancing act being done when one treats the Algerian War (in a textbook), very much reminding me of Descombe's "compromise."

Indeed Berstein in the interview with the author referred to the study of World War Two (in particular Vichy) as an exception or having a unique place in the program. It is one of the only aspects of contemporary history that is studied separately. He justifies this position by describing the Second World War as a "coupure chronologique importante" (an important chronological break), leading to the "renversement de puissances" (reconfiguration of power) and creating a "nouvelle configuration" (new configuration) and, lastly, giving rise to "problèmes ethiques" (ethical problems). Berstein said that not studying the Second World War would pose a problem of "connaissance historique" (historical knowledge) but "surtout" (above all) a "problème civique" (civic problem) because for him "c'est là que les problèmes de mémoire representent les plus lourds enjeux" (that is where what is most at stake memorially). Interestingly he attaches more importance to the civic problem than that of knowledge—supporting the argument of this book that history lessons are still very important for socialization and ultimately identity. Elsewhere in the interview he spoke of the way history classes can be seen to "modeler en quelque sorte la connaissance historique qu'ont les futurs citoyens des événements du passé" (forge in some way the historical knowledge that future citizens have of the past; Berstein 2000). While the Second World War is more important in world and French history than the Algerian War, I do not think the above reasons given to justify the exceptional place given to the study of the Second World War in *terminale* apply exclusively to that conflict. Indeed the Algerian War could be described in virtually the same way, opening up the possibility of another program where the Algerian War would have a different, more central place; were that what one wanted. At present, and so far, it is not, arguably due to the fact that the past (a knowledge of which is to a large extent acquired by the study of history) is essential to present identity.

The Teacher Link

Teacher Choices and the Change in Program

Overall there is relatively little difference between what is supposed to be taught and what is actually taught. Most teachers do similar things in class in like manner and for similar amounts of time, and these lessons given by teachers clearly correspond to what is supposed to be taught.

However, in practice there is also a certain amount of choice on the part of the teacher as to what to teach. A lot of teachers in my sample insisted on this point when talking about how they decided what to teach. For one: "Ca me paraît important. C'est l'un de mes choix" (It seems important to me. It's one of my choices; Teacher 17). She also said: "J'y passe le temps qu'il faut passer, je crois . . . parce que je crois que c'est important, donc plus que ce que me disent les programmes ou les inspecteurs" (I spend the necessary time, I think . . . because I believe that it's important, so more than what the program or the inspectors tell me to do). Another teacher stated:

> Bien entendu, pour la guerre d'Indochine et pour la guerre d'Algérie on est amené à faire peut-être un peu plus que le programme officiel prévoit pour des raisons un peu d'instruction civique, enfin de formation des élèves . . . à leur rappeler . . . enfin leur apprendre quelque chose qu'ils connaissent mal. (Of course, for the war in Indochina or the Algerian War we are led to do perhaps a bit more than the official program specifies for reasons of civic instruction, or educating the pupils . . . remind them . . . or teach them something that they know little about; Teacher 4.)

This choice can be especially where to study the war or how long to spend on the war. Often choosing one subject inevitably means sacrificing another. Teachers frequently talked of spending more time on the Algerian War being "to the detriment" of other subjects and certain teachers said that they would not have time to finish the program due to the choices they had made (insisting on one part of the program; not necessarily the Algerian War).

In the group talking about the 1997-1998 year the maximum time spent on the war was six hours, the minimum was thirty minutes, and the average was two and a half hours. There is a large homogeneity (and influence of the State-prescribed link) because most teachers hover very close to the average time spent (although this does not rule out significant differences between minimum and maximum times). In the group talking about the 1998-1999 year the maximum time spent on the war was three hours, the minimum was thirty minutes, and the average was one and a half hours. Despite teachers' insistence that it is they who decide what to teach, there is for most teachers' classes surprisingly little difference between program, textbook, and classroom contents in terms of the sort of information that is given (especially in terms of what is taught rather than for how long or where). Nonetheless, there is scope for initiative on the part of individual teachers, and, as my research shows, such shifts in emphasis can tell us important things about the personal and societal factors that may influence the application of ministerial directives within specific classrooms. Furthermore, such factors that motivate teachers to do more on the Algerian War (or pupils to be more interested in the subject) are in themselves ultimately taken into consideration in the State-prescribed link, for example in terms of the desire not to aggravate conflictual memories, as was shown in the previous section.

This book argues that there is not sufficient wider societal pressure to study the war in considerable depth, so that what is imposed is a very partial consideration of the Algerian War. Yet, we have seen that individual teachers have a certain degree of freedom to study the Algerian War in more or less detail than the program dictates. What makes teachers do significantly more? Interestingly of the small sample of teachers that I interviewed the determining factor is overwhelmingly being a *pied-noir* or of "pied-noir origin." This is true for three of the four teachers who did significantly more than their colleagues. One of these teachers (Teacher 6) had lived in Mostaganem in Algeria. She claimed that her uncle had been killed on 1 November 1954, and was therefore one of the first victims of the war. Her father had also been killed by the FLN in 1957. Her family had a vineyard in Algeria until Algerian independence in 1962. Another teacher was born in Oranie and then lived in Algiers until 1962. They lived in Bab-El-Oued and had therefore experienced firsthand the "semaine des barricades" (when barricades were erected in the area to protest against de Gaulle's Algerian policy). The teacher who was of "pied-noir origin" was a man whose mother was a *pied-noir*. His grandfather had been a pilot in Air-Africa. He had two uncles who were members of the OAS. The other teacher who also did a lot on the Algerian War in class, but who was not of "pied-noir" origin, had been in Algeria with her husband "en coopération" and said that during the Algerian War she had had "une mauvaise conscience" (a troubled conscience).[32]

Before the change in program (that came into effect in September 1998) one of these teachers did six hours on the Algerian War, two did five hours, and the other one did three and a half hours. This kind of interest makes the teachers do more than can easily be taught in the program (about two hours) where a lot of teachers stop and significantly more than what need be done (perhaps one hour). Here we can see a clear example of the way the process of transmission of memory can be more pluralistic than a view that claims the program is simply imposed. In this instance this is clearly linked to groups and a quite distinctive group memory. We can note that in the teacher sample *pied-noir* origin led to more interest in the subject and in the pupil sample *Maghrebi* origin will be seen to lead to increased interest in the subject. However this choice by individual teachers to spend more time on the Algerian War, while it exists, is still in an environment where significant imposition takes place and is fairly marginal given the amount of teachers susceptible to exercise it and the degree of deviance.

At the opposite end of the scale, if we group the teachers according to school, then it is clear that the two teachers in School A and two of the three teachers interviewed (the other being "pied-noir" and doing the war in detail) at School B do similar things in class and considerably less than others. This could be seen in the time they spent in class on the war and their general comments on teaching the conflict. Both these schools are "prestigious" schools fairly centrally located in Lyon where, very importantly in this commentator's opinion, there are fewer pupils of North-African origin than in other schools. Perhaps teachers in such schools are also under more pressure to provide very good results at the *baccalauréat* and therefore stick to the program and are more influenced by preparing the pupils for the examination. Such issues seemed to be evident in the comments of the teacher quoted above (Teacher 5) who said that his pupils would criticize him if he spent a lot of time on the Algerian War since this was not a subject they would have to address in the *baccalauréat* examination.

This point links in to the central question of "demand" for the subject. Teachers, for example, answer pupil questions but only if there actually are questions. Often teachers insisted on this point. While they described the lesson as being very teacher-centered they also said that they answered questions that they were asked. As one teacher said: "On est amené à préciser certains points en fonction des questions des élèves . . . ça ne me guide pas, j'ai mon cours préparé mais ça peut m'amener à aller plus loin" (We are led to clarify certain points as a function of the pupils' questions . . . that doesn't guide me, I've got my class prepared but it can lead me to go further; Teacher 17). The ethnic makeup of the school was also something mentioned in a lot of interviews. For example one teacher stated:

> Dans la banlieue où j'enseigne il y a près de vingt pour cent des élèves qui sont d'origine maghrébine. Et je pense que ce n'est pas inintéressant de leur apprendre ce morceau de leur histoire qui est aussi notre histoire. (In the suburbs where I teach nearly twenty percent of the pupils are of Maghrebian descent. And I think it's interesting to teach them this passage of their history that is also our history; Teacher 1.)

Another teacher, this time at School B, said: "En général les élèves écoutent mais en fait ne se sentent pas concernés . . . parce que, bon pour eux, c'est à la fois trop vieux et puis leur famille souvent n'est pas concernée par le phénomène" (In general the pupils listen but in fact they don't feel affected . . . be-

cause, for them, it is both too distant in time and their family often is not concerned by the phenomenon; Teacher 5). Below and in chapter 3 we will discuss
the definite change in memory linked to generational change but here we can
note that for this teacher at least, interest in the subject depends to a large extent
on family (and sometimes therefore ethnicity). One teacher in an interview mentioned how the pupils in two secondary schools where he had worked differed
and therefore his approach to the Algerian War had changed. He did not describe
exactly how his approach had altered but he said:

> J'avais des élèves au début des années 80 qui étaient aussi bien intéressés mais il
> y en avait aussi pas mal qui étaient d'origine maghrébine . . . d'origine algé-
> rienne . . . Et puis j'ai changé de lycée et dans le lycée où je suis il y a peu de
> maghrébins, donc l'approche n'est pas la même, évidemment. (At the beginning
> of the 1980s I had pupils who were also interested but there were a good number
> who were of Maghrebian descent . . . Algerian descent . . . And then I changed
> high school and in the school where I now teach there are few Maghrebians, so
> the approach is not the same, obviously; Teacher 2.)

Indeed the present is also important in other ways in understanding classroom
content. Numerous teachers mentioned the present as a justification for studying
various elements of the war. One example of this was the study of *harkis*.
Teacher 12 said she studied the *harkis* in lesson and mentioned current affairs in
this choice as well as a "lieu" (site): the Duchère (district of Lyon) and a stele
(the Oran Monument to the Dead, that was brought back from Algeria to Lyon at
the initiative of *pieds-noirs* who fled Algeria and settled in the Duchère). Another teacher said:

> J'en ai parlé parce que c'est un problème qui revient encore maintenant. Ça ils
> ont été très sensibles. Je crois qu'ils ne savaient pas finalement très bien ce que
> c'était. Je crois qu'ils ne savaient pas. Donc j'en ai parlé. J'ai expliqué ce que
> c'était exactement que les harkis, pourquoi leur situation était particulièrement
> difficile et injuste. (I talked about it because it's a problem that is still current.
> They were very sensitive to this. I don't think they really knew much about it. I
> don't think they knew. So I talked about it. I explained who the *harkis* were, and
> why their situation was particularly difficult and unjust; Teacher 17.)

Another teacher mentioned the demonstration that ended tragically at the metro
station Charonne and current affairs: during the Papon trial there had been a lot
of media coverage of this event from the Algerian War, prompting her to do it in
more detail than other years. A third teacher mentioned recent books on the
events of the night of 17 October 1961 that convinced him to spend more time
on this subject in future. Furthermore the rise of the French Front National (National Front) was also cited as a reason to spend time on a study of the Algerian
War in history classes by teachers. On the link between the Algerian conflict and
the rise of the FN one teacher said:

Si je m'écoutais pour faire du bachotage, pour mieux préparer, je réduirais. Mais je pense que c'est utile pour leur formation, pour comprendre en fait comment peuvent réagir leurs compratiotes face à des problèmes qui peuvent resurgir sous un autre forme comme par exemple la montée du Front National. (If I listened to myself to cram, to prepare better, I would do less. But I think that it's useful for their education, to understand in fact how their compatriots can react to problems that can re-emerge in another form like for example the rise of the National Front; Teacher 5.)

The civil war in Algeria was also mentioned by several teachers throughout different interviews. Clearly then the present influences what is taught.

Having identified that what is taught is indeed a memory of sorts, between memory and history, let us turn to the practical translation of the program to study these points and see how this is the case. As can be seen from the above figures on time spent in class on the Algerian War, there is a significant difference between the amount of time spent in the period 1989-1998 and in the post-1998 program. Changing the whole program in 1998 has significantly changed the way the Algerian War is taught by making teaching the Algerian War even more dependent on the choices of teachers and causing its study to be increasingly to the detriment of other parts of the program. The change in program was at the centre of the B interview questions and was therefore discussed at length in the interviews with teachers. The general consensus was that there has been even more of a move away from a factual history to a broader history that is more general and more synthesized.

The program is longer because of the reintroduction of World War Two in the *terminale* program and indeed increases in size every year because of the "De 1939 *à nos jours*" (From 1939 to the *Present Day*) emphasis that means there is more to do every year in order to study "until the present day" (therefore significantly more so than in 1983). The program was also made more general by the introduction of very general chapters e.g. four country/system models. On the change in program, one teacher stated: "on nous demande d'insister sur les grandes périodes de manière beaucoup plus générale. Donc en fait on nous demande de rentrer moins dans les détails" (we are asked to focus on long periods in a much more general fashion. So in fact we are asked to go into less detail). She also said: "Sur la décolonisation on devrait aller plus vite. La guerre d'Algérie on devrait la citer que comme exemple de guerre coloniale mais sans vraiment rentrer dans les détails" (We should go more quickly on the topic of decolonization. The Algerian War should be cited only as an example of a colonial war without really going into detail; Teacher 11). Another teacher said: "Moi je sais que cette année je m'appesantis moins sur, disons sur les détails, enfin les détails, sur les points particuliers. Et la guerre d'Algérie, si on l'étudie, on entre dans le particulier" (I know that this year I dwell less on, let's say details, or on particular points. And to study the Algerian War we need to go into particulars; Teacher 12). These points are fully supported by another teacher when he said: "On demande aux élèves de retenir de moins en moins une histoire factuelle mais beaucoup plus des évolutions globales" (We require the students less and less to remember a factual history, rather much more global evolutions; Teacher 14). In fact all the teachers interviewed after the change in program make these points.

For one teacher an example of what was dropped consisted of what happened in the rue d'Isly in Algiers on 26 March 1962:

> Je n'en parle plus. Avant, les autres années, j'en parlais mais là je n'en parle plus. Je n'ai pas le temps . . . Manque de temps. Pour que les élèves puissent comprendre il faudrait rentrer plus dans le détail. Je ne peux plus. Moi je ne le fais plus. (I don't talk about it anymore. Before, in previous years, I spoke about it but no longer. I don't have time . . . Lack of time. In order for the pupils to understand we would need to go into more detail. I can't. I don't do it anymore; Teacher 17.)

A further example of something dropped by her was the bombing in 1958 of Sakhiet-Sidi-Youssef in Tunisia by the French air force, that resulted in numerous deaths (children being amongst the victims). Another teacher also said that the change in program would lead to fewer events from the war being studied. When asked whether it would be possible in 1998-1999 to continue to study the Algerian War in its own right she replied:

> Moi je pense que non. Je pense que ça va être très difficile de garder la guerre d'Algérie en elle-même . . . Je suis à peu près sûre que je vais la traiter de manière très, très rapide et que je n'aborderai pas toutes les questions que j'abordais auparavant. Donc de manière pas satisfaisante. (I don't think so. I think it will be very difficult to keep the Algerian War as such . . . I am pretty sure that I'm going to deal with it very, very quickly and that I won't cover all the questions that I covered previously. So in an unsatisfactory fashion; Teacher 15.)

How and Where the War is Taught

Arguably the way the Algerian War is taught—qualitative aspects of the question—is more important, for example, than how long is spent on the war—quantitative aspects of the question—although there is clearly a link between the two. The program is inevitably described as long and demanding. Above all we need to note that the Algerian War is taught in *terminale*, a year that differs from *seconde* or *première*.[33] All teachers said that the lessons were conducted as a "Cours Magistral" so the teacher lectures and the pupils write. Teachers said that in other years different teaching practices were possible that allowed teacher and pupil to spend more time on subjects (since there is no national examination to prepare for there is less of a time constraint). Other teachers also mentioned the "utility" of the classes: "On essaie au maximum que ce qui est fait en classe soit utile/utilisable" (We try as much as possible to ensure that what is done in class can be used; Teacher 1). This means that teachers try to make classroom content relevant to answering examination questions. The way the Algerian War is taught also depends on the *série*:

> Le problème des Terminales S est que le coefficient d'Histoire-Géographie à l'examen/au bac est relativement faible, donc ils vont minimiser leurs efforts et ils préfèrent qu'on leur présente un matériel tout fait qui n'est plus qu'à réutiliser. Donc on peut bien essayer d'illustrer le cours par soit quelques extraits de bande vidéo, soit en essayant de leur indiquer des films ou des lectures ou des références mais on n'a pas le temps de les utiliser en classe. Deux heures c'est très, très court. On a juste le temps de faire le tour de la question à peu près mais on ne peut pas approfondir. (The problem with pupils in Terminale S is that the weighting for History-Geography in the exam is relatively low, so they minimize their efforts and they prefer that we present "ready-assembled" material that can be reused. So we can try and illustrate the class either by extracts from videos, or trying to tell them about films, readings, or references to pursue but we can't use them in class. Two hours is very, very short. We only have time to conduct an approximate overview but we can't go into depth; Teacher 5)

Although this teacher is talking about the *série* S (scientific students) his comments effectively also (to a slightly lesser degree) apply to other *séries* and the *terminale* year in general. The comments on the attitude of the students, the problem of time, the inability to go into detail, and not being able to use support documents echo what was said by other teachers.

Crucial to understanding how the Algerian War is taught and what is taught is the question of the detail that is given on the Algerian War and the fact that most points are just mentioned without sufficient explanation. To a large extent this is linked to the nature and aims of the program. For one teacher the aim of the lessons was to show the "étapes" (stages) in the war (Teacher 2). This is fairly evident in teachers' discourse when they stick to a chronology. One teacher brought some documents to the interview, one of which was a chronology of the Algerian conflict taken from *Le Monde* in 1992. He talked me through the chronology and pinpointed the elements he did or did not do in class. Broadly speaking, and this applies to all the teachers in the sample, if the emphasis is put on the stages of the war then very little is done before 1954 (perhaps Sétif 8 May 1945), and then 1954 is studied as the "déclenchement" (start) of the war, 1955 and 1956 constitute an "enlisement" (worsening) in the war, 1957 is important for the battle of Algiers and 1958 is studied for de Gaulle's return to power. The lessons show that 1959 included de Gaulle's speech on "autodétermination" (self-determination), in 1960 de Gaulle speaks of an "Algérie algérienne" (Algerian Algeria) that leads to certain reactions including the "semaine des barricades" (week of barricades), 1961 brings a referendum and more reactions including the OAS and the putsch, and in 1962 there are negotiations, the "accords d'Evian" (Evian Peace Accords), and independence.

In this way the details of the war, so to speak, are not studied, but the student should understand the development of the war. The stages of the war are studied in so far as the lessons should show how a relatively small insurrection led to independence and, importantly, how over the years peace was achieved (insisting on the role of de Gaulle). As the teacher who talked me through the chronology said: "Il y a beaucoup de choses qui passent à la trappe . . . qui sont souvent évacuées" (There are a lot of things that are dropped . . . that are often left out; Teacher 10). In the chronology he gave me, elements of the war not studied but in the chronology included December 1954, Creation of the "Mouvement National Algérien" (MNA: a nationalist movement rivaling the FLN); 19 May 1955, Decision to call up again soldiers who had already done their military service; 6 February 1956, "La journée des tomates;" 18 May 1956, Palestro; 30 September 1956, Terrorist attacks in Algiers including one on the Milk-bar; 22 October 1956, Hijacking of Ben Bella et al.; 29 May 1957, Melouza; 8 February 1958, Sakhiet-Sidi-Youssef; 1960 Jeanson trial and the "Manifeste des 121;" 8 February 1962, Charonne; 26 March 1962, La rue d'Isly. While that does not mean that all of the other elements included in the chronology were studied, it does show how many significant events of the war are not covered in class. It also shows how much of what is left out includes to a large extent the most violent and ultimately most occluded aspects of the war. In the elements of the war studied by that particular teacher, while there was an emphasis on explaining the overall development of the war (in the way explained above) there was also a lot of insistence on de Gaulle. Another teacher described the lessons as "general history:"

> On fait toujours un cours en fonction de l'épreuve du baccalauréat possible. Donc, on les prépare à tels types de sujets et aussi au fait que c'est un cours d'histoire générale donc on ne rentre pas dans les détails extrêmement précis sur la guerre d'Algérie. (The content of a class is always related to possible end of year examinations. So, we prepare them for certain types of subjects and also cover general history so we don't go into very much detail on the Algerian War; Teacher 3.)

One teacher, after the change in program, seemed particularly unhappy with the way in which the new program meant she had to examine history in *terminale* and particularly the Algerian War. She said: "Il faut dire tout, parler de tout, mais sans rien approfondir, ça reste très, très superficiel" (We are supposed to say everything, talk about everything, but without going into detail, it's very, very superficial; Teacher 16). This is inherently linked to the problem of time, a point that was mentioned by all teachers throughout all interviews. All teachers have to go extremely quickly. As we have seen, spending more time on one subject is to the detriment of others and teachers often do not finish the program. This determines the lecture-style form of the lesson. It also dictates whether sources can or cannot be used. This is true for written documents or video but also for the question of inviting veterans into class. Most importantly of all it means that no details or explanation can be given.

In this way while many teachers said that they did study points I asked them about in my interview questions (included in the appendices), more often than not this treatment was qualified as "citer" (cite), "indiquer" (indicate), "mentionner" (mention), "signaler" (signal) or "évoquer" (evoke). Such words are very dominant in teachers' discourse and undoubtedly mean that details are not given. As one teacher said: "la mémoire n'est pas vraiment, je trouve, transmise dans la mesure où c'est évoquée mais cc n'est pas véritablement expliquée" (memory isn't really, in my opinion, transmitted in so far as it's evoked but it's not really explained; Teacher 16). Only a limited number of points are dealt with in class and those that are talked about are not done in sufficient detail so that they are understood. This corresponds to the result of history classes, but is not true of knowledge obtained from the family. These points will be discussed further below in the "Pupil Link" section.

One question can be examined in particular to grasp the importance of only mentioning things: torture during the Algerian War. Indeed this aspect of the war was one example given by a teacher to illustrate the way points were only mentioned without going into detail. When asked about how long he spent on the war, he said:

> On ne peut pas rentrer dans les détails, on peut juste voir les mécanismes et des indications et on ne peut pas rentrer dans les détails ni des opérations militaires ni en fait de tel ou tel détail significatif comme par exemple le rôle de la torture. On parle du problème de la torture mais on le cite en passant, on n'cst pas obligé d'aller plus loin. (We can't go into detail, we can only look at mechanisms and indications and wc can't go into thc details of the military operations or in fact this or that significant detail like for example the role of torture. We talk about the problem of torture but we cite it in passing, we don't have to go further; Teacher 5.)

Teachers when asked about torture, in the B sample, sometimes seemed a little ill at ease. This can bc seen in different reactions. It can be heard, as one teacher replied to the question on torture with "Ah!" or seen, as teachers look uncomfortable. It can also be discerned in the content of what is said on torture as teachers immediately insist that there were excesses on both the French and Algerian sides (and while this is undoubtedly true, one has the impression that the phrase is a way to relativize or justify torture). It can also be seen in incoherent answers. One teacher started her answer by insisting on thc importance of studying torture (by making reference to the scale of its use and to the accusations of torture leveled against the leader of the French National Front in the 1980s) and then finished by saying that she just mentioned this question in class. Another started by saying that she did not study torture but then later said that she told the students that the Algerian War had been a very hard war and for a long time torture had been a taboo subject. Beyond this ill-ease in answering the question in the interview, one teacher (out of seven) said she did not talk about it in class. Three teachers described it as being a quick treatment. The other three dealt with it in more depth (though they were all talking about the period before the change in program). Textbooks' treatment of torture has already been described in this book and amounted in 1998 editions of textbooks to one or two lines and a document.

Also of key importance is where the Algerian War is examined. The program very much dictates what kind of information is given on the Algerian War as it is "used" to illustrate wider phenomena. As one teacher stated: "Elle est toujours vue au travers de quelque chose" (It is always seen through something else; Teacher 7). The place of the Algerian War in the program has very important consequences on the sort of information that is given (and also that which is not). For example in the section on the French Fourth and Fifth Republics:

> On fait une étude assez précise des événements de mai 1958 et on essaie de montrer l'enjeu du changement de gouvernement. Donc on parle beaucoup des problèmes algériens mais aussi des problèmes institutionnels en même temps. C'est donc plutôt comme à-ce-stade-là un morceau de l'histoire politique française. Ensuite on revient sur la question de la guerre d'Algérie quand on étudie la politique du général de Gaulle jusqu'en 1962, et donc c'est pareil, on voit les principales étapes mais au milieu d'une analyse des réalisations gaullistes à-ce-moment-là. (We do quite a detailed study of the events of May 1958 and we try to demonstrate what is at stake in the change of government. So we talk a lot about Algerian problems but also institutional problems at the same time. So at that stage it's more like a part of French political history. Then we come back to the question of the Algerian War when we study the policy of General de Gaulle up to 1962, and so it's the same thing, we look at the main stages (of the war) but in the context of an analysis of Gaullist actions at that time; Teacher 1.)

Another teacher stated:

> Lorsque je la traite dans le cadre de la décolonisation je vois en quoi l'Algérie est un exemple de décolonisation. Quand je la traite dans la Quatrième et la Cinquième Républiques je vois en quoi l'Algérie a été un facteur politique d'évolution pour la Quatrième et la Cinquième Républiques. En quoi par exemple elle a précipité la fin de la Quatrième ou le début de la Cinquième. Comment le général de Gaulle l'a traitée. Ce n'est pas du tout la même optique. (When I deal with it in the Decolonization chapter, I look at how Algeria is an example of a decolonization movement. When I deal with it in the chapters on the Fourth and Fifth Republics I show how Algeria was a political factor in the evolution of the Fourth and Fifth Republics. How, for example, it hastened the end of the Fourth Republic and the beginning of the Fifth. How General de Gaulle dealt with it. It's a completely different point of view; Teacher 14.)

The problem with viewing the Algerian War in these chapters is that it means only certain information is used to illustrate these wider phenomena and it is not the Algerian conflict that is studied in its own right. The Algerian War is somewhat lost in these vast chapters. This is why (and how) in *terminale* classes there is only a very partial study of the war. Only certain aspects of the war are studied and others are never studied. The study is not only partial but also broken up into different parts. As Paul Fournier said about textbooks: "Le cadrage dispersé aboutit donc à une absence de réflexion sur l'ensemble du problème de la guerre d'Algérie" (The broken-up framework thus leads to a lack of reflection on the overall nature of the Algerian War).[34] Certain elements of the war can easily be and are avoided.

In the French Fourth and Fifth Republics much of what is done on the Algerian War in the period 1958-1962 to a large extent concerns de Gaulle. It can however also be noted that even when the Algerian War is studied in the chapter on decolonization de Gaulle's policy is also studied to the detriment of other elements. For one teacher the second of her two hours revolved around de Gaulle (Teacher 11). For all teachers in the B sample de Gaulle was said to be central. When asked whether she studied de Gaulle one teacher said: "La politique de de Gaulle. Evidemment. Elle est au cœur du programme. Les institutions et tout ça" (De Gaulle's policy. Of course. It's at the heart of the program. Institutions and all that; Teacher 12). For another de Gaulle's policy "chapeaute le reste" (heads the rest): "C'est la politique gaulliste qui est le chapeau du chapitre sur la guerre d'Algérie" (It's the study of Gaullist policy that heads the chapter on the Algerian War; Teacher 13). This was also a point made by Teacher 2 (and other teachers, e.g., Teacher 10) in the A sample:

> surtout je leur montre comment de Gaulle essaie de résoudre le problème par petites touches . . . surtout comment de Gaulle ayant vu que finalement il n'était pas possible, du moins, en 1958/59 lorsqu'il est au pouvoir de garder l'Algérie, comment il va faire évoluer les différents niveaux d'opinion vers l'indépendance—que ce soit l'opinion métropolitaine, que ce soit l'armée qu'il faut reprendre en main, bon pour les pieds-noirs c'est difficile de leur faire admettre évidemment et puis par petites touches comment on arrive aux accords d'Evian. (above all I show them how de Gaulle tries to solve the problem step by step . . . especially how de Gaulle, having seen that in the end it wasn't possible to keep Algeria, at least, in 1958/59 when he is in power, how he manages to get different opinion groups to come around to support independence— whether it's metropolitan opinion, the army that needs to be towed in; well, for the *pieds-noirs* it's difficult to get them to support it, but little by little how we get to the Evian agreement; Teacher 2.)

As was very clear in one teacher interview (supported by others), the study essentially focused on de Gaulle and used other events to illustrate de Gaulle. Other events are "integrated" into a study of de Gaulle's policy. For one teacher the study of de Gaulle was central and so the first thing on the list that she said she studied was de Gaulle's policy, and then other things on the list were mentioned to illustrate the reaction to de Gaulle in France and Algeria (especially for her the putsch, during which certain generals in the French army tried to oppose de Gaulle by the threat of force; and the OAS, a group that also used force to oppose de Gaulle's abandonment of Algeria). This can also be seen by the use of sources in classes, i.e., predominantly de Gaulle's speeches. For example one teacher said: "on lit des morceaux de discours ensemble" (we read excerpts of speeches together; Teacher 17). This seems to be common. Teacher 14 said he used video as a source and that this was a de Gaulle speech and linked to Article Sixteen of the Constitution during the putsch. Teacher 4 said that he used a de Gaulle document as a "texte de réflexion" (text on which to reflect). Teachers 1 and 10 also said they used video footage of 13 May 1958; and the latter also used a video from the CNDP ("Centre National de Documentation Péda-gogique:" National Pedagogical Documentary Centre) on de Gaulle's press con-ference in which he talked of "une Algérie algérienne." We saw in the previous section the way that if questions are set at the *baccalauréat* linked to the Alge-rian War this very often takes the form of a textual commentary of a de Gaulle source. Unsurprisingly the interviews conducted with pupils showed that they were particularly strong on de Gaulle's change in policy but very weak on most other aspects of the Algerian War. This will be shown below.

The way the lesson can be created around de Gaulle's policy is very impor-tant in understanding how the program "works" and "operates" and similarly ultimately how narratives are created. It is important to note that history (espe-cially in history classes) is used to "show" things and that what is shown is the result of varied agendas, choices, and aims. This is reflected in teachers' dis-courses by the much used phrase "je montre" (I show). If they want to show what de Gaulle's policy was, then that means mentioning the policy, the reac-tions to this policy and not other things. In my B interviews teachers did not for the most part study the following items given on the list proposed in the inter-view: "les porteurs de valise" (French resistance to the Algerian War), "les luttes internes au sein du FLN" (division and in-fighting in the FLN), the massacre at the end of the war in "la rue d'Isly" in Algiers, the military side to the war or only very briefly mentioned many points (see above for an idea of the scale of "mentioning"). Perhaps to a large extent this is because the above items do not directly illustrate what is to be shown. This argument could be linked to the gen-eral values linked to the war. Robert Frank has, for example, argued that the Al-gerian War does not convey the same values as does a commemoration of World War Two, that is, especially the Resistance. This explains to some extent why the war has been so difficult to commemorate and it might also be argued that it is not as "studiable" as World War Two. This however need not necessarily be the case. If more of an effort were made, perhaps values and lessons could be found that are to be transmitted, for example, the way conscripts did not follow the putsch; or the vicious circle created by terrorism/torture so well described by Albert Camus. This would only be possible after considerable dialogue.

In terms of decolonization, the emphasis is essentially put on the origins of the Algerian War. Teachers, in the interviews, said that they did the origins of the war in detail and this is something also present in textbooks. Unfortunately however the study "a un aspect de catalogue" (is like a catalogue; Teacher 1). For one teacher (Teacher 16) the beginning of the lesson was "les causes de la décolonisation" (the causes of decolonization) i.e. in general. On different na-tionalist movements in Algeria before 1954 one teacher said: "je les évoque . . . rapidement . . . parce que c'est compliqué en fait" (I evoke them . . . quickly . . . because it's actually quite complicated; Teacher 17) while another said "on ne peut pas rentrer dans les détails, ce n'est pas possible" (we can't go into detail, it's not possible; Teacher 11). Teacher 14 did not examine the reform of 1947[35] because it was too complicated, did not spend much time at all on nationalist movements and only cited Sétif; but he did do inequality in Algerian society, the impact of World War Two, and other decolonizations. Given the place of the Algerian War in the program it is perfectly understandable that teachers cannot go into significant detail on the origins of the Algerian War. The amount of detail done on decolonizations in general and on Algeria in particular is one thing that separates teachers who spend (or rather spent, since they were talking about the period before the 1998 reform) a lot of time on the Algerian War (Teacher 15 and Teacher 13) and those who do/did not.

The Pupil Link

History classes are in relative terms an important source of information on the Algerian War for young people. By including the Algerian conflict in *terminale* all pupils who take the *baccalauréat général* are virtually guaranteed to obtain some information on the war, whereas via other vectors they may or may not. In general memories of the Algerian War are not significantly transmitted by other vectors, as will be argued in other chapters of this book. However, in absolute terms not much information is transmitted in history classes because the Algerian War is only partially studied. The fact that its treatment is not a detailed study emerged clearly in the pupil interviews. For one pupil: "Il n'y a pas un point spécifique qu'on développe bien, comme la guerre d'Algérie, ce serait intéressant de plus en parler" (There isn't a specific point that we develop a lot, like the Algerian War, it would be interesting to talk more about it; Pupil 6). For another: "On ne fait pas de l'histoire événementielle" (We don't do factual history; Pupil 1).

Such treatment of the war in class leads to a general lack of detailed knowledge on the part of the pupils and no real understanding. Often when asked a question on a particular point—for example, what was the OAS?—they may have heard of it (at best) but know little about it. Perhaps it was something "cited" or "mentioned" by the teacher. As one teacher noted, explaining how a historical reality could be deformed: "Ce n'est pas parce qu'on la déforme sciemment, mais parce qu'on simplifie tellement pour aller vite que comme eux ils simplifient sur notre simplification il risque d'avoir des confusions voire des contresens" (It's not because we deliberately deform it, rather because we simplify so much in order to go quickly, and since they simplify our simplification, there's a danger of confusion or even misinterpretation; Teacher 1). His point was confirmed during the pupil interviews. One pupil, trying to answer a question on a specific event in the interview, referred to the lesson plan but could only state: "Il y a juste la date. On ne sait pas ce qui s'est passé" (There is just the date. We don't know what happened then; Pupil 6).[36] There is little understanding on the part of pupils if their knowledge comes from the classroom. Furthermore even if points are mentioned in class there is some loss from the teacher to the pupil, for example, perhaps pupils do not take good notes. While this is the case for history classes, it is not true of knowledge obtained from the family.

Since the Algerian War is not studied in depth pupil knowledge of what might be called "details" is very weak. Pupils were unsure (and usually knew nothing) of what happened at the "métro Charonne" on 8 February 1962 and at "la rue d'Isly" on 26 March 1962; French resistance to the Algerian War; internal division in the FLN; the massacre in Paris on 17 October 1961; the military aspects of the war; and the "semaine des barricades" (during which *pieds-noirs* blocked parts of Algiers to oppose de Gaulle). Conversely, the OAS was usually at least recognized, pupils could usually explain the exodus in 1962, and they could also explain what the Evian Peace Accords were. They knew the dates marking the beginning and the end of the war and the length of the conflict and they understood the 1961 putsch. A possible explanation of why pupils have this knowledge but no knowledge of other aspects of the war can be found in the place of de Gaulle and the study of the reactions to his policy identified in the previous section. We should also note that the above knowledge does not include the least glorious aspects of the war. One exception however was the bombing of Sakhiet-Sidi-Youssef, which was well known by Pupil 2, Pupil 11, and Pupil 10 (the first two of whom are of Algerian origin), a possible reason being the importance in the program of showing in class the internationalization of the conflict point that was mentioned by teachers.

Therefore the study of the Algerian War in *terminale* is very partial. Overall it is not a study of the aspects of the war that do not "help to tell bigger stories," a situation that in my opinion inhibits significant transmission of the memory of the Algerian War through classes in *terminale*. Numerous examples of confusion in the interviews demonstrate that information is not effectively transmitted: most pupils could not remember things, had to use their notes to answer questions, and confused names or events. There are also numerous instances of pupils guessing, that often translated into phrases such as "il doit y en avoir" (the must be)—for example on whether there are books or films on the Algerian War—or "il a dû y en avoir" (there must have been)—for example on whether there was censorship during the period of the Algerian hostilities. The fact that the Algerian War is studied in wider subjects makes a comparative study possible and perhaps incites students to draw parallels. Faced with gaps in their knowledge, it is a logical reaction on the part of pupils. Furthermore, the answer to the question in the interview on Sakhiet-Sidi-Youssef given by Teacher 11's three pupils was only possible with notes, so we can also identify a loss of information from teacher to pupil and question what pupils actually leave the class with. Indeed in *terminale* pupils finish with notes. They also equate the time spent on the Algerian conflict and the importance of the subject with the amount of notes they have.

The arguably weak impact in absolute terms of history classes can also be explained by the way the lessons are given. We have seen how classes are very much lecture-based and involve little discussion—teachers speak and the pupils take notes. One pupil in particular accurately summarized the way the war is taught when she mentioned that:

> Le programme c'est sûr qu'il est chargé, qu'il y a beaucoup de choses, énormé-
> ment; on a peu d'heures. Donc les profs ils font le maximum. Ils éssaient d'aller
> le plus rapidement possible. On ne peut pas avoir toutes les précisions qu'on
> veut . . . Ils traitent les choses en général, donnent une vue globale. C'est vrai
> que pour avoir plus de précisions il faut par soi-même . . . aller lire des manuels .
> . . se documenter plus précisement. (It's true that the program is demanding, that
> there are a lot of things to cover, a huge amount; in little time. So the teachers do
> as much as possible. They try to go as quickly as possible. We can't have all the
> precisions that we would like . . . They approach things in a general fashion,
> give a global perspective. It's true that to go into more background one has one-
> self to . . . go and read textbooks . . . read oneself in a more targeted way; Pupil
> 2.)

Pupils therefore echoed teachers throughout the interviews by mentioning the lack of time and the length of the program. Pupil 3 said: "nous on écoute, on prend des notes parce qu'il y a que ça à faire, on prend des notes" (we listen, we take notes because that's all there is to do, take notes). One teacher mentioned how the program is adapted to good pupils who take good notes. He said: "Il est beaucoup trop lourd, beaucoup trop étendu par rapport au temps qu'on a pour l'enseigner; ce qui oblige à courir tout le temps, toujours très rapide, donc à être très souvent, quasiment tout le temps, magistral" (It's much too packed, much too long compared to the time we have to teach it; which compels us to always go very quickly, always flat out, so often, almost always lecturing; Teacher 1).

Broadly speaking, pupil knowledge corresponds to what teachers say they do in class, but there is some loss from teacher to pupil as pupils are unable to talk about aspects of the Algerian War that teachers said were done in class. To some extent this is inevitable, but it could largely be due to teachers "mention-ing" points but not giving sufficient explanations. It is also the result of what is imposed by the program since the program largely dictates what is taught and in what detail. However there are inherent limits to the class. If too few details are done in class then pupils have no understanding of the Algerian War due to lack of explanation. Alternatively, if too many details were given then perhaps pupils understanding would suffer due to being drowned in a sea of facts to memorize. Clearly history in *terminale* has to be selective; a memory of sorts. Despite the lack of detailed knowledge mentioned above, all pupils are relatively strong on two things in particular: the origins of decolonization and de Gaulle's Algerian policy. We can also remark that not all students have the same knowledge: per-haps the pupils with the most knowledge were the group of Pupil 8, Pupil 9 and Pupil 12, who are all of Algerian origin. We can state that pupils whose grand-parents are from Algeria seem to have more knowledge than others, perhaps not only due to information gained from the family but also, to a very large extent, increased interest in the subject.

The interviews conducted with pupils showed that they were particularly strong on de Gaulle's change in policy but very weak on most other aspects of the Algerian War. One pupil when asked when in the year they had done the Algerian War in class said: "c'est en arrivant avec Charles de Gaulle qu'on a parlé de son rôle avec la guerre d'Algérie" (it's when we got to Charles de Gaulle that we talked about his role concerning the Algerian War; Pupil 4 whose teacher is Teacher 1 who studied the war mainly in the French Fourth and Fifth Republics rather than in Decolonization). She was also able to talk about de Gaulle's policy, mentioning it on several occasions during the interview, but was much weaker on other questions. In another interview, when asked whether there were any things that they had done in class that I had not mentioned in my interview questions one of the pupils said: "Vous, vous n'avez pas beaucoup parlé de la politique de de Gaulle; nous c'est ce qu'on a bien vu ça" (You didn't talk much about de Gaulle's policy, whereas we looked at that a lot; Pupil 6 who is a pupil of Teacher 11). In another interview, the pupils said: "ce n'était pas particulièrement sur l'Algérie, c'était global" (it wasn't particularly about Algeria, it was global), "on n'a pas fait un cours spécial sur la guerre d'Algérie" (we didn't do a separate class on the Algerian War), "on l'a pas étudiée en tant que telle" (we didn't study it as such; Pupil 8); "Pourquoi on a parlé de la guerre d'Algérie? C'est pour parler de de Gaulle. Ce n'est pas la guerre d'Algérie en soi" (Why did we talk about the Algerian War? It was to look at de Gaulle. It's not the Algerian War in itself; Pupil 12; both he and Pupil 8 are in the same class with Teacher 3 who spent two or three hours on the Algerian War). Another pupil also talked of the way the war is not done in its own right. When explaining why she will study it for the *baccalauréat* she said: "Il y a toujours une relation à la guerre d'Algérie, ou alors la politique de de Gaulle face à cette guerre, ou alors qu'est-ce que la décolonisation" (There is always a relation to the Algerian War, either de Gaulle's policy towards this war, or decolonization; Pupil 11). Surely though there is more to the Algerian War than that since the result of this placing of the Algerian conflict is her description of it as being on "les périphéries" (the periphery).

The interviews with pupils also showed that they were particularly strong on the origins of the war compared to other questions on the Algerian War. Sometimes this tended to be the origins of decolonization in general but not of the Algerian War in particular. For one pupil (Pupil 11) there seemed to be a difference between what she herself thought, therefore had learned from other sources, and what she had been told in class. Accordingly she said: "Les origines, du moins comme on nous l'explique en cours, les origines elles sont vagues" (The origins, at least how they were explained in class, the origins are vague). I interpret her comments as meaning that in class they had insisted mainly on the origins of decolonization in the world rather than on the Algerian War in particular. Another pupil, Pupil 1, spoke of decolonization in general, without mentioning anything specific to Algeria. She stated that the French had asked all colonies to supply soldiers during World War Two and in return had promised to liberate colonies, yet this promise had not been kept. So Algerians (although if we had been talking of another decolonization she presumably would have said other people) had wanted independence. She also spoke of the influence of other decolonizations, for example, British. She did not mention the Algerian population, economy, or political situation. Such pupil knowledge can be explained by the fact that the Algerian War is studied in decolonization in general in the program. Decolonization is a possible examination question that necessitates this type of knowledge. However we can also note that Pupil 10 in her notes and the group of Pupil 8, Pupil 9 and Pupil 12 were very good on the origins of the Algerian War.

We can also state that generally the military side of the war and the least glorious aspects of the conflict are not studied in class. For Pupil 4: "Côté militaire on n'en a pas trop parlé" (We didn't talk much about the military side). None of the pupils said they had studied the military side of the war in class. Teachers, in interviews, said that the military side of the war was something that they did not cover in class or only a little. One teacher in particular, Teacher 17, said this was an aspect of the Algerian War that she no longer studied. She said that previously she had used maps of Kabylie and the Aurès and had explained the difference between fighting in towns and in the country. She had not done a great deal before but it had been more than now and since the 1998 reform of the program. The way the military side of the war is not studied may however be linked to the nature itself of the war. Although there were military operations that mobilized soldiers in what is now referred to as a war, much of the Algerian conflict was a political war. It was a "revolutionary war" (as Indo-China had been) in so far as the enemy was hard to identify, blending into the population like Mao Zedong's "fish in water," and used terror (often in terrorist attacks) to achieve their goals. The army became involved in a wide range of activities including political, economic, and psychological action. We have seen in this book how such factors can constitute a barrier to memory, as other commentators have argued.

Other examples of what we might call minimization or underestimation of the war include the question of the number of French soldiers who were *appelés* (conscripts) or *rappelés* (reenlisted). Pupils were fairly weak on this point and generally surprised by the real number. Their weakness on this question was however less clear-cut than it had been on other issues. Pupil 1 had no idea of the number of French young men who had been sent to Algeria and when pressed to put forward a figure suggested a maximum of ten thousand. The group of Teacher 11's three pupils disagreed amongst themselves at first and when one of the three suggested "millions" the others were surprised. Pupil 2 did not know. Nonetheless, teachers often said that this was something they covered in class. Another stark example of the minimization of the Algerian War came from Pupil 5 when she said: "La France n'était pas brutale avec les Algériens" (France was not brutal with Algerians). This could be linked to her parents' choice of coming to France. More examples of the underestimation of aspects of the war include the way pupils sometimes knew Ben Bella's name but not the fact that he had been hijacked in a plane by the French air force (Pupil 6 and Pupil 7 in one of the groups, Pupil 10 and the group of Teacher 3's three pupils). Similarly Pupil 2 and Pupil 3 had heard of Sakhiet-Sidi-Youssef but did not mention deaths.

Harkis were named but their massacre was not referred to by the group of Teacher 11's three pupils. This pupil knowledge corresponds to what was said during the teacher interviews on class content.

Another result of the partial study of the Algerian conflict in *terminale* is the minimization of the stakes of the war, as shown in pupils' lack of understanding of what the term "the memory of the Algerian War" means. While most scholarly work has shown memories of the war to have been occluded and repressed, pupils seem to have no understanding of these concepts. Again pupils talk in general but not in particular on the war in Algeria. They say for example that we must remember and not forget in order not to make the same mistakes as in the past—very much resembling Nora's description of "duty-memory." Such opinions may have been expressed in class concerning the Second World War and are used by pupils for all cases of memory. Pupil 11 however answered this question very well in the interview. Some pupils were also able to link the Algerian War and its problematic memory with current tensions in France, for example, the group of Pupil 5, Pupil 6, and Pupil 7. Lastly it might be advanced that the Algerian conflict is something they have heard a little about outside of (before) class and that they know is not talked about much.

Conclusion

The Algerian War is not significantly present in the *terminale* history course—in the program and examination questions, reflected in textbooks—and is becoming less and less present. This is in part since the program in *terminale* is an integral part of the *école* in the *République* and these history lessons play an important role in creating cohesion in society by reference to the past; difficult or impossible on a subject such as the Algerian War due to the continuing presence in the classroom (and society) of different mutually hostile memories of the Algerian War. Such points were evident in the classroom at both the level of teachers and pupils and their interest in or approach to the subject. Another explanation of the partial small study of the war can be found in the overall memory of the Algerian War and the lack of a "collective national memory" and continuing existence of fragmented group and individual memories. Identity is central to this debate as is shown in much theoretical work on memory, which concerns all French children and in many ways the Algerian War cannot be, or at least is not, isolated and studied in depth in respect of the principles of the Republic: in favor of universalism and against communities and difference. Yet teachers do have some room for maneuver, providing evidence of a more pluralistic model of collective memory. It is possible but difficult to spend more time on the Algerian War, often to the detriment of other aspects of the program. Pupils too can take more or less interest in the Algerian War. Yet eighty percent of pupils think that too little is said about the Algerian War in schools.[37] Consequently the education system fails in some of the objectives it has set itself and conflicting memories that circulate in society—for example in families or in the media—cannot be challenged by history.

Notes

1. Henry Rousso, *Le Syndrome de Vichy* (Paris: Seuil, 1987), 253.

2. Eric Hobsbawm and Terrence Ranger, eds., *The Invention of Tradition* (Cambridge: Cambridge University Press, 1992).

3. Vincent Descombes, *Le Même et l'autre* (Paris: Les Editions de Minuit, 1979), 17.

4. The first "affaire du foulard" occurred in autumn 1989 when four girls were suspended from a school in Creil near Paris for wearing a headscarf. After frenzied media coverage and polemic the matter was provisionally settled by a ruling by the State Council that meant conflicts were negotiated at the local level. Throughout the 1990s this ruling held under growing strain until a firmer line was taken in 2004 as part of a "secular renewal" and reinvigoration of France's republican and secular principles, when all ostentatious religious signs were banned from State schools.

5. Inspectors literally visit classes and inspect what is being done in the classroom.

6. Primary oral sources were used and include eighteen interviews conducted in Lyon with secondary school history teachers. These interviews were conducted between February 1998 and June 1999. Interviews were also conducted with twelve pupils and two historians. The teachers worked in six secondary schools in or very near Lyon, and the pupils were drawn from four of these schools. The teachers varied in terms of age, gender, family involvement in the Algerian War, and qualifications (CAPES or *agrégation*). Of the twelve pupils, seven were of Algerian origin and one other had a father who had fought in the war, pointing to the importance of family history to memories of the Algerian War. Pupils were found through teachers making an announcement in class leaving it up to pupils to volunteer. Teachers were found initially through professional contacts and subsequently through word of mouth. The interviews were taped and generally lasted between half an hour and three quarters of an hour. Twelve pupils were interviewed in 1999 in eight interviews. The interviews with teachers were split into two sample groups which I will call A and B. Ten teachers were interviewed with the first set of questions and eight with the second. The interview questions used can be found in the appendices of this book. This chapter also draws on written sources such as textbooks and examination questions.

7. Quoted in Geneviève Pastor, "L'enseignement de la guerre d'Algérie en classe de terminale. Instructions officielles et sujets au baccalauréat en France," in *Mémoire et enseignement de la guerre d'Algérie: actes du colloque, 13-14 mars 1992, Paris*, vol. 2, (Paris: Institut du Monde arabe/Ligue de l'enseignement, 1993), 419.

8. Cited in Pastor, "L'enseignement de la guerre," 424.

9. Serge Berstein and Dominique Borne, "L'enseignement de l'histoire au lycée," *Vingtième Siècle*, no. 49 (January-March 1996): 142.

10. Pierre Kerleroux and Herbert Tisson, "Entretien avec Serge Berstein et Gilbert Gaudin sur les programmes d'histoire et de géographie," *Historiens et Géographes*, no. 348 (May-June 1995): 46.

11. Berstein and Borne, "L'enseignement de l'histoire au lycée," 141-42.

12. Extract from the *Bulletin officiel de l'Education Nationale*, 29 June 1995, reproduced in *Annabac sujets 2000 Histoire-Géographie L, ES, S* (Paris: Hatier, 1999), 19.

13. Michel Winock, "La Guerre d'Algérie," *Libération*, 26 June 1984, 22-24.

14. The high number of total questions is explained by the fact that at that time there were numerous *académies* within France where different questions were set.

15. Dominique Borne, "L'Histoire du vingtième siècle au lycée. Le nouveau programme de terminale," *Vingtième Siècle*, no. 21 (January-March 1989): 102.

16. Joël Cornette and Jean-Noël Luc, "Bac-Génération 84. L'Enseignement du temps présent en terminale," *Vingtième Siècle*, no. 6 (April-June 1985): 126.

17. See Guy Pervillé and Paul Fournier, "La guerre d'Algérie dans les manuels scolaires de Terminale," *Historiens et Géographes*, no. 308 (March 1986): 893-97 and 897-898 respectively; and *Mémoire et enseignement de la guerre d'Algérie: actes du colloque, 13-14 mars 1992, Paris*, vol. 2 (Paris: Institut du Monde arabe/Ligue de l'enseignement, 1993).

18. Henri Gibelin, "Pour en finir avec la querelle des manuels," *Les Cahiers Pédagogiques*, no. 369 (December 1998): 13.

19. Pierre Milza and Serge Berstein, eds., *De 1939 à nos jours* (Paris: Hatier, 1983/4), 250.

20. Pierre Milza and Serge Berstein, *Histoire Terminale* (Paris: Hatier, 1993), 203.

21. Pervillé and Fournier, "La guerre d'Algérie dans les manuels scolaires de Terminale," 898.

22. "Doyen de l'Inspection Générale" (therefore the head *Inspecteur*, author of the 1989 program) and co-chairman between the early 1990s and 1998 with Serge Berstein of the history GTD (therefore coauthor of the 1990s programs).

23. Borne, "L'Histoire du vingtième siècle au lycée," 104.

24. Berstein and Borne, "L'enseignement de l'histoire au lycée," 136.

25. Jean Peyrot, "L'enseignement de l'Histoire et la démocratie," *Historiens et Géographes*, no. 353 (June-July 1996): 11.

26. Jean Peyrot, "A quoi sert l'enseignement de l'histoire et de la géographie?" *Historiens et Géographes*, no. 297 (December 1983): 285 and 286 respectively.

27. Jean-Pierre Rioux, "A quoi servent les cours d'histoire?" *L'Histoire*, no. 202 (September 1996): 50.

28. Jean Peyrot, "Aux chocs de la vie," *Historiens et Géographes*, no. 328 (July-August 1990): 10.

29. Michel Wieviorka, "La production institutionnelle du racisme," *Hommes et Migrations*, no. 1211 (January-February 1998): 14.

30. Borne, "L'Histoire du vingtième siècle au lycée," 104.

31. Descombes, *Le Même et l'autre*.

32. "En coopération" is linked to military service and meant working in another country for the French State rather than being a soldier in France.

33. In the French education system pupils pass through *seconde, première* to then finish their secondary education in *terminale*.

34. Paul Fournier, "La guerre d'Algérie dans les manuels scolaires de Terminale," *Historiens et Géographes*, no. 308 (March 1986): 899.

35. A reform passed by the Ramadier government. It created an assembly in Algeria with two electoral colleges of equal size. Elections were loaded in favor of the settlers since although they numbered less than one million their votes elected the same number of representatives as those of the Muslims did, who numbered nine million.

36. The question related to what happened during the battle of Algiers and the notes (included in the appendices) read "Janvier 57-Septembre 57: 'bataille d'Alger:' victoire militaire pour les Français mais désastre politique" (January 57-September 57: Battle of Algiers: military victory for the French but political disaster).

37. Alain Coulon, *Connaissance de la guerre d'Algérie. Trente ans après: enquête auprès des jeunes Français de 17 à 30 ans* (Paris: Université de Paris VIII, 1993), 23.

Chapter Three

The Family: Discussing the War Years

Introduction

Since we have posited that "collective memory" is above all transmission of memory via the school, the family, and the media, we now need to understand the extent of transmission of memories within the "private sphere" of families. In the French Republic there is a particularly strong division between the "public sphere" of the State education system and the "private sphere" of the family, crucial, for example, to any understanding of debates since 1989 on the "affaires du foulard" (Islamic veil "affairs").[1] For Paul Thompson: "Telling family history undoubtedly goes on, but we have scarcely studied how it happens."[2] Maurice Halbwachs focused on the family as one group that creates a collective memory and provides individual (family) group members with the "social frames of memory" of time, language, and space. For Halbwachs memory is socially constructed, and there are as many collective memories as there are groups and institutions in society: "Every collective memory requires the support of a group delimited in space and time."[3] Thus "Family recollections in fact develop . . . in the consciousness of various members of the domestic group."[4] Families clearly play an important role in socializing individuals and in identity construction. For Halbwachs:

> today, each family has its proper mentality, its memories which it alone commemorates, and its secrets that are revealed only to its members. But these memories, as in the religious traditions of the family of antiquity, consist not only of a series of individual images of the past. They are at the same time models, examples, and elements of teaching. They express the general attitude of the group; they not only reproduce its history but also define its nature and its qualities and weaknesses . . . the various elements of this type that are retained from

the past provide a framework for family memory, which it tries to preserve intact, and which, so to speak, is the traditional armor of the family.[5]

Family transmission of memories of the Algerian War is a particularly important subject since conscription was used during the conflict. A whole generation of young men fought in Algeria. Most families in France have a grandfather, a father, a husband, a brother, or another member of the family who fought in North Africa. Millions of French men were drafted to fight in Algeria, for up to twenty-seven months. These men are currently of retirement age in France. Also, Algeria was a "colonie de peuplement" (populated colony) so there are also over one million settlers and their descendants in France as well as hundreds of thousands of Algerians, their children and grandchildren. In the previous chapter, we saw the difficulties and the shortcomings in the education system. Nonetheless we saw that in relative terms history classes are an important vector of memory. This is especially true of the Algerian War given the weakness, even absence, of other vectors of memory. All pupils interviewed stated that the teacher and history classes were a very important source of information on the Algerian War. Yet other vectors of memory—such as the family—exist. Indeed, they inevitably influence schools. As Jean-Pierre Rioux said in the interview in Paris:

> L'école républicaine en France ne pense pas qu'il faille privilégier la guerre d'Algérie au détriment d'autres événements pour aussi ne pas prendre le risque, parce que ça l'école ne veut pas, d'envenimer les conflits de mémoire qui existent et dont on peut prendre compte en classe, c'est évident, pour toujours les ramener à des éléments de connaissance et d'acquisition de connaissance par tous les élèves sur un phénomène comme la guerre d'Algérie. (The French Republican school system does not believe that the Algerian War should be focused on to the detriment of other events also in order to avoid the risk, because the school authorities do not want to do this, of aggravating memory conflicts that exist and are there in class, obviously, in order to always bring discussion back to elements of knowledge and knowledge acquisition by all students on a phenomenon like the Algerian War; Rioux 2000.)

In the previous chapter, we saw that teachers have a certain amount of room for maneuver in the way they interpret the program and what they do exactly in class. While in general they tend to do very similar things, some fascinating differences have been noted—especially the choice to do more or less on the Algerian War. These choices are linked closely to teachers' family history. Those teachers who did more in my sample tended to be of *pied-noir* origin but in a larger sample might be shown to have broader scientific, personal or sociological motivations. We also saw that the ethnic makeup of the class could influence what takes place in the classroom, through, for example, questions from pupils. In addition, seven of the twelve pupils who were interviewed for this project were of Algerian background, indicating more interest in the subject from this group. In this chapter we will focus in more depth on the family vector of memory. To what extent are memories circulating in classes from pupils? Are pupils learning much about the Algerian War from their families? How does this information obtained from the family compare with what is learnt in the classroom? How, if at all, do "individual" and family "group" memories fit into the "common" memory of the school history program? A particularly important area concerns ethnic minorities and transmission of memory. While we will consider transmission of memory in all of the groups to emerge from the war, particular attention will be given to two groups: the *harkis*—Algerians who fought in the French army—and *beurs*—young French people of North African descent. This is because, as we will see in this chapter in particular, of all of the groups— *beurs*, *harkis*, *pieds noirs*, and conscripts—these are the two that have most struggled to find a place or make a home in France. Racism is a significant problem in French society. Since the 1980s the far-right National Front party has campaigned on a resolutely anti-immigrant stance, with considerable electoral success. Racism can take a number of forms and be measured in a number of ways. All indicate that there is a significant amount of discrimination in contemporary French society along racial lines, leading to significant exclusion of ethnic minorities in the French Republic. Algerians and their descendants are particularly disadvantaged in this respect. There is apparent disagreement and confusion in existing literature concerning the extent of family transmission of memory on the Algerian War as we saw in our review of Critical Literature. The apparent paradox can be resolved if we accept that little transmission of memory in the family can lead to activism. One form of activism is writing, including "historical fiction."

We will see that a bricolage of theories of collective memory can best explain the extent of family transmission of memory—we can draw on Halbwachs as well as the more obvious Freud. Halbwachs indicates the importance of memories to the functioning of the family as a group; by providing cohesion. Cohesion in this context could be within the family by avoiding discussion of topics that could bring shame on members of the family, or by avoiding divisive memories that could exclude the family from wider society. Yet the silence and repression we encounter can also be understood through reference to "repression" of memories by individuals due to shame and trauma, hence our reference to Freud. The trauma of certain events may have led to an absolute inability to tackle certain issues. Also the activism/pluralism model of collective memory can also help understand how individuals deal with "occlusion" of memories and silence from their elders or society more generally. Consequently, the silence on the topic of the Algerian War within families may lead family members to actively seek out memories, explanations for the silence, and ways to overcome it.

Harkis is a generic term used to describe Algerian soldiers who fought for the French army during the Algerian War—the correct term is "forces supplétives" (supplementary forces). In fact *harkis* were only one of many groups— *groupes d'auto défense, moghazins*, etc.—but *harkis* is the term commonly used in France to refer to all of these groups. In 1957 there were 42,000 "supplétifs" in the French army and by 1958 this figure had risen to 88,000.[6] At the end of the war the soldiers were disarmed and abandoned. Many were then massacred by Algerians, while others escaped in dramatic conditions and in France were confined to camps for decades. By the late 1980s there were about 450,000 "Français musulmans" in France.[7] As we saw in the introduction, they are currently active in the public sphere. *Harkis* are studied in particular depth since the "silence of the fathers" is particularly prevalent here, and the position of this group in France has been particularly difficult. *Harkis* have been excluded from French society in very important ways. They were exiled within French Algeria, as they were forced to leave their fertile lands during the colonial period by settlers. They were literally torn from their compatriots, and even family members, by the war itself, as they chose (or were forced), for a myriad of reasons, to fight in the French army. They were then exiled to France due to a very real fear of persecution in Algeria in 1962, where they subsequently were marginalized in very important ways, to the extent that they are only just being integrated into French society, yet are still officially unable to return to Algeria.

Beurs is a term that has often been used in France to describe young people of Algerian descent—children of North African immigrants.[8] By the early 1980s Algerians were the largest nationality group, numbering some 800,000 people. As Ross shows, the narratives of modernization and decolonization are usually erroneously separated in France, usually by forgetting one of them, with serious consequences for stereotypes of immigrant workers and their descendants. Yamina Benguigui's documentary *Mémoires d'Immigrés* (Immigrant Memories) explicitly sets out to challenge this forgetting by discovering and promoting a "Maghrebian heritage" through a process of oral history that recovers silenced memories of immigration, and attempts to link the generations by showing the younger generations (as well as broader French society) how and why their parents or grandparents came to France and under what conditions. Although in the 1950s and 1960s immigration to France operated predominantly on a "single male rotation system," with male workers working temporarily in France, family immigration developed strongly in the 1960s and 1970s. Immigrants therefore ceased to be solely on the margins of French society and thus ignored, and so French society was presented with a number of new challenges—revolving around how to deal with cultural difference in housing, schools etc. In the 1980s the children of the workers who had come to France predominantly in the 1950s and 1960s reached school age in significant numbers. The "Marche des Beurs" of 1983 represented a huge increase in visibility in children of North African immigrants in France. The "Marche des Beurs" was literally a walk undertaken by children of Algerian immigrants and *harkis*. It started from Marseilles and Lyon and finished in Paris, where at its end 60,000 people marched. It was a "marche pour l'égalité, contre le racisme" (walk for equality, against racism).[9] The term has been challenged in the 1990s for a variety of reasons.[10] While it originally allowed a word used negatively to be instilled with new value, therefore negating the damage the original word Arab could cause, it was subsequently recuperated by the media and the government and so its meaning changed and it could no longer perform the same function. Other uses of "verlan" (back slang) have followed, such as *rebeu*. Ethnicity is always a difficult area to discuss, as we balance a need to differentiate to better describe and understand with a need to avoid categorizing or stereotyping whole groups.[11] Furthermore it is incredibly difficult to talk of communities or "ethnic groups" in France. The term we will use the most needs to be young people of Algerian descent, for which the shorthand *beur* will be used.

History Classes and the Family

History Classes

In the previous chapter we examined school transmission of memories. One way that the specificity of this vector of memory can be observed is in differences between a history class and a testimony. Quantitatively two out of eighteen teachers had ever invited veterans of the Algerian War, although one of the two did not speak exclusively about this colonial war. None had done so during the period when the interviews with teachers took place (between September 1997 and June 1999). This seems to me to be a rather low figure, all the more so when compared with the number of World War Two testimonies. A first reason for the low number of classroom testimonies from veterans of the Algerian War is the problem, already mentioned above, of time in *terminale*. One particularly telling example of the current race against the program is the practicability of inviting veterans to the school.

One of the two teachers who had invited a veteran of the Algerian War to school had done so over ten years ago. The meeting involved a veteran and an Algerian to get two viewpoints on the war and lasted two hours. Above all, the discussion created a lot of interest and a lot of questions—notably on the everyday life in Algeria and feelings and opinions at the time of the war. That meeting took place twice in the early 1980s and according to the teacher has not been done recently since:

> Ca ne s'est plus reproduit parce que justement dans les anciens programmes on avait plus de temps, et donc comme on avait moins de temps dans ces programmes, ça ne s'est pas fait. (It was not repeated precisely because in the former programs we had more time, so since we have less time in these programs we didn't do it again; Teacher 4.)

Indeed, the *terminale* year is very different from other years as can be seen from the fact that even the testimonies on World War Two were done in *première* or *troisième*. The problem of time has been aggravated by the reform to the program that came into effect in September 1998. The practicalities of inviting a veteran might also be problematic as veterans have to be organized in associations, to be able to be contacted, and to agree to come to the school. One teacher also mentioned that the Algerian War is still a very delicate subject to talk about.

Another referred to the problem of subjectivity and said she did not really want someone in class whose experience would make him particularly partial. A last interesting point to note is the impact on teachers of wider society that arguably means that teachers might not even think to invite a veteran of the Algerian War as they might a veteran of World War Two. Perhaps this is because the war was for such a long time not referred to as "une guerre" (a war). One teacher, for example, said: "Je n'y ai jamais songé" (I've never thought about it; Teacher 14). Another teacher said: "Je n'ai même jamais pensé à le faire" (I've never even thought to do it; Teacher 17).

Interestingly, even the second of the teachers who had invited someone who gave a testimony on the Algerian War, when asked: "Est-ce qu'un ancien combattant est venu à un moment donné parler aux élèves?" (Has a veteran ever come to talk to the pupils) replied: "Je ne fais pas venir d'anciens combattants de l'Algérie" (I don't invite veterans of the Algerian War) before mentioning that the person who had come was Hélie de Saint Marc, that is, an important figure from the war in Algeria. This answer can perhaps be explained by the fact that the testimony was aimed at explaining how an officer could disobey his orders and so he was invited as a French army officer rather than exclusively as a veteran of the Algerian War. He also spoke at length in the testimony of the war in Indo-China. This subject however is inherently linked to the Algerian conflict and so de Saint Marc spoke for three quarters of an hour on the Algerian War in a testimony of two hours. The teacher had prepared the visit by spending a little more time on the years 1960-1961 (during the Algerian conflict) to explain the reasons for the April 1961 putsch. It might also be true that de Saint Marc is not exactly an "ancien combattant" (veteran), a term that makes one think more of *appelés* and *rappelés* (conscripts). As the teacher said, de Saint Marc had come:

> non pas en tant, je dirais personnellement . . . en tant qu'ancien combattant d'Algérie, mais en tant que officier de l'armée française revolté contre le général de Gaulle, parce que ça permet de comprendre les hésitations, parfois même peut-être les contradictions du général de Gaulle et comment un officier de l'armée française qui normalement est au service de l'Etat, peut à un certain moment en conscience se révolter contre l'Etat. Et ça c'est très intéressant. (not as, I would say myself . . . not as a veteran of the Algerian War, rather as an officer in the French army who revolted against the General de Gaulle, because it allows us to understand the hesitations, even the contradictions of General de Gaulle and how an officer in the French army who is ordinarily a servant of the State can consciously revolt against the State at a certain time. That is very interesting; Teacher 18.)

We can note that the teacher had invited de Saint Marc due to his "sympathie personnelle" (personal liking) for the man and since he respected this person who had been "fidèle à sa conscience" (true to himself). He was able to come once a year for four or five years until 1997 because he lives in Lyon. The pupils had found the testimony fascinating and had asked a lot of questions. Lastly we can state that the insistence on de Gaulle's hesitations and contradictions mentioned in the quotation above are not at all evident in textbooks' description of de Gaulle's Algerian policy. Nor are notions of rebellion and disobeying the State.

None of the pupils had been in a class in *terminale* where a veteran of the Algerian War had spoken. One pupil had however been in a class in *troisième*[12] where a veteran of the Algerian War had been invited. That particular pupil (Pupil 11, who is of Algerian origin) had received a lot of information from her grandfather who had actively fought against the French in Algeria (he was in her words a "maquisard," therefore a member of the FLN). She learnt a lot however from the testimony since it gave her a different point of view to that previously received. In that lesson there had been two people who gave testimonies: one on the Second World War, the other on the Algerian War. For the latter it was a French soldier (an *appelé*) who was also a *pied-noir*. He spoke for an hour and a half and talked about everyday life: "le vécu." Qualitatively we can note that the information given in class and that given through an oral testimony is radically different. One teacher explained the difference between the teacher's lesson and the veteran's testimony in the following terms:

C'est le positionnement par rapport à l'élève. Nous quand on est face à l'élève on est un enseignant qui avons des connaissances . . . qui apportons des connaissances à l'élève. Là ils auraient quelqu'un qui a vécu le fait dont il parle et donc ils ont une tendance à avoir un intérêt redoublé et à poser des questions souvent plus précises qu'ils pourraient nous poser à nous. Et c'est pour ça que c'est intéressant. (It's the position in relation to the pupil. In the pupils' eyes we are teachers who possess a certain amount of knowledge . . . who transmit knowledge to the pupils. Here however would be someone who has lived through what he's talking about so there tends to be much more interest and more detailed questions than they could ask us. That's why it's interesting; Teacher 13.)

We can note that the teacher who said this had not been able to invite a veteran of the Algerian War to give a testimony in class, but would have liked to. It was not possible due to time and practical considerations. He said in the interview that he would have liked to invite a man called Bernard Gerland, who has written a monologue that he repeats on his experience as a soldier. This is a fascinating and very memorable account that I was lucky enough to see in a theater in Lyon in 1997. It is however a hard-hitting recital as, after a somewhat positive introduction to his time in Algeria, he suddenly begins to describe how he executed a prisoner in a "corvée de bois" (illicit summary execution after interrogation). Clearly he has never recovered from this act. Both of the teachers who had invited people who gave testimonies on the Algerian War (Teacher 4 and Teacher 18) said that those meetings had gone very well. They gave rise to a lot of interest and a lot of questions. The difference between a lesson and a testimony is also in part shown in pupil comments on lessons as compared to testimonies since all but two of the twelve pupils interviewed had at some point (usually *première* but sometimes *troisième*) heard a testimony on World War Two, the Resistance, or deportation. Pupils when describing testimonies described them as

being "parlant" (hard hitting) in the sense that "ça illustre bien" (it illustrates
things well; Pupil 9), "réel" (real), "émouvant" (moving), "intéressant" (interesting) etc.

The difference between World War Two and Algeria on this point is fascinating and very important too. The relatively high number of testimonies seen on
World War Two shows the current importance attributed to transmitting information on World War Two from generation to generation. Again the Algerian
War can be seen to be overshadowed by the memory of World War Two. Once
again we see how there has been a considerable investment by French society in
Franco-German reconciliation, whereas concerning the Algerian War there is
insufficient "volontarisme de mémoire" (desire to foster memory) to conduct a
more sustained "work of memory" that could go a long way to reconciling
France and Algeria and elements within each of these societies. Pupil comments
also show the importance in terms of transmission of the "Centre d'Histoire de la
Résistance et de la Déportation" (CHRD) in Lyon. Many of the testimonies
given on the Second World War reflected in their content the concerns of this
History Center and would seem to have been organized with the help of or
through the CHRD. Clearly the existence of museums and other historical centers is important for the transmission of memory, and while an exhaustive study
of museology for the Second World War and Algeria cannot be undertaken here,
it can nonetheless be said that the Algerian War does not benefit from the same
museological interest as the Second World War. This is important in so far as a
museum can be a *lieu de mémoire* (site of memory).

Therefore it can be argued that the kind of information and the impact of the
vectors differ. This is in part due to the fact that in the context of a class it is
clear that pupils are not necessarily receptive to information. This was mentioned
in particular by two teachers. One of them pointed to the fact that it is important
to note that the Algerian War is taught in *terminale*—a different year than *seconde* or *première* (the two years before *terminale* in French secondary education). He said:

> Globalement vous avez en terminale les élèves assez passifs. Ils sont passifs
> parce que la clef c'est le baccalauréat, donc leur attitude c'est une attitude de
> consommateur. Ils écrivent, ils écrivent, ils écrivent sans beaucoup d'esprit cri-
> tique, ils sont là pour digérer une matière qu'on leur donne. Leur but est un but
> utilitaire, c'est d'avoir la meilleure note possible au baccalauréat (On the whole
> pupils in *terminale* are quite passive. They are passive because the goal is the
> *baccalauréat*, so they have a "consumer" attitude. They write and write and
> write without much critical reflection, they are there to digest a subject that we
> dispense. Their objective is a utilitarian objective, it's to get the best mark pos-
> sible at the *baccalauréat*; Teacher 3).

This comment gives us a good indication of the setup of the lesson: clearly one
in which the teacher lectures and the pupils write. Beyond the transmission of
the memory of the Algerian War, it shows the inherent limits of any transmission
of memory through history classes in *terminale*. Students are not in class to de-

bate or discuss but to follow a predetermined program, take notes, and regurgitate this "knowledge" in an examination.

The attitude of the pupils also depends on the *série*. One teacher in particular said that in Terminale S the pupils, due to the weak weighting of history in this *série*, minimized their efforts. Here again pupils are in class to pass an examination and want to take notes to "use" in the examination, which might be seen as a fairly narrow definition of "teaching" and "education." History is weighted lowest for science students. For them history is weighted three while mathematics is weighted nine. History is weighted four for Literature students and five for economics/social science students. There is very little understanding on the part of pupils whose knowledge comes from the classroom. Only a limited number of points are dealt with in history class and those that are talked about are not done in sufficient detail so that they are understood. To some extent classes are inherently limited and there are things that are simply impossible. However the limits of class are also to a certain extent imposed by choices.

This knowledge corresponds to the result of history classes, but is not true of knowledge obtained from the family. One particularly interesting way that this can be seen is on the question of torture in the Algerian War. Before looking at the findings of the interviews with pupils concerning the family however, we can note that in a 1985 survey about the teaching of history, the Algerian War when taught autonomously (rather than in the Decolonization chapter) was "un sujet chaud" (a delicate subject), and these reactions noted by teachers were principally attributed to family history:

> Qu'est-ce qui motive les réactions des élèves? D'abord, l'histoire familiale (dans quarante-quatre pour cent des cas). Explique-t-elle le poids des guerres—1939-45, Algérie—dans l'ordre des préoccupations? (What dictates the reactions of the pupils? Firstly, family history [in forty-four percent of cases]. Does it explain the place of wars—1939-45, Algeria—in the hierarchy of concerns?)[13]

Family history is therefore to be expected to be important in motivating the reactions of pupils in class. The interviews conducted with pupils for this book support this statement. Torture is one aspect of the Algerian War that is not done in detail in class. Either the subject had not been done at all or it certainly had not been memorable. For one pupil: "Il n'y a pas fait référence" (He didn't refer to it; Pupil 2 on Teacher 1's class). She went on to say that the massacre in Sétif on 8 May 1945 was "le seul événement dont il nous avait parlé où les Français avaient fait du mal à l'Algérie" (the only event that he talked to us about where the French had hurt Algeria). For another: "On n'a pas vu ça" (We didn't do that; Pupil 7 on Teacher 11's class). For others the subject had been done quickly in a minimum of words. One pupil's notes read "jan 57-sep 57: mission de nettoyage d'Alger, mais par quelles méthodes!! (sur le style de la Gestapo=désastre politique=grand bruit.)" (Jan 57-Sep 57: mission to clean up Algiers, but by what methods!! [like the Gestapo=political disaster=lots of noise]). Two other students told me that the subject was not essential and that the Algerian War was not like Vichy/World War Two. Pupil 8 said: "Ce n'est pas quelque chose d'essentiel" (It's not something essential) and Pupil 12 mentioned that for torture during World War Two: "c'était autre chose . . . c'était de la vraie torture ça" (that was something else . . . that was really torture that was). The subject had clearly not been done in sufficient detail and was therefore underestimated in turn by pupils. None of the pupils interviewed had gained any detailed information on torture in class because the subject had at best been covered very quickly in one or two sentences.

Concerning the theoretical work on memory studied earlier in this book, the treatment of torture in class, the model for which also comes from the program and textbooks, certainly indicates difficulty treating the subject as it is repressed and occluded and not openly discussed or faced up to. Ross in her book *Fast Cars, Clean Bodies*, can perhaps be of help here. She states that: "Torture in the Algerian war strove to 'leave no traces'—which is to say, to immobilize time, or to function as an ahistorical structural system."[14] This may explain part of the difficulty of teaching about torture. Ross provides a fascinating account of the growing obsession with hygiene and cleanliness (in housekeeping) in mainland France during the period of the Algerian War, in a rapidly changing France, while in Algeria raged a "sale guerre" (dirty war). A main reason why this war was "dirty" was the use of torture which even if it was "artisinal" to begin with soon "industrialized" and "modernized."

The Family

However, two pupils had obtained significant information from their family on torture so we can compare this information to what we know is transmitted in history classes. Three important points emerge from this comparison: firstly, much more detailed information can come from the family than from the classroom; secondly, the information from the family can be controversial or divisive; and thirdly, the children whose family came from North Africa sometimes never talked of the Algerian War, but in some cases they did (particularly if family links with Algeria were still strong). Firstly Pupil 2, who is of Algerian origin, said that in class: "On n'en a pas trop parlé" (we didn't speak about it much). However in her family her mother, mother's uncles and grandmother talked about the Algerian War, especially in Algeria. According to her mother, villagers often helped the FLN so the French took the food from the village and regrouped populations. She was able to give a very detailed description of this treatment: "regroupement" (population roundups). She described this as follows:

> Les résistants ils venaient souvent la nuit pour venir chercher la nourriture. Donc ma mère elle m'a dit qu'ils prenaient la population, enfin les gens du village, et ils les amenaient dans des endroits et ils les entassaient tous ensemble. Ils leur disaient "vous restez là, comme ça on est sûrs que les autres ils ne viendront pas chercher la nourriture chez vous." Donc elle m'a dit, ça c'était ma grande-mère aussi, elle m'a dit: "ils nous prenaient et ils nous mettaient avec les enfants et

tout dans des petites maisons et ils nous entassaient tous les uns sur les autres."
Elle me racontait des anecdotes: elle me disait qu'il y en avait qui se pissaient . .
. qui se urinaient les uns sur les autres tellement c'était difficile. Et donc ils les
laissaient là pendant la nuit. (Resistance fighters often came at night to get sup-
plies of food. So my mother told me that they took the population, or rather the
people from the village, and they led them away to places where they put them
all together. They said "you stay there, so that we know that the others won't
come to get food from your house." So she said to me, this was my grandmother
too, she said: "they took us and they put us with the children in small houses and
they piled us on top of each other." She told me anecdotes: she told me that
there were people who pissed . . . who urinated on each other since it was so difficult. And so they left them there all night; Pupil 2.)

She also knew about torture and described the use of electricity, suspending people from rafters, and rape. Members of her family had been tortured. She said
these were subjects that it was not easy to talk about. There was a stark difference between her answer given to the question on torture in the interview and her
answers to other questions. On this subject she was able to provide a significant
amount of relevant information to support her answer. She talked for a long time.
Also fascinating is the way she talks of "resistance fighters" (FLN) and "collaborators" (people who worked with the French). Such descriptions highlight the
tremendous division caused by the war, including in families: indeed she talked
of her uncle "collaborating" but her grandfather "resisting." Clearly such reflections on a colonial past that ended barely decades ago can still be divisive and
uncomfortable in the present.

Secondly, for another pupil (Pupil 1), who is also of Algerian origin (but
more distant as her grandfather was the son of a settler who left Algeria before
the war), there was a stark difference in the quality of information received from
the family (grandmother) and the class. In history classes torture had been studied but they had not spent much time on it. She said: "On indique que la France
n'avait pas hesité à utiliser la torture, les moyens violents" (It was indicated that
France had not hesitated in using torture, violent means). She also said: "On
nous a dit qu'on a beaucoup utilisé la torture et que ça avait choqué quand même
à la fin certains Français, parce qu'ils n'étaient pas au courant pendant" (We
were also told that torture was extensively used and this had nonetheless shocked
some French people at the end of the conflict, because they weren't aware of it
during the war). She could not remember why the French army had used torture
although this had perhaps been mentioned in class. Her grandmother however
had given her a real example of violence during the war. Pupil 1 had asked her
grandmother a question (her grandfather is dead) while she was revising history
to prepare for a test to talk about the Second World War (on the Occupation:
"What was life like during the Occupation?") but the conversation had also
drifted onto the Algerian War. The grandmother had been told by her neighbor,
who had been a conscript in Algeria and had driven such trucks, that the French
collected people in trucks whom they suspected of resisting and threw them off a
cliff into the sea. This is the kind of information that cannot be obtained from a

class. It can be noted that this kind of information is possibly divisive in so far as it concerns different sections of French society that were opposed in the past and also concerns a period during which terrible actions were performed in France's name.

Lastly, a third pupil's comments can be described here. Pupil 11, whose grandfather participated in the FLN in the Algerian War, had also obtained a lot of information from the family, members of which had died during the Algerian War. It is of course highly noteworthy that two of these three examples of pupils who had gained information from their families (notably on torture) are *beurs* and have strong links with Algeria. The other also has a family history linked to Algeria. We can also note the difference in terms of memory between France and Algeria that other studies have shown—basically, for France, scholars talk of repression whereas for Algeria scholars talk of memories of the war being hon-ored.[15] Unlike the other two pupils, for Pupil 11 it is better not to speak of such things: "Je crois qu'il vaut mieux cacher les choses horribles, pas heurter les âmes sensibles" (I think it's better to hide horrible things, not to shock sensitive people). In class on torture they had done very little, perhaps even nothing. Again we can see how this subject is still very divisive as she talks of her grand-father's lifelong (since the Algerian War) "hantisse de l'Etat français, l'armée française" (obsessive fear of the French State and the French army). Apparently she often talks with her grandfather: "Il aime en parler mais il a besoin d'en par-ler" (He likes to talk about it but he needs to talk about it). It is important to note that he was described by Pupil 11 as a "grand maquisard" (resistance hero, FLN). Perhaps this is a good example of the way if the past is glorious and serves present purposes then it is discussed. This was not however easy due to trauma since he had lost members of his family in the war including his brother.

This claimed involvement in resistance activities during the Algerian War reminds us of the French memory of World War Two in the first few decades after that conflict. The claim that members of the family resisted the French in Algeria could be compared to the mythified French portrayal of the French Re-sistance to the Nazi occupier. Faced with such narratives, a "critical distance" can be argued to be needed in order to understand and take into account the role of selective memory in a group's construction of present identity. However, be-yond the important fact that the sample interviewed for this book is extremely limited and there do not seem to be many secondary sources on this question, we can note that reference was also made in the interviews to members of the family collaborating (see Pupil 2) and that Pupil 11 thought it was better not to talk of such things and therefore cannot be said to have particularly sought to impose a glorified view of her family history on the interviewer. Nonetheless, a wider study might show more evidence of a mythified Resistance to the French in Al-geria and this is certainly a delicate, yet fascinating area to investigate further. There are many other aspects of the Algerian War which have echoes of World War Two. Whatever the answer to the questions, by not studying in more depth the Algerian War in order not to aggravate or reactivate divisive individual and group memories of the Algerian conflict, State authorities are very wary of such (potential) memories.

More generally on the family we can note that not all families of *beurs* where the grandparents had experience of the Algerian War talked of this period. In families where the parents come from Algeria there is not always discussion. Pupil 8, Pupil 9, and Pupil 12 said that they did not talk much with their grandparents. Pupil 12's great uncle had served five years of prison during the Algerian War and did not talk about it since it was too difficult. He said that he talked a little with his father because his father had not lived through the Algerian War. Pupil 9 said: "ils n'en parlent pas" (they don' talk about it) and "je n'en parle pas" (I don't talk about it) and Pupil 8 said "on ne s'implique pas trop" (we don't get involved) and "ça fait partie du passé" (it's the past). Beyond my sample, one example of little family transmission is given in a fascinating edition of the review *Hommes et Migrations* on "Les Harkis et leurs enfants" (*Harkis* and their children). In this we can read:

> Fréquemment, de la part d'un ex-supplétif, c'est le silence qui accueille toute question portant sur la nature des opérations auxquelles il lui fut donné de participer durant la guerre d'Algérie. Que les questions soient posées par les enfants ou par un étranger ne change pas grande chose à l'affaire . . . Toutefois on aurait tort de mettre ce silence sur le compte d'une démarche d'autocensure résultant d'un sentiment de culpabilité. En effet, on peut retrouver la même discretion chez les Algériens ayant adhéré au FLN. (Often, one is confronted with silence from *harkis* when a question is asked about the operations they participated in during the Algerian War. It matters little whether the questions are asked by a child or a stranger . . . However it would be wrong to account for this silence by reference to feelings of shame. Actually, one can find the same silence amongst Algerians who belonged to the FLN.)[16]

Interestingly Roux in this quotation talks of the silence of both *harkis* and ex-FLN members (in France). A last example can be given here of lack of transmission of memory through the family in this group. It appears in another edition of *Hommes et Migrations*, in an interview with the son (at the time in *terminale*) of a man who was at the Paris demonstration that took place on 17 October 1961. In it the interviewer asks: "Et ton père, te parle-t-il souvent du 17 octobre 1961?" (And your father, does he talk to you often about 17 October 1961?) The interviewee answers:

> Non, il n'est pas trop revenu dessus. Parce que je pense que c'est quelque chose qu'on a peut-être envie . . . pas d'oublier, parce que ça restera, mais . . . on n'aime pas trop parler des mauvaises expériences. (No, he's not talked about it much. Because I think it's something that one wants to . . . not to forget, because you can't, but . . . we don't like to talk about bad experiences.)[17]

This reminds us of what we know about families of *appelés* or *rappelés* (conscripts). All families that have members who lived through the Algerian War have difficulty talking about their experiences during the conflict. Our knowledge of their memory comes from sources such as Bertrand Tavernier's film *La Guerre sans nom* (The War Without a Name) and Claire Mauss-Copeaux's book *Appelés en guerre d'Algérie* (Conscripts and the Algerian War). In this last study the author states: "aujourd'hui beaucoup ne veulent pas en parler à leurs enfants" (today many do not want to talk about it with their children).[18] When commenting on the fact that in only one of the thirty-nine interviews that she conducted was a conscript's child present, she says: "Ils se disent en général plus réticents à partager leurs souvenirs avec leurs enfants et reconnaissent leur refus obstiné de répondre à leurs questions" (In general they say they are more reticent to share their recollections with their children and admit to their stubborn refusal to answer their questions on this topic).[19] In this group of people there is very little discussion on the Algerian War. Stora's work can also be useful in understanding family transmission for conscripts. In his television series *Les Années algériennes* (The Algerian Years) a conscript (Mr. J-M Linné) is questioned. The dialogue is as follows:

> Interviewer: Vous avez des enfants? (Do you have children?)
> Linné: J'ai trois enfants. J'ai six petits-enfants. (I have three children. I have six grandchildren)
> Interviewer: Vous leur en dites quoi de la guerre d'Algérie? (What do you say to them about the Algerian War?)
> Linné: Je n'en parle jamais. (I never talk about it)

Furthermore it is very unlikely that within families of other groups, for example, "opinion métropolitaine" (French domestic public opinion) that have few links to Algeria much information is transmitted. What is meant by this group is French public opinion in mainland France during the Algerian conflict. These are people who lived through the conflict, but were not involved in the war, despite some potential knowledge of it or even a distant member of the family or friends serving in the army in Algeria. In this group we may find lack of interest for the subject and very little information to be transmitted.

To sum up, there are therefore families that do not discuss the Algerian War. Due to the limits of this sample it is impossible here to state with certainty exact numbers. However we can say that if information is obtained from the family it is very detailed and much richer than information obtained from the class. It can also be the kind of information that is never discussed in the classroom. We can also state that in some families information is transmitted. In our sample, families from Algeria seemed to discuss the war the most, and particularly if they had retained strong links with other family members still in Algeria. This would seem to be information that is given since it is not shameful to those who tell the story and supports what they want to say. However we must note that not all families transmit information and that if this does not happen it can be because such memories are painful. Furthermore if they did talk about it, this communication can also be fairly superficial. Pupil 5 said that she spoke with her grandmother about the Algerian War but that this often equated to looking at photos and "se rémemorer des gens" (remembering people). She said that she received "des informations mais pas beaucoup, beaucoup" (some information, but not a lot). This could be supported by what we know about families of *pieds-noirs*. One teacher whom I interviewed who is *pied-noir* (Teacher 17) said that *pieds-noirs* spoke about Algeria in their families but only of the good things about the colonial period. Let us now look at some of these issues to emerge from the case study in more detail. In particular we will consult a wide corpus of secondary sources to have a more representative view of the extent of family transmission of memory in families from North Africa.

Harkis: Family Silence and Activism

As we saw in the Introduction, *harkis*—Algerian soldiers who fought for the French army—were one group whose exodus from Algeria was particularly fraught with difficulty and traumatic. In 1999, Jordi and Hamoumou, authors of *Les harkis, une mémoire enfouie* (The *Harkis*: Repressed Memories), described the place of the *harkis* in French collective memory as follows:

> Depuis trente-six ans (aussi), la France—ou pour le moins une très grande majo-rité de Français—ne les voit pas. "Harkis, connais pas!" semble un leitmotiv bien commode pour oublier la présence française en Algérie, pour évacuer les drames et les tensions provoqués par la guerre, pour respecter les sensibilités historiques et sans doute les histoires officielles." (For thirty-six years (also), France—or at least the vast majority of French people—does not see them. "*Harkis*, never heard of them!" seems to be a very convenient leitmotiv to forget French presence in Algeria, to neutralize the dramas and the tensions the war created, to respect historical sensibilities and without doubt official histories.)[20]

Group/national cohesion and self interest were important then in explaining the marginalized place of the *harkis* in French memory. Silence on the topic or feigned ignorance feeds into a broader process of forgetting that allows the trauma of the war to be (provisionally) overcome by ignoring it. For Laurent Muller, author of *Le Silence des harkis* (Silence of the *Harkis*): "L'Algérie, la France, comme les Français musulmans eux-mêmes, ont intérêt à entretenir le silence et l'oubli" (Algeria and France, as well as French Muslims themselves, have something to gain from maintaining the silence and the forgetting).[21] The history of the *harkis* is linked to dishonor for the army and a dark episode of Gaullism in so far as the French army used the *harkis* to fight its dirty war and then abandoned them and stood by as they were massacred. Forgetting divisive elements of the past once again goes hand in hand with nation building. Obvi-ously though this nation is inherently exclusionary and built on unsure founda-tions. The *harkis* and their descendants are the main losers here, although the cohesion of wider French society has been weakened by this approach to manag-ing divisive memories. The title of Stora's book *La Gangrène et l'oubli* (Gan-grene and Forgetting) accurately captures what is at work here: forgetting leading to the perpetuation of the division of the time since it is marginalized and cannot be addressed, hence over time it operates like a gangrene or a cancer on the wider French society.

The wider silence in French society is very much reflected in families. In the case of the *harkis*, the evidence of little transmission of memory through the family is rather overwhelming. Muller refers to "des silences qui continuent à planer au sein de la plupart de ces familles" (silences that continue to hang over most of these families).[22] The second part of his study is described as an attempt to "analyse(r) un élément commun et caractéristique de la majeure partie des familles d'anciens harkis: le silence du père au sujet de son passé" (analyze a common element, typical of most families of *harkis*: the silence of the father concerning his past).[23] For Kara, in the households of *harkis* there is/was what he describes as a "silence assourdissant" (a deafening silence).[24] Similarly, Jordi and Hamoumou entitle a chapter in their work "Histoire refusée et mémoire re-foulée" (denied history and repressed memory) and describe "une histoire tue autant que refusée" (a history not told as well as denied) and "une mémoire re-foulée et un dialogue difficile" (a repressed memory and difficult dialogue).[25] Many examples are given of children of *harkis* whose fathers never talked of the war.

Abrial also provides some excellent data on family transmission of memory of the Algerian War in *harki* families. For example, in a highly detailed dis-course analysis of lapses in her interview corpus material, the past and family history is an element of interviewee discourse where silences abound. In addition to:

> la mise en relation des silences et de la famille . . . On constate en effet qu'ils s'attardent spécifiquement sur le passé et l'histoire de la famille . . . Les inter-ruptions se forment autour d'un axe significatif: celui du passé et de la manière dont se gère ce passé à l'intérieur de la cellule familiale. (the relationship bet-ween silences and the family . . . We find in effect that they specifically dwell on the past and the history of the family . . . The lapses occur around a signifi-cant axis: that of the past and the way this past is managed within the family cell.)[26]

However, little transmission of memory has led to activism that has forced greater recognition of the *harkis* by French society. This in itself is an indication of the shortcomings of and damage caused by the model of simply trying to ig-nore a traumatic and difficult past. Mohamed Kara, author of *Les tentations du repli communautaire* (The Temptation of the Community), puts it thus: "autant les parents se sont tu . . . autant le fils aujourd'hui se rebellent" (the more the parents have not talked . . . the more the son today rebels).[27] Psychological rea-sons may explain "memory activism." Kara attributes quite a lot of importance to such factors, since he relies heavily on Erving Goffman's work *Stigma*. One senses that for Kara militant activism needs to be understood in relation a psy-chological need in so far as "c'est le regard des autres qui dit qui vous êtes" (it is the Other who tells you who you are) and "Ils œuvrent dans le cadre associatif à une valorization du groupe" (They work in the associative sphere to add value to the group) in a "mouvement de réappropriation de l'histoire" (movement to re-appropriate history) in a "parcours identitaire" (search for identity).[28] For as Abrial reminds us:

> L'intégration à la française, batie autour de l'héritage républicain, a toujours eu pour but de faire accéder les individus au rang de citoyens. Le cas des harkis semble symptomatique; il montre que la réussite de l'intégration n'est jamais acquise au seul fait de la nationalité; d'autres dimensions telles que la reconnaissance de l'histoire et de la culture des individus intervenant dans le processus. (The French model of integration, built around the Republican heritage, has always sought to make individuals into citizens. The case of the *harkis* appears to be symptomatic; it shows that successful integration is not simply a function of nationality; other elements such as recognition of one's history and culture also count.)[29]

This is an excellent point. Recognition of one's history in French history and an integration of individual, family, and group histories into the wider dominant French history is crucial to a sense of feeling French and being accepted as such. There is undoubtedly an abundance of evidence of activism by children of *harkis* that can take various forms and has evolved over the years. Examples of forms of activism vary from hostage taking and violence to militancy in associations. Muller states that there are about four hundred and fifty associations of *harkis* in France, of which one third are presided over by members of the second generation. Revolts perhaps most dramatically took place in Narbonne during the summer of 1991, but there were also important revolts in 1975, 1987, 1992, and 1997. Jordi and Hamoumou describe the activism of children of *harkis* as follows:

> Depuis trente-six ans, épisodiquement, des hommes et des femmes barrent les routes, font des grèves de la faim, s'enchaînent aux grilles de préfectures ou de ministères, pour attirer sur eux le regard des autorités et celui des "autres Français." Pour demander réparation aussi, pour qu'on reconnaisse leur place dans l'histoire de France, pour être enfin traités comme tout citoyen français. (For thirty-six years, periodically, some men and women block roads, go on hunger strike, chain themselves to the gates of prefectures or ministries, to attract the attention of authorities and of "other French people." To try and obtain compensation, to secure recognition of their place in French history, lastly to be finally treated as French citizens.)[30]

Stéphanie Abrial's work is very useful in understanding social agency and *harki* collective memory due to the typology of activism that she constructs from her sample of twenty-five interviewees. She claims that "harki identity" for a young person can be either "proclamée" (proclaimed), "structurée" (structured) or "absente" (absent). She differentiates between what she terms "les apolotiques" (apoliticals) and "les conventionnels" (conventionals) on the one hand, and the "protestataires" (protestors) and the "porte-paroles" (spokespeople) on the other.

The "apolotiques" and "conventionnels" have both distanced themselves from the history of the parents.[31]

One can also obtain a better idea of the activities of harkis from *Le Monde*. It is very interesting to note that despite significant media coverage (1991: 105 articles on the *harkis*)[32] their situation improved little throughout the 1990s. Debate in 1991 focused upon revolts by children of *harkis* that began in May and continued all summer. Whereas media coverage initially focused on the revolts and their political ramifications (concentrating predominantly on financial measures) not until early August was the issue of this marginalized memory addressed.[33] On the other hand, associations have recently succeeded in obtaining a "journée nationale d'hommage aux harkis" (national day of homage to *harkis*), celebrated for the first time in 2001.[34]

Harkis have recently attempted to try France for "crimes against humanity." According to the journalist Philippe Bernard they wanted to "saisir l'occasion de tenter de sortir de quarante ans d'oubli" (seize the chance to emerge from forty years of being forgotten). For Muller the aim of children of *harkis* can be to "mieux faire connaître le sort de leurs parents" (better raise awareness of the fate of their parents).[35] Associations enable members to be with people, to be listened to, and to act together. For Abrial: "Il s'agit de s'impliquer dans un organisme offrant la possibilité d'être 'visualizés' par *l'extérieur* et réconfortés à *l'intérieur*" (The objective is to become involved in a group that offers the possibility to be "visualized" *by others* and comforted *within*).[36] In her sample, eleven of the twenty-five interviewees belong to an association. Omar, an interviewee (President of an association of children of *harkis*) insists on the way associations allow "representation" in the areas of defending one's rights, acting as a counterforce and also in personal revenge. There is a clear division across generational lines in this movement, that is perhaps unsurprising and mirrors generational differences that one encounters in the broader Maghrebian community.[37] For example, it is evidenced in the work of Soraya Nini or Yamina Benguigui whose work emphasizes the gulf between the generations: broadly speaking a first generation that defers to French society and does not want to draw attention to itself, and younger generations who feel much more able to speak out and challenge injustice or discrimination.

Beurs: Family Memory and Activism, 17 October 1961

In broader literature, there is overwhelming evidence of lack of transmission of memory in families who migrated from Algeria. Ahmed Boubeker in his work *Familles de l'intégration* (Integration and Families) speaks of "les banlieues de l'antimémoire" (antimemory suburbs). He argues that there is "Une génération sans mémoire illustrant, selon une chronique nationale des violences urbaines, la décomposition des familles immigrées" (A generation without memory illustrating, by way of a national chronicle of urban violence, the break up of immigrant families).[38] The lack of memory is inherently linked to the *banlieue* itself—

housing projects that explicitly aimed to break down cleavages in social groups. They are "lieux sans histoire, sans mémoire, 'non-lieux'" (sites without history, without memory, "non-places").[39] Hastily built in the 1950s and 1960s to respond to housing shortages during the postwar reconstruction and the "trente glorieuses" (thirty glorious years of economic growth), these once "modern" mass housing projects on the outskirts of French cities have gradually been abandoned by anyone who had the means to leave and have disintegrated physically, culturally, socially, and economically. These suburbs are now inhabited mainly by immigrants and their families. Boubeker therefore asserts that these suburbs preclude and lack memory and history, and are consequently linked to the disintegration of immigrant families.

A project that took place from 1995 in the Isère, organized by the ADATE (Association dauphinoise pour l'accueil des travailleurs étrangers: Dauphinois Association for Insertion of Foreign Workers) entitled "Chemins de travers" (Cross Pathways) on the topic of the memory of immigrants to the area also showed the lack of transmission of memories in migrant families. One of the cultural actions undertaken involved showing a film about the history of the migrants, that sparked reactions from children of immigrants: "Ces trente à quarante ans de silence, cette parole des hommes si rarement entendue, cette transmission difficile au sein de la famille, ce fossé entre les vieux migrants et les jeunes beurs où la communication ne passe pas: la réconciliation est difficile entre deux générations" (These thirty to forty years of silence, this speech of men so rarely heard, this difficult transmission within families, this divide between aged migrants and young *beurs* where communication fails: reconciliation is difficult between the two generations).[40] Here we see the way that there has been such a long period of silence on the topic, due largely to the difficulty of the subject, that a huge divide has been created across the generations, with younger generations ignorant of the experiences of their elders.

A conference held in December 2000 entitled "Mémoires de l'immigration algérienne: La guerre d'Algérie en France" (Memories of Algerian Immigrants: the Algerian War in France) also showed the lack of transmission of memory amongst Algerian immigrants. For Ali Mekki: "De cette histoire, ces jeunes ne savent rien, et s'ils ne savent rien c'est qu'on ne leur a rien dit, rien enseigné, ni les parents, ni l'école" (These young people know nothing about this history, they know nothing because neither parents nor teachers have said anything to them about it, nor taught them it).[41] The organizers interestingly identify the institutions of the school and the family as the main areas where young people can learn about history. Both are judged to be failing to transmit these memories. Similarly, in testimony published in an article in Le Monde in 2002 of an Algerian family, Sakina, daughter of Dahbia, states that: "J'ai pris conscience que beaucoup de pères algériens meurent en France sans léguer aucune histoire. Ensuite, pour nous, c'est le vide, car à la différence de nos parents, nous n'avons rien laissé en Algérie. Or, nous avons trop souvent intégré le silence des manuels scolaires et l'indifférence de la société française vis-à-vis de cette histoire" (I realized that a lot of Algerian fathers die in France without bequeathing any history. Then, for us, there's an empty space, because unlike our parents, we left nothing in Algeria. Yet, we have been too willing to take on board the silence of textbooks and French society's indifference to this history).[42] The idea of "bequeathing history" linked to the wider concept of heritage conveys well the depth of experience here: a strong sense of (family) history is crucial to an individual and group sense of belonging and identity. The emptiness that results from the silence is crushing. Again schools and the family are identified as the main potential sources of information on the Algerian War and are found wanting. Similar testimony appeared in *Le Nouvel Observateur* in 2001 in a dossier entitled "Où vont les beurs?" (What Future for the *Beurs*?) where Norredine Iznasni declared:

> Mes parents ne m'ont jamais raconté leur guerre d'Algérie, ni les rafles du 17 octobre 1961, avant que je le leur demande il y a quatre ans. Toute cette douleur immense, ces familles explosées par la guerre l'ont gardée pour elles. Et leurs petits-enfants, ceux qui ont sifflé "la Marseillaise" le 6 octobre, ne se sont même pas rendu compte des conséquences que cela aurait dans la période actuelle. S'ils n'ont pas compris l'importance symbolique de ce match, c'est qu'on ne leur a rien dit de l'Algérie d'avant, de la torture, de la guerre. (My parents never told me about their experiences during the Algerian War, nor about the roundup of 17 October 1961, until I asked them four years ago. These families torn apart by the war kept to themselves all of that immense pain. And their grandchildren, those who booed during the national anthem on 6 October, didn't even realize the consequences their actions would have in the present context. They didn't understand the symbolic importance of this match because they've not been told anything about colonial Algeria, about torture, or the war.)[43]

There are a number of important points here. Again young people have not been told anything about Algeria or the war. Families and individuals have had no outlet for their considerable pain. The allusion to 6 October relates to a soccer match between France and Algeria held in 2001 where young French of Algerian origin controversially booed the national anthem (and later invaded the pitch resulting in the match not being finished). The match had been anticipated by many commentators as an opportunity to reconcile the two nations—much as the 1998 French World Cup victory with its ethnically diverse team was viewed as a celebration of French multiculturalism. In both cases, the idealistic image and rhetoric are not reflected in any actual reality.

Another example of the lack of transmission of memories of the Algerian War in the Algerian-immigrant community in France can be found in Benjamin Stora's documentary *Les Années algériennes* (The Algerian Years) when Farid Aïchoune talks about the memory of 17 October 1961. In that year he was nine years old and was arrested on 18 October. He said:

> Il y avait une mémoire mais une fois que la guerre elle a été finie c'est basta. Il y avait un mot d'ordre que les Algériens disaient . . . "Sept ans ça suffit" donc les gens conservaient à l'intérieur d'eux-mêmes un certain nombre de souvenirs mais n'aimaient pas trop en faire état. Une sorte de pudeur quoi. (There were

memories but once the war was over it was enough, period. There was a term that Algerians used . . . "Seven years is long enough" so people kept a certain number of memories inside them but didn't like to talk about them. Like a sort of modesty.)[44]

A further example of the absence of family transmission in this group was given in an issue of *Quo Vadis* in an interview with Mohamed Hocine, founder of the "Comité contre la Double peine" (Committee Against Double Punishment) and his family. This committee was a pressure group that campaigned against a law that allowed (until recently) people of foreign nationality to be expelled from France if they were convicted of a crime. The subject of the conversation was principally how and why his parents had come to France that led to a discussion of his father's experience during the Algerian War, including his participation in the October 1961 demonstration. The overall impression given was one of the discovery for the first time by Hocine of his father's history as if this kind of discussion had never taken place before despite the age of the participants. Hocine said:

> Il y a beaucoup de jeunes qui ne connaissent pas l'histoire de leurs parents. Ils nous ont engendrés, ils nous ont vu grandir, ils savent tout sur nous, et nous on ne sait rien sur eux. (There are a lot of young people who don't know the history of their parents. They bore us, they saw us grow, they know everything about us, yet we don't know anything about them.)[45]

Families are thus split across the generations due to a lack of understanding of the older generation by young people resulting from not knowing about the history of the parents. The consequences of such ignorance are very important to an understanding of contemporary French society. The lack of discussion of the Algerian War in families from Algeria has clearly led to a generational split in such families. It has caused a lot of pain for those that lived through the war and have not been able to share their experiences, thus repressing those memories. Generally young people and the families have not been able to establish narratives of belonging in French society.

For Mekki: "Dans ce silence, des milliers d'enfants issus de l'immigration grandissent et se heurtent de plein fouet à cette histoire qui va conditionner à jamais le regard porté sur eux et qu'ils ont d'eux-mêmes" (Thousands of young people of immigrant descent are growing up in this atmosphere of silence and they are squarely affected by this history that continually shapes the view society holds of them and their own self image).[46] The history of the war, that is not discussed or understood, does however affect the children of people from Algeria since it feeds into anti-Arab racism prevalent in France and it shapes the view that they have of themselves. In both instances, the silence needs to be broken so that such views can be actively challenged and reworked. The consequences of so much silence on this important topic are also discussed in an article published in *Le Monde* in 2002 entitled "Immigrés et harkis face à face" (Immigrants and

Harkis Face to Face) that claims that: "Le silence de leurs parents sur les déchirures de la guerre pèse sur les enfants nés en France" (The silence of their parents about the injuries caused by the war weighs on the children born in France) since:

> si ces "héritiers" se heurtent au silence de leurs parents, c'est que la mémoire de ces derniers est de l'ordre de l'intransmissible, car trop paradoxale, aussi bien chez les harkis que chez les immigrés: mémoire de prétendus "collabos" abandonnés par la France chez les uns, mémoire d'Algériens venus faire leur vie chez l'ancien colonisateur chez les autres. "Le silence des parents est un paramètre dans le malaise des enfants." (these "inheritors" are confronted with the silence of their parents because their parents' memories cannot be transmitted, because they are too paradoxical, amongst *harkis* as well as immigrants: memories of supposed "collaborators" abandoned by France for one group, memories of Algerians who migrated to the former colonial power for the others. "The silence of the parents is a factor in the problems of the children.")[47]

Children are therefore suffering from this silence. A new idea is introduced here: that these memories cannot be transmitted because they are too paradoxical. Farid Aïchoune makes the same point about the difficult contradictions of Algerian immigrant history: "Ces jeunes dont les grands-parents ont milité dans les rangs du FLN ne savant pas grande-chose de la guerre d'Algérie . . . Crainte d'avouer à leurs enfants que leur combat a été en grande partie dévoyé? Certainement. Mais, surtout, comment dire aux siens que l'on s'est battu pour l'indépendance de l'Algérie pour finalement choisir de vivre en France? La démarche est douloureuse: évoquer la guerre, c'est faire revivre un déchirement, un échec" (These young people whose grandparents were militants in the FLN know very little about the Algerian War . . . Is this through fear of admitting to their children that their battle has to a large extent gone astray? Definitely. But, above all, how can one tell one's siblings that one fought for the independence of Algeria only to end up choosing to live in France? It's a painful process: the act of bringing up the war amounts to reliving a divorce, a failure).[48]

In another project, "Les fils de la mémoire et de l'oubli" (Sons of Memory and Forgetting), whose findings were published in the same volume *Villes, patrimoines, mémoires*, Lela Bencharif and Virginie Milliot discovered former colonial soldiers who all had the same difficulty in discussing their own history:

> Le silence et l'oubli se sont déposés avec tant de force sur ces vies, qu'il est dans certains cas impossible de faire remonter à la surface ce qui a été enfoui, de retrouver le chemin du souvenir et du récit. Certains refusent—"A quoi bon?"—, pourquoi raconter une histoire que l'on ne se raconte pas même à soi . . . ? Cette absence de reconnaissance, cette invisibilité historique les a murés dans un silence qui bloque toute possibilité de transmission. (Silence and forgetting have taken such hold of these lives, that in certain cases it is impossible to recover what has been repressed, to reopen pathways towards remembering and voice. Certain people refuse—"What's the point?"—, why share a history that

one does not tell oneself . . . ? This absence of recognition, this historical invisibility has isolated them in a silence that prohibits any chance of transmission.)[49]

Here an even stronger argument is made that transmission is impossible: it is too hard. Memories have been repressed for so long that voicing them is impossible. One solution to this problem may reside in wider society. If as Halbwachs has shown, the "frames of memory" for individuals and groups are to be found in society, then wider French society can make it easier for these families to discuss the Algerian War. For Philippe Bernard: "Intégrer les Français, enfants d'Algériens, suppose d'inscrire l'histoire de l'immigration et celle de la guerre d'Algérie dans l'histoire nationale. D'autant que cette histoire est rarement transmise par les parents immigrés, mal armés pour le faire et empêtrés dans les contradictions de leur propre parcours. Donner un sens au fait que les 'beurs' sont aujourd'hui français à part entière exige la mise au clair de l'histoire coloniale et en particulier de la guerre d'Algérie, y compris ses épisodes les plus ambigus ou les plus détestables" (A requirement in order to integrate French children of Algerian origin is to include the history of immigration and of the Algerian War into national history. All the more important since this history is rarely transmitted by immigrant parents, ill-disposed to be able to do it and caught up in the contradictions of their own journey).[50]

Another approach to overcome the clear difficulties that families have in discussing the Algerian War consists of activism. Indeed, it would seem to be the case that a lack of transmission of memory through the family can itself lead to "memory activism." This emerges above all in the work of Yamina Benguigui or *beur* writers. Benguigui in her documentary *Mémoires d'Immigrés* (Memories of Immigrants) explicitly set out to tell the story of the first generation whose role in the history of France has been neglected in France.[51] Benguigui begins her documentary: "Qu'avez-vous fait de mon père? Qu'avez-vous fait de ma mère? Qu'avez-vous fait de mes parents, pour qu'ils soient aussi muets? Que leur avez-vous dit, pour qu'ils n'aient pas voulu nous enraciner sur cette terre, où nous sommes nés? Qui sommes-nous, aujourd'hui? Des immigrés? Des Français d'origine étrangère? Des musulmans?" (What have you done to my father? What have you done to my mother? What have you done to my parents, to make them so silent? What did you say to them, to make them not want to ground us in this land, where we were born? Who are we today? Immigrants? No! Children of immigrants? French of foreign descent? Muslims?).[52] Her documentary consists of a quest to answer these questions by reconstructing the memory of Maghrebian immigration. For Sylvie Durmelat she is a "memory entrepreneur" and she would be one of the people Catherine Wihtol de Wenden refers to as "opérateurs de la mémoire" (memory operators).[53] The structure of the documentary (the fathers, the mothers, the children) shows the gendered nature of the migrant experience and the importance of generation. Throughout the documentary it is clear that there has been a generational breakdown in transmission of family history. However, Benguigui's concern is more the history of migration, a topic that is less problematic than the Algerian War in itself.

In fact, Stora and Liauzu both allude to this type of activism. Faced with family silence children whose parents came from Algeria are more curious and may well try outside of the family to discover their past. An example is given by Bernard as follows:

> Abdel Aïssou, président du Mouvement des droits civiques, compare la démar-che des beurs à celle des jeunes juifs de l'après-guerre, en bute de silence de leurs parents sur la Shoah. "Chez moi, la guerre était comme un cadavre dans un placard. On n'en parlait jamais. Un jour, j'ai découvert combien mes parents avaient souffert." (Abdel Aïssou, President of the Movement for Civic Rights, compares the approach of the *beurs* to that of young Jews after the Second World War, frustrated by the silence from their parents about the Shoah. "In my family, the war was like a skeleton in the closet. We never talked about it. One day, I discovered how much my parents had suffered.")[54]

The impact of this activism is more what is at stake in differences between Liauzu and Stora. How widespread is this "work of memory" and what are the possibilities of any counter-narratives to challenge dominant narratives of the Algerian War? For Claude Liauzu in an article in 1999:

> La "Marche des Beurs" de 1983 a ouvert une nouvelle phase. Au delà de l'action directement politique, un travail culturel, une quête identitaire ont été engagés. Ils sont à l'origine de la création de l'association "Au nom de la mé-moire," du livre et du film de Yamina Benguigui, *Mémoires d'immigrés*, de pu-blications, etc. Mais cela concerne-t-il la majorité? Dans les situations d'anomie, dans les banlieues en déréliction, dans les familles désagrégées, ce qui l'emporte c'est sans doute l'impossibilité d'accéder à une mémoire, de se reconnaître et d'être reconnu dans l'histoire enseignée. (The "Marche des Beurs" in 1983 inau-gurated a new phase. Beyond the directly political action, a cultural project, a search for identity have been begun. They have given rise to the creation of the association "Au nom de la mémoire" [In the Name of Memory], to the book and the film by Yamina Benguigui entitled *Mémoires d'immigrés* [Immigrant Memories], to publications, etc. But does this involve the majority? In situations of anomy, in run down housing estates, in broken up families, what certainly oc-curs is the impossibility of reaching or obtaining a memory, of recognizing and being recognized in the history that is taught.)[55]

There are a number of strong points here. A search for identity has been taking place since the 1980s, but it is to some extent a minority pursuit and one that struggles to compete with the dominant narratives of school history, for example. Furthermore, integration and globalization are also additional threats to an emerging "counter narrative." Michèle Tribalat's work shows the extent of inte-gration of young people of immigrant origin in France.[56] In some ways integrat-ing to France entails adopting the views and opinions of the dominant society. And for Hargreaves:

> The generation that was most closely involved in the Algerian conflict is now nearing or has entered old age. In the political as in the cultural sphere, it is

gradually being displaced by younger generations with no direct memories of the colonial era and its bloody end. These new generations are less narrowly concerned with the national frames of reference that were fundamental to the French presence in Algeria and the struggle for independence.[57]

So for young people the Franco-Algerian perspective is no longer the only point of reference. If this is the case, it further limits the amount of "memory activism" one would expect from *beurs* on the Algerian War. Begag concurs when he states that: "c'est en France que la grande majorité d'entre eux va désormais vivre; le processus d'enracinement et d'acculturation est en marche. Il a été largement consolidé par la production d'une culture immigrée de France" (The vast majority of them from now on are going to live in France; the process of taking root and acculturation is underway. It has been considerably consolidated by the production of an immigrant culture in France).[58] For Begag, a process of acculturation is underway, that depends on cultural production, but again this production is much wider than any link to the Algerian War: more globalized than a Franco-Algerian perspective. However, we need to recognize that migration from Algeria was directly concerned by the Algerian War, and the legacy of the war has clearly affected this group, therefore cultural production at some stage is going to need to address this topic, even if in the short term wider more consensual concerns are the initial entry point (history of immigration, colonial soldiers in the World Wars, "world music").

Nonetheless, there have clearly been successes, notably surrounding the events of 17 October 1961, as was shown in the introduction to this book. We can note the existence of groups such as "Au nom de la mémoire" (In the Name of Memory)[59] led by individuals such as Anne Tristan, Agnès Denis, and Mehdi Lallaoui. In 1991 they published the book *Le silence du fleuve* (The Silence of the River). Also, we can note the association "17 octobre 1961: contre l'oubli" (17 October 1961: Against Forgetting)[60] whose honorary committee includes Jean-Luc Einaudi, Francis Jeanson, Pierre Vidal-Naquet, and Madeleine Rebérioux. Their stated aims include attempting to obtain official recognition of the massacre of 17 October 1961, and the French State's acknowledgement that it was a crime against humanity; the creation of a site of memory ("lieu de souvenir") in honor of those who died that evening, and unhindered access to archives. They have attempted to achieve these aims through exhibitions, demonstrations/commemorations, publishing a book, symposia, petitions, and their website—that includes amongst other things testimonies, documents, a bibliography, and a filmography. This group however is made up essentially of intellectuals who opposed the Algerian War. One area however where we do find challenges to dominant narratives of the Algerian War is literature. For the reasons given above, stronger challenges seem to be emerging from the children of *harkis* than from the *beurs*.

Literature: the Work of Memory and Representing

Films and literature have been a privileged vector of memory for both children of *harkis* and *beurs*. While, as we have already seen, there is some disagreement as to the real ability of children of migrants to challenge dominant narratives in France, such narratives have been written. As we will see in this section, novels by children of *beurs* were far more numerous than those of children of *harkis* in the 1980s and 1990s, with only one notable novel during that period dealing with the history of the *harkis*—Mehdi Charef's *Le Harki de Meriem* (The *Harki* from Meriem). Yet in recent years there would appear to be an emerging corpus of novels by children of *harkis*. For example, Hadjila Kemoum's *Mohand le harki* (Mohand the *Harki*), Zahia Rahmani's *Moze* and Dalila Kerchouche's *Mon père ce harki* (My Father the *Harki*) were all published in 2003. The unifying theme is a search for identity. Kerchouche literally retraces her family's journey to and early years in France in an attempt to better understand her family history, and particularly to make some sense of her father's suicide. Clearly one of the ways in which memories of this conflict are transmitted and contested is in literature. We can speculate that this approach to the inclusion of children of *harkis* and *beurs* has focused on achieving voice and generating memories—an approach that contrasts with more common and direct socioeconomic or violent tactics of intervention—and that such tactics of intervention will facilitate (long term) the inclusion of these groups due to the way "inclusion" functions in France— namely the tremendous importance of history and memory to national identity. Throughout this book we have seen examples of how a common memory and history foster identity in the present, by providing a group narrative that generates a sense of group belonging.

Writing on Algeria by all the groups involved in the war has in fact been prolific. Philip Dine has argued convincingly that it is precisely a failure of historiography that explains the sheer scale of fictional and filmic narratives of the Algerian War.[61] Stora has identified over two thousand books on the war in Algeria published in France between 1956 and 1996.[62] We were also able to gauge the amount of written scholarship and testimony written on the war in our survey of historiography earlier in this book. Written testimonies in particular have been one very important way that many individuals who participated in the Algerian War have employed to communicate their experiences of the conflict. Writing can be seen as healing trauma (in a Freudian perspective), as an example of agency in collective memory (in a pluralist perspective), and as constructing memories that provide group cohesion in the present (in a Halbwachsian perspective). It constitutes a vector of memory and on a personal level aids in the working through of difficult memories resulting from a traumatic past. Literature, and history—"historical fiction"—also function(s) as a discourse. For a number of reasons, children of *harkis* and *beurs* have felt the need to write. The writing of children of *harkis* and *beurs* often sets out to challenge dominant discourses. Each of the three understandings of memory is therefore relevant, and each functions on different levels—from personal to group, and from national to international.

Stora in an article in *Libération* in 1992 highlighted the importance of films and literature to collective memory, since he felt that a very long period of mourning was coming to an end due to a sudden rush of films on Indo-China and Algeria.[63] He talked of "l'homme du Sud" (people from the South) who it would seem have allowed an opening to take place in two ways: firstly in their country of origin by letting film makers actually work in Algeria and secondly in France by the research, filmmaking, or book-writing of people whose parents came from Algeria and who have provided a lot of the impetus for studying this period of French history (by doing it themselves). In a later article, Stora identifies several works of fiction that constitute "traces de guerre dans les gisements littéraires" (traces of war in literary heritage).[64] These are Nabile Farès's trilogy, Nacer Kettane's *Le Sourire de Brahim* (Brahim's Smile), Mohamed Kenzi's *La Menthe sauvage* (Wild Mint), Leïla Sebbar's *Le chinois vert d'Afrique* (The Green Chinaman from Africa), Mehdi Charef's *Le harki de Meriem* (The *Harki* from Meriem), Tassadit Imache's *Une fille sans histoire* (A Girl Without a History), and Paul Smaïl's *Vivre me tue* (Living Kills Me). Particular attention is also given in this article to the representations of the events of 17 October 1961.

Alec Hargreaves's work on *Beur* narratives was groundbreaking. He identified the role of narratives in transmitting memories outside of the Algerian community, particularly after 1985 and concerning memories of the events of 17 October 1961. He speaks of the tensions that can be found in *beur* authors' work between success within France and respect for North African heritage. In many ways *beurs* are torn between France and Algeria. For Hargreaves "The battleground over which their struggle is waged is one of identity rather than of territory."[65] These kinds of tensions are, for example, present in the work of Bouzid and Sakinna Boukhedenna.[66] Neither of these authors can feel at home in France or Algeria and want to escape to a third make-believe place where they could settle. For Hargreaves:

> *Beur* novels generally take the form of a bildungsroman, where the central thread is the youthful protagonist's search for a sense of direction in life amid the conflicting cultural imperatives to which he or she is subjected.[67]

Hargreaves also shows the place of migrant memories in *beur* literature. He originally tackled this question in his seminal work *Immigration and Identity in Beur Fiction*. This search for identity for children whose parents are from Algeria involves addressing the topic of the war in Algeria. For Hargreaves:

> The Algerian war has gripped the imagination of several Beur writers in ways which have taken them significantly beyond the bounds of autobiography, but important underlying parallels with their own experiences are none the less present.[68]

Works examined included Tassadit Imaches's *Le Rouge à lèvres* (Lipstick), Mehdi Charef's *Le Harki de Meriem* (The *Harki* from Meriem), Nacer Kettane's *Le*

Sourire de Brahim (Brahim's Smile), Mehdi Lallaoui's *La Colline aux oliviers* (The Olivegrove Hill) and Ahmed Kelouaz's *Celui qui regarde le soleil en face* (Looking Straight into the Sun). Hargreaves also explains that "Some of the earliest childhood memories of Beur authors date back to the politically explosive years of the Algerian war. The personal impact of those events is depicted in heavily autobiographical novels."[69] In addition to the novels cited above, Hargreaves identifies two more works that fall into this category: Kamel Zemouri's *Le jardin de l'intrus* (The Intruder's Garden), and Tassadit Imache's *Une fille sans histoire* (A Girl Without History). Memory is shown to be central to these novels since "Personal identity involves a complex mixture of memory and desire, which interface with each other across the present" and "No human being can have a satisfactory sense of personal identity without knowing something of where s/he comes from . . . Equally important is an ideological motivation conditioned by a vision of the future."[70] These are all very important points. A sense of history does feed into identity, and individuals do need this sense of belonging. Narratives of belonging draw on elements of the past. In more recent work Hargreaves identifies a:

> recent upsurge of interest in migrant memories (that) is intimately connected with the generational structure of the family, which makes it a key site for the transmission of memory . . . Until recently, the memories of Algerian migrants were almost wholly absent from the public sphere. They have entered that sphere mainly through a growing body of literary, cinematic and historical work by second-generation members of the Algerian minority in France. The most frequently evoked episode in the history of colonial migration is the savage repression of the demonstration of October 17, 1961.[71]

Richard Derderian also examines recent ethnic minority memory through the lense of cultural production. He "explores how the memories of second-generation North Africans in France, often cast as the chief victims of the so-called Algeria syndrome, offer a much needed challenge to the conflict's cloistered remembering" concluding that "the memory work of second-generation North Africans plays an important role in fostering a greater awareness of the true complexity of the French past."[72] A wide range of "memory-charged cultural initiatives" since the mid-1970s are examined—theater companies, music groups, films, and television documentaries showing that "the children of Algerian workers have actively laid claim to a shared past."[73]

The difficulties in representing this history are however considerable. Derderian correctly identifies "the considerable weight of official forms of amnesia" since "It is the sheer accumulated weight of established ways of remembering the conflict . . . that stifles or diminishes the influence of counternarratives."[74] It seems clear that while writing can help individuals to construct identities and to work through difficult issues, the small number of such works inevitably struggles to counter the powerful dominant narratives of, for instance, the school system or the media. Similar issues are explored in a review in *Le Monde* of the film "Vivre au paradis" (Living in Paradise), where we learn that:

Bouriem Guerdjou ne répugne pas aux grands mots, il parle volontiers de mis-
sions qu'il s'est assignées: rendre justice à la génération de ses parents en évo-
quant leurs conditions d'existence lors de leur arrivée en France; rendre justice,
aussi, aux victimes du massacre du 17 octobre; et redonner un sens
d'appartenance à la deuxième génération, lui offrir une possibilité de se trouver
des racines. Il raconte . . . que, alors qu'il travaillait au film, ce sont ceux-là
mêmes dont il évoque le souvenir qui lui déconseillaient de montrer le bidonville ou le drame du 17 octobre. "On me disait de ne pas reparler de tout ça, de
faire plutôt 'une histoire française.'" (Bouriem Guerdjou is not scared of telling
things the way they are, he readily talks about the aims he has set himself: to obtain justice for his parents' generation by representing and voicing the conditions they endured when they arrived in France; also to obtain justice for the victims of the massacre perpetrated on 17 October; and to give a sense of belonging
to the second generation, give them a chance of finding their roots. He says . . .
that when he was working on the film, it was those whose memories he was
evoking that advised him not to show the *bidonville* or the drama of 17 October.
"I was told not to talk about all of that stuff again, rather to tell 'a French
story.'")[75]

So Guerdjou is very aware of the importance of narratives and representations of
the history of the Algerian War and migration. They can provide a sense of belonging and crucial roots for the second generation, as well as helping shape
French perceptions of Algerian migrants by making them more aware of their
conditions and their contribution to French society. However, this is no easy
task. This brief survey of literature by children of Algerian migrants and *harkis*
shows that literature is one way in which dominant narratives of the Algerian
War are challenged. While it is true, as Liauzu has pointed out, that the vast majority of children of migrants are unable to write novels, one can expect such
narratives to have a long term effect in France, given the importance of history
and memory to French national identity. As Hargreaves points out "While the
third generation now emerging among the Algerian minority is far removed in
time from the colonial era, its future in France clearly remains heavily conditioned by the legacy of that period."[76]

Conclusion

We have seen that on the whole there is relatively little family transmission of
memory of the Algerian War in the "private sphere" of the family in France.
Although in our small case study some pupils had found out very detailed information about the Algerian War from the family, others had not and wider reading indicates that on the whole there is much silence in families on this topic.
The little transmission of memory affects all groups involved in the Algerian
War, but seems to be particularly painfully felt for children of foreign origin
whose sense of belonging and efforts at making France "home" are particularly
challenging. Historical memory is crucial to constructing a sense of belonging in

France. Racism and discrimination against Algerians and their descendants make belonging for this group problematic. Silence on the topic of the history of the family (during the Algerian War) and the experiences of migration further compound this lack of identity and belonging. It is not insignificant that the majority of the pupils who volunteered in Lyon to be interviewed for this project were of North African descent, indicating greater interest in this topic than in other groups; perhaps also reflecting frustration with the amount they have learnt or heard from other sources. Lack of transmission of memories can easily be explained—by a lack of social frames of memory (including as we will see throughout this book in the "public sphere" of the State education system and the media), shame (for conscripts this might be the question of torture; for *harkis* their activities during the war and choice of siding with France; for immigrants the decision to live and settle in France, the former colonial power), a desire to integrate and move on, etc. We need therefore to refer to different theories of collective memory: a Freudian model that emphasizes the difficultly of working through traumatic events and repression and occlusion of memories resulting from "narrative failure;" a Halbwachsian model of memory that emphasizes the importance of social frames of memory, but also the role of memories in supporting the family; and a pluralist model that better allows for action when faced with silence. In two groups, this family silence has led to considerable activism—the *harkis* and the *beurs*. There is disagreement amongst scholars on the impact of this activism. I believe that this activism does have a long term effect, for individuals, groups, and the French nation as a whole, but this impact should not be exaggerated—what dominates is still silence on this topic for the majority of people.

There are clear reasons why these two groups have been involved in activism while others have not. As Nora points out:

> What is today commonly called memory, in the sense in which people speak of working-class memory, Occitanian memory, or female memory, in fact marks the advent of historical consciousness of defunct traditions, the reconstructive recovery of phenomena from which we are separated and which are most directly of interest to those who think of themselves as descendants and heirs of such traditions. Official history felt no need to take account of these traditions because the "national group" was generally constructed by stifling them or reducing them to silence, or because they did not emerge as such into history. Now that such groups are being incorporated into national history, however, they feel an urgent need to reconstruct their traditions with whatever means are available, from the most ad hoc to the most scientific because for each group tradition is part of its identity. The group's memory is in fact its history.[77]

While there may be much silence in families, one result can be activism, possibly in the form of narratives that challenge dominant discourses. It would seem that this activism is the product of a minority, but it can be expected that in future memories will spread beyond the few. Both *beur* and children of *harkis* are referring to the Algerian War in their cultural production. It is to be expected that in future more memories will be (re)constructed.

Family transmission of memory therefore is in many ways different from the other vectors of memory. We have been able to contrast memories that are transmitted through classes with direct memories from veterans and family members. The latter, if transmitted, are qualitatively far richer. Family memories influence the educative vector of memory in so far as educative authorities do not want to "envenimer les conflits de mémoire qui existent et dont on peut prendre compte en classe" (aggravate memory conflicts that exist and that are there in class; Rioux 2000). Yet this means that there is often too great a difference between personal (family) history and wider national history. As such, the wider public "frame of memory" does not include Algerian memories. As Kristen Ross has argued, in contemporary France the Algerian War appears to be "ancient history" when in fact it transpired recently and still affects many people in France. One way or another, memories are *used*. The State education system uses memory and history to create a national memory culture that emphasizes commonality and omits difference. Private memories are used differently to form more subjective identities.

Notes

1. In autumn 1989 four pupils were suspended from a school in Creil, near Paris, for wearing veils in class ("foulards"). For demographic reasons linked to the increasing arrival and settlement of families from North Africa to France in the 1960s and 1970s, the 1980s were the decade that children of migrants from North Africa entered secondary schools in large numbers and the secular French school system was confronted with the challenge of managing greater diversity than it previously had. At the heart of the "affair" were the concept of secularism and the role of the State school system in the Republic. In 1990, the State Council judged that veils were only a problem if "ostentatious" and an example of "proselytism." This was to be determined at the local level of schools and individual cases. The whole "affair" generated huge amounts of discussion in the media. Throughout the 1990s the issue periodically reemerged, but generally was handled through negotiation at the local level. Jacques Chirac said in 2003 that "for more than a century, the Republic and schools have developed together concomitantly" and that "the Republican school, that cements the nation, is the source of French identity:" Speech by President Chirac on 20 November 2003 at the opening of the "National Debate on Schools" quoted in Dominique Borne and Jean-Paul Delahaye, "La laïcité dans l'enseignement: problématique et enjeux," *Regards sur l'actualité*, no. 298 (February 2004): 25. At the end of 2003 President Chirac declared himself in favor of a "sursaut laïque" (strong secular renewal). On 15 March 2004 "The Law on the Veil" was passed, banning all religious signs, voted 494/36. It entered into application at the beginning of school year on 2 September 2004.

2. Paul Thompson, "Believe it or not: rethinking the historical interpretation of memory," www3.baylor.edu/Oral_History/Thompson.pdf.

3. Maurice Halbwachs, *On Collective Memory*, edited and translated by Lewis A. Coser (Chicago and London: University of Chicago Press, 1992), 84.

4. Halbwachs, *On Collective Memory*, 54.

5. Halbwachs, *On Collective Memory*, 59.

6. Catherine Wihtol de Wenden, "La Vie associative des harkis," *Migrations Société* 1, no. 5-6 (October-December 1989): 12.

7. Wihtol de Wenden, "Vie associative des harkis:" 12.

8. See Alec G. Hargreaves, *Immigration, "Race" and Ethnicity in Contemporary France* (London and New York: Routledge, 1995) for a discussion of the meaning(s) and use(s) of the term "beur."

9. Benjamin Stora, *La Gangrène et l'oubli: la mémoire de la guerre d'Algérie* (Paris: Editions La Découverte, 1992), 347.

10. For example evident in the title of Soraya Nini's novel *Ils disent que je suis une beurette* (Paris: Fixot, 1993).

11. It is particularly important to differentiate between self-ascribed ethnicity (how one defines one's own ethnicity) and categorization (ethnicity defined from the exterior) to try and avoid wrongly categorizing or stereotyping whole groups of people.

12. *Troisième* corresponds in Britain to GCSE ("General Certificate of Secondary Education") fourth or fifth year or Australian Year 9 and 10.

13. Joël Cornette and Jean-Noël Luc, "Bac-Génération 84. L'Enseignement du temps présent en terminale," *Vingtième Siècle*, no. 6 (April-June 1985): 126.

14. Kristen Ross, *Fast Cars, Clean Bodies: Decolonization and the Reordering of French Culture* (Cambridge, Mass., and London: the MIT Press, 1995), 122.

15. See Jean-Pierre Rioux, "Trous de mémoire" and Hassan Remaoun, "Un seul héros, le peuple" and "L'Histoire confisquée," *Télérama hors série*, 1995: 90-93.

16. Michel Roux, "Le Poids de l'Histoire," *Hommes et Migrations*, no. 1135 (September 1990): 24/25.

17. Camille Marchaut, "Cela me fait mal au cœur qu'on oublie ça," *Hommes et Migrations*, no. 1219 (May-June 1999): 62.

18. Claire Mauss-Copeaux, *Appelés en Algérie: la parole confisquée* (Paris: Hachette, 1999), 52/53.

19. Mauss-Copeaux, *Appelés en Algérie*, 61.

20. Jean-Jacques Jordi and Mohand Hamoumou, *Les harkis, une mémoire enfouie* (Paris: Autrement, 1999), 11.

21. Laurent Muller, *Le silence des harkis* (Paris: L'Harmattan, 1999), 9.

22. Muller, *Le silence des harkis*, 16.

23. Muller, *Le silence des harkis*, 73.

24. Mohamed Kara, *Les tentations du repli communautaire* (Paris: L'Harmattan, 1997), 118.

25. Jordi and Hamoumou, *Les harkis*, 115 and 120 respectively.

26. Stéphanie Abrial, *Les enfants de harkis* (Paris: L'Harmattan, 2001), 116.

27. Kara, *Les tentations du repli communautaire*, 158.

28. Kara, *Les tentations du repli communautaire*, 168 and 162 respectively.

29. Abrial, *Les enfants de harkis*, 73.

30. Jordi and Hamoumou, *Les harkis*, 11.

31. See Stéphanie Abrial, *Les enfants de harkis*, especially Chapter 6.

32. I draw on the *Index analytique du Monde* for a quantitative study (1977, 1981-1982, 1984-1986, 1991, 1996, 1998-1999, 2000-2001) of the nature of mention of the Algerian War in *Le Monde*.

33. See for example "L'histoire des harkis est refoulée depuis 30 ans," *Le Monde*, 7 August 1991, 1; "Sociologue M. Hamoumou expose occultation franco-algérienne du problème harki (entretien)," *Le Monde*, 7 August 1991, 7.

34. "Jacques Chirac demande une journée d'hommage aux harkis," *Le Monde héb-domadaire*, 17 February 2001, 10.

35. Muller, *Le Silence des harkis*, 20.

36. Abrial, *Les enfants de harkis*, 158.

37. It is of course important to distinguish between *harkis* and their descendants and *immigrés*. Although one would question the existence of such communities, individuals in both groups nonetheless can be mutually hostile, despite sharing certain commonalities.

38. Ahmed Boubeker, *Familles de l'intégration* (Paris: Stock, 1999), 156.

39. Boubeker, *Familles de l'intégration*, 160

40. "ADATE: hommage aux pères," in *Villes, patrimoines, mémoires—Actions culturelles et patrimoines urbains en Rhône-Alpes* (Lyon: Editions La Passe du Vent, 2000), 63.

41. Ali Mekki, "Opening Remarks," *Zaàma*, special issue, 2002, 6.

42. Philippe Bernard, "Mémoire d'Algérie, mémoire d'en France," *Le Monde*, 19 March 2002.

43. "Où vont les beurs?" *Le Nouvel Observateur*, no. 1930, 2 November 2001.

44. Farid Aïchoune, interviewed in *Les Années algériennes,* Benjamin Stora et al., volume three "Je ne regrette rien," produced by Antenne 2, Première Génération, Ina enterprise, 1991.

45. "D'Octobre 1961 à la Double peine," interview with the Hocine family, in a special issue of *Quo Vadis* entitled "Douce France: La Saga du mouvement beur," (autumn-winter 1993): 79.

46. Ali Mekki, "Introduction," *Zaàma*, special issue, 2002, 3.

47. Philippe Bernard, "Immigrés et harkis face à face," *Le Monde*, 30 June-1 July 2002, 18.

48. Farid Aïchoune, "On leur a volé leur histoire," *Le Nouvel Observateur*, 1-7 November 2001, 22.

49. Lela Bencharif and Virginie Milliot "Les zones d'ombre du patrimoine," in *Villes, patrimoines, mémoires*, 66-67.

50. Philippe Bernard, "Du match France-Algérie au 17 octobre 1961," *Le Monde*, 26 October 2001, 16.

51. See Yamina Benguigui, "L'héritage de l'exil," *Qantara*, no. 30, (Winter 1998-1999): 32-33.

52. Yamina Benguigui, *Mémoires d'immigrés, l'héritage maghrébin* (Paris: Albin Michel, 1997), 9-10.

53. Sylvie Durmelat, "Yamina Benguigui as 'Memory Entrepreneur,'" in *Women, Immigration and Identities in France*, ed. Jane Freedman and Carrie Tarr (Oxford & New York: Berg, 2000), 171-88. Catherine Wihtol de Wenden, "La Génération suivante entre intégration républicaine et clientélisme ethnique," *Modern and Contemporary France* 8, no. 2 (May 2000): 239.

54. Philippe Bernard, "L'Algérie de la deuxième mémoire IV. Un seul pays, deux histoires," *Le Monde*, 20 March 1992, 5.

55. Claude Liauzu, "Voyage à travers la mémoire et l'amnésie: le 17 octobre 1961," *Hommes et Migrations*, no. 1219 (May-June 1999): 61.

56. Michèle Tribalat, *Faire France: Une enquête sur les immigrés et leurs enfants* (Paris: La Découverte, 1995).

57. Alec G. Hargreaves, "France and Algeria 1962-2002: turning the page?" *Modern and Contemporary France* 10, no. 4 (2002): 445.

58. Azouz Begag, "Les relations France-Algérie vues de la diaspora algérienne," *Modern and Contemporary France* 10, no. 4 (2002): 481.

59. Au nom de la mémoire, Boîte postale 82, 95873 Bezons Cedex.

60. http://17octobre1961.free.fr/pages/association.htm

61. Philip Dine, *Images of the Algerian War: French Fiction and Film, 1954-1962* (Oxford: Clarendon Press/OUP, 1994). He also examined writing on Algeria in the 1990s in Philip Dine, "(Still) *A la recherche de l'Algérie perdue*: French Fiction and Film, 1992-2001," *Historical Reflections* vol. 28, no. 2, (summer 2002): 255-75.

62. Benjamin Stora, *Le dictionnaire des livres de la guerre d'Algérie 1955-1996* (Paris: L'Harmattan, 1996). In his work *La Gangrène et l'oubli* he estimated that seventy percent of the works published between 1962 and 1982 were written by those who opposed Algerian independence; Stora, *La Gangrène et l'oubli*, 239.

63. Benjamin Stora, "Indochine, Algérie, autorisations de retour," *Libération*, 30 April-1 May 1992, 5.

64. Stora, "Jeunes et représentations," 364-65.

65. Alec G. Hargreaves, "Resistance and Identity in *Beur* narratives," *Modern Fiction Studies* 35, no. 1 (spring 1989): 93.

66. Sakinna Boukhedenna, *Journal. "Nationalité: immigré(e)."* (Paris: Mercure de France, 1983); Bouzid, *La Marche* (Paris: Sindbad, 1984).

67. Hargreaves, "Resistance and Identity in *Beur* narratives," 93.

68. Alec G. Hargreaves, *Immigration and Identity in Beur Fiction* (Oxford: Berg, 1997), 62-63.

69. Hargreaves, *Immigration and Identity in Beur Fiction*, 86.

70. Hargreaves, *Immigration and Identity in Beur Fiction*, 144 and 152.

71. Alec G. Hargreaves, "Generating Migrant Memories," in *Memory, Identity and Nostalgia* ed. Patricia ME Lorcin (Syracuse, NY: Syracuse Press, forthcoming).

72. See Richard L. Derderian, "Algeria as a *lieu de mémoire*: Ethnic Minority Memory and National Identity in Contemporary France," *Radical History Review*, no. 83, (spring 2002): 29-30.

73. Derderian, "Algeria as a *lieu de mémoire*:" 34.

74. Derderian, "Algeria as a *lieu de mémoire*:" 29 and 32.

75. Jean-Michel Frodon, "Bourlem Guerdjou, messager de justice," *Le Monde*, 3 March 1999, 34.

76. Hargreaves, "Generating Migrant Memories," forthcoming.

77. Pierre Nora, ed., *Realms of Memory* (New York: Columbia University Press, 1996-1998), 626.

Chapter Four

The Media: Reporting the War
Forty Years On

Introduction

The mass media now play a crucial role in informing and shaping public consciousness on many issues. A tremendous amount of our understanding of the world is influenced by what we read, watch, or hear in the media. This is no less true concerning our understanding of the past. The media are a vector of memory[1] in so far as they construct representations of the past—in terms of choices concerning what is represented, how, where, when, and how often. Memories are transmitted through the media and literally made collective. Benedict Anderson showed the importance of the development of the print media in allowing us to imagine the nation in his book *Imagined Communities*. National communities are imagined since we will never meet all of the other members of the community yet we imagine the characteristics of the group, largely through reference to the media. Surveys into what French children know about history are regularly conducted in France, time and again highlighting the importance of the media in the transmission of historical memories. Philippe Joutard calls this an "école parallèle" (parallel schooling) since "l'école est loin d'avoir le monopole d'accès à l'histoire . . . A plus forte raison aujourd'hui" (schools do not have a monopoly on access to history, far from it . . . Even less so today).[2] For Pierre Nora, editor of the hugely influential multivolume French cultural history *Les Lieux de mémoire* (Realms of Memory), in France "le modèle traditionnel a éclaté" (the traditional model of commemoration has shattered) as history has accelerated[3] and the old unitary order has been superseded by "une multiplicité d'initiatives décentrées où se croisent et chevauchent le médiatique, le touristique, le ludique et le promotionnel" (a multitude of devolved initiatives where the media, tourism, entertainment, and promotional interests all cross and overlap) where the State's role is "plus incitative que directrice" (more as facilitator than director).[4] Indeed, for Nora:

> We have seen the end of societies that had long assured the transmission and conservation of collectively remembered values, whether through churches or schools, the family or the state . . . Indeed, we have seen the tremendous dilation of our very mode of historical perception, which, with the help of the media, has substituted for a memory entwined in the intimacy of a collective heritage the ephemeral film of current events.[5]

Whereas we can see the family as an intermediary group between the individual and bigger collectivities, the media can operate at the national—in some cases international—level. Pierre Bourdieu has analyzed the media in *On Television and Journalism*. For Bourdieu, artists, writers, scholars and journalists are "the holders of the (quasi) monopoly of the instruments of diffusion" and his work aims "to show how the journalistic field produces and imposes on the public a very particular vision of the political field, a vision that is grounded in the very structure of the journalistic field and in journalists' specific interests produced in and by that field."[6] In terms of collective memory, for Konrad Jarausch the media (and historians and politicians) operate in a public arena and create a memory culture where individual and group memories merge into public memory:

> When projected into the public arena, the diverse individual stories and competing collective recollections lead to the creation of a memory culture that defines how a country deals with its own past. In this intellectual debate about the meaning of prior events, the print and electronic media select certain dramatic images and voices, amplify their intensity, and broadcast their messages to a wider audience that wants to be entertained and have its sentiments reinforced rather than challenged.[7]

The media therefore play an important role in the creation of a memory culture by providing an arena for intellectual debate about the past, albeit one that may be limited in its possibilities. Béatrice Fleury-Vilatte also highlights the importance of the media in shaping and disseminating historical representations in her study of the televisual memory of the Algerian War when she states that the media:

> posent néanmoins, à partir d'un point du vue informatif, un regard sur la société environnante qui en est d'emblée une interprétation, non une restitution. Intermédiaire entre le fait et son énoncé, entre le référent et le référé, entre l'énonciateur et le récepteur, ces documents sont un lieu de médiation dont l'étude permet d'approcher la nature des différents enjeux (politiques, sociaux, individuels, communautaires) que concentre l'histoire racontée, et ceci avec d'autant plus d'intérêt que le support accueillant cet énoncé est lui-même tout particulièrement convoité. (nevertheless they adopt, from the standpoint of informing society, a view of the surrounding society that is first and foremost an interpretation, not a restitution. These documents are an intermediary between

the fact and its utterance, the referent and that which it denotes, between the speaker and the receiver; they mediate and their study allows us to understand the nature of the different stakes [political, social, individual and community-based] that are related to the history told, all the more so since this representation is particularly avidly desired.)[8]

Interestingly, it was during the Algerian War that televisions became increasingly part of French households. Virtually all households had acquired a television set by the late 1960s, yet even in 1963 there was only one State-controlled television channel. Between 1960 and 1967 the number of television sets in France more than quadrupled from two million to nine million.[9] De Gaulle used the emerging audiovisual culture to talk directly to the people. Radios were important to conscripts as seen in the role of transistor radios during the 1961 putsch.[10] During the Algerian War, the media played an important, yet in significant ways contradictory role in informing French society about the conflict. On the one hand censorship and State control meant that the media were an organ of the government, on the other hand important material about the war was able to be published. There was censorship yet French society was informed about the war—in a whole host of books (such as Henri Alleg's *La Question* [The Question] or Pierre-Henri Simon's *Contre la Torture* [Against Torture]) and articles about the war in reviews such as *Les Temps Modernes* or *Esprit* and magazines/newspapers such as *France Observateur*, *L'Express*, or *Le Monde*. These people, publishing houses, and reviews all courageously resisted the government and the State. Indeed such publications were castigated by military authorities as being "la presse défaitiste" (the defeatist press). Given that *Le Monde* will be the subject of our case study of media transmission of memory, we can note that during the Algerian War the newspaper's editor—Hubert Beuve-Méry writing under the pseudonym Sirius wrote several editorials criticizing French conduct in Algeria. For example, referring to the issues raised in Simon's book *Contre la Torture* he wrote "Dès maintenant, les Français doivent savoir qu'ils n'ont plus tout à fait le droit de condamner dans les mêmes termes qu'il y a dix ans les destructeurs d'Oradour, et les tortionnaires de la Gestapo" (As of now, French people need to know that they no longer have the right to condemn in the same way as ten years ago those who destroyed the village of Oradour or Gestapo torturers).[11] For Benjamin Stora "l'information circulait malgré tout" (information still managed to circulate) and "la société sait, mais se contente de partager le secret d'une guerre non déclarée" (society knew, but was content to buy into the lie of a non-declared war).[12] For Pierre Vidal-Naquet, intellectual and anticolonial militant, this can be explained as follows:

> Les espérances que nous avions de créer un vrai mouvement d'opinion comparable à l'affaire Dreyfus, qui était notre référence quasi obligatoire, n'ont pas été couronnées de succès. Il y a bien eu, en 1957, un mouvement d'opinion dont on trouve trace dans la presse. Malgré tout, après le retour au pouvoir du général de Gaulle, en qui beaucoup faisaient confiance pour résoudre les problèmes, on a eu l'impression d'un édredon, d'une sorte d'oreiller de silence. Et nous nous

sommes trouvés, effectivement, minoritaires. (Our hopes of creating a real political movement comparable to the Dreyfus Affair, that was our almost obliga-
tory reference point, were not altogether successful. There was, in 1957, a shift
in public opinion, traces of which can be found in the Press of the time. All the
same, after the return to power of de Gaulle, whom many people expected
would resolve the problems; one had the impression of an eiderdown, a sort of
comfort blanket of silence. And we found ourselves, effectively, in the minority.)[13]

The media were more circumspect concerning the events of 17 October 1961—
when dozens of Algerians were massacred in central Paris. Didier Daeninckx, in
his detective novel *Meurtres pour mémoire* (Murders for Memory)—a thriller,
the genre that as Philip Dine has argued is the "prevailing discourse now associated with the popular commemoration of the Algerian war"[14]—after a graphic
account of the massacre, describes, in a passage heavy with irony, the media
coverage of that night's events as follows:

> Le lendemain, Mercredi 18 octobre 1961, les journaux tiraient sur la grève de la
> SNCF et de la RATP, pour l'augmentation des salaires. Seul *Paris Jour* consa-
> crait l'ensemble de sa "Une" aux événements de la nuit précédente: "LES AL-
> GÉRIENS MAÎTRES DE PARIS PENDANT TROIS HEURES." (The follo-
> wing day, Wednesday 18 October 1961, the papers ran headlines on the strikes
> by the SNCF [trains] and the RATP [subway], over wage increases. Only the
> newspaper *Paris Jour* devoted its front page to the events of the previous
> night with the headline: "ALGERIANS MASTERS OF PARIS FOR THREE
> HOURS.")[15]

Jürgen Habermas is one theorist who has been particularly attentive to questions
of collective memory and the media. In the 1980s in Germany the *Historiker-
streit* (Historians' Debate) mobilized the mass media in discussions of Germany's past.[16] He, and other intellectuals, used the media in a very intervention-
ist fashion to publicly "debate" various interpretations of German history related
to the Nazi period. Habermas has insisted on the importance of the "Public
Sphere" and the role of the media in creating a public sphere. He links the media
to Theodor Adorno's concept of "Working Off the Past"—publicly conducted
ethical-political self-understanding.[17] For Habermas Germans need to work-
through the Nazi legacy in the public sphere. Memory is performed in the public
sphere, impacting upon individuals since Habermas believes that "subjective
identities in Germany take form partly in relation to the prevailing terms of public discussion and debate about the nation's Nazi past."[18] So the extent and nature of media coverage of a topic will influence individual and group remembering, by providing "the frames of memory" (such as the words we use, the content
of memories, or the timing of our remembrance). Media coverage will influence
how individuals, families, associations, and other groups remember. This critical
memory-work can be linked to Paul Ricœur's "work of memory," explicitly referred to by editorialists at *Le Monde* in statements defending their 2000-2001
coverage of the French army's use of torture during the Algerian War since for

them: "c'est au travers de récits comme celui de Mme Ighilahriz que se fait et se refait l'indispensable 'travail de mémoire,' pour reprendre l'expression du philosophe Paul Ricœur, l'inlassable répétition de la 'représentation des choses passées,' ce qui doit être transmis de génération en génération, contre l'oubli qui n'est pas l'absence du souvenir, mais l'oblitération par la banalisation" (it is through testimony like that of Mrs Ighilahriz that the necessary "work of memory" is performed and repeated, to use the term coined by the philosopher Paul Ricœur, the untiring repetition of the "representation of past events," that which must be transmitted from generation to generation, working against forgetting, that is not an absence of memory, rather obliteration by trivialization).[19] Paul Ricœur published his influential work on memory entitled *La mémoire, l'histoire, l'oubli* (Memory, History and Forgetting) in 2000 in which he undertook a phenomenology of memory, an epistemology of history, and a hermeneutics of forgetting.[20]

For Jay Winter, coeditor of *War and Remembrance in the Twentieth Century*, collective memory needs to be understood in terms of agency, and I will argue in this chapter that journalists are agents themselves and the media has been an important place where other agents (activists) have played out "memory battles." Other commentators on collective memory, such as Paula Hamilton have also pointed to the increasing importance of the media (and popular culture) to collective remembering and historical representations.[21] Indeed, newspapers sometimes themselves equate media coverage and memory directly, as is evidenced in the following title resuming and referring to the 2001 media polemic surrounding the French army's use of torture during the Algerian War: "La mémoire de la torture pendant la guerre d'Algérie refait surface" (The Memory of Torture During the Algerian War Resurfaces).[22] The media play an important role in "producing meanings" and are part of the "culture industries."[23]

The media in recent years have been at the center of renewed examination by French society of the Algerian War. Throughout 2000 more and more media coverage appeared in France on one of the most taboo aspects of the Algerian War: the French army's use of torture.[24] Until this mediatic event the subject of torture was very rarely evoked and its discussion was limited to periodic eruptions such as the publication (in the early 1970s) of General Massu's *La Vraie bataille d'Alger* (The Real Battle of Algiers) or discussion (in the early 1980s) of Jean-Marie Le Pen's activities in Algeria. Media "debate" continued into 2001 and only tailed off in 2002. French radio and television also discussed the question. This media coverage lasted two years and has been described as a "very polemical and mediatized reactivation of the memory of the Algerian war."[25] The coverage began in *Le Monde* when the paper first published the testimony of Louisette Ighilahriz.[26] She described how she had been tortured by French forces and alleged that high ranking French army officers had been present, specifically Generals Jacques Massu and Marcel Bigeard—the former headed the Tenth Division of the French Paratroopers during the Battle of Algiers in 1957. In response they also published their own viewpoints in the paper, and over time other officers such as Generals Maurice Schmitt and Paul Aussaresses—the latter published *Services Spéciaux: Algérie 1955-1957* (Special Services: Algeria 1955-1957) in 2001—were also accused of human rights' violations.[27]

Previous work on the role of the media in the construction of French collective memory of the Algerian War focused on newspaper coverage of the twentieth anniversary of the end of the war and televisual memory of the war.[28] More recently discussion has focused on the "media debate" of 2000/2001, with two different positions emerging. Analyses of the significance of this media coverage however diverge. For some the media coverage constituted a step "towards a new history." They claim that the media coverage allowed a working through of repressed memories, somewhat in a Freudian perspective.[29] This position broadly corresponds to the view of journalists at *Le Monde* and/or those who signed "L'appel des Douze" (Petition of Twelve).[30] For instance, one journalist stated that:

> Jamais en plus de quarante ans de militantisme, leur protestation n'avait reçu pareil écho . . . Appelés ou engagés, ils éprouvent aujourd'hui le besoin de se libérer des cauchemars de leurs années algériennes. "On leur a offert un divan," résume Madeleine Rebérioux, historienne, cosignataire de l'appel. (Their protest had never received so much attention as this in more than forty years of activism . . . Conscripts or volunteers, they now feel the need to free themselves from their nightmares arising from their time in Algeria. "We offered them a space for therapy," as Madeleine Rebérioux, historian, cosignatory of the petition, puts it.)[31]

For others it is more an example of "memory battles" taking place in the present.[32] This view of the media debate would seem to draw predominantly on a pluralist understanding of collective memory, in which various groups compete for a place in the collective memory.

The "media event" therefore raises numerous fascinating issues that this chapter will begin to explore. What role do the media play in the construction of collective memory? (How) do the media, in a Halbwachsian perspective, provide a "social frame" for group and individual memories? In our case study, did the media coverage allow repressed memories to be worked through in a Freudian perspective? Beyond a quantitative and qualitative study of articles—that does indicate what is represented/remembered and to what extent—how can we analyze media reception? What specific characteristics does this vector of memory have in relation to others? To what extent is the media able to provide "discussion" of the past or any sustained coverage of history? What was represented? Why did this coverage take place when it did? For while most commentators acknowledge the importance of the media to collective memory, few have analyzed it. This chapter focuses above all on the French daily newspaper *Le Monde*.[33] The study is diachronic and synchronic, qualitative and quantitative. I draw on the *Index analytique du Monde* (Index of *Le Monde*) for the quantitative study (1977, 1981-1982, 1984-1986, 1991, 1998-1999, 2000-2001) and printouts of articles for December 2000, as well as January, April, June, and November 2001 for the qualitative study. As part of the synchronic study, we also focus on a number of articles published in June 2001 in two other French daily newspapers: *Libération* and *Le Figaro*.[34] The qualitative study pays particular attention to the themes, style, and language of media reporting about the Algerian War.

According to secondary school teachers, the Algerian War is "ancient history" for pupils. As we saw in a previous chapter the Algerian War is not significantly present in the *terminale* (final year of high school) history course—in the program and examination questions, reflected in textbooks—and is becoming increasingly absent. Teachers are unable to go into a great deal of detail in class—they are unlikely to be able to invite veterans to school to give testimony, to show films, or to focus *per se* on the Algerian War—and they therefore cover the topic quickly in the much broader topics of the history of the French Fourth and Fifth Republics, Decolonization, or de Gaulle's presidency. Pupil knowledge of the Algerian War reflects the "State-prescribed" and "Teacher" links in this educational chain, since their understanding of the conflict is fragmented and superficial. 80 percent of pupils think that too little is said about the Algerian War in schools.[35] Let us therefore begin this chapter by looking in greater detail at what pupils in interviews identified as sources of information on the Algerian War, outside of class.

Pupils and Historical Learning—Various Vectors of Memory

Pupils in interviews stated that the main sources of information used to prepare for the *baccalauréat* examination are the lesson notes and the textbook.[36] More generally, in terms of all sources of information on the Algerian War for young people, we can state that the role of teachers and the textbook is very important and more consequential than the role of other sources. However, as we have seen, the potential impact (although not realized at present) of other sources such as the family is greater than the present inherently limited impact of classes. The important role of education in shaping young people's historical memory has also been shown in various opinion polls in which it can be seen that answers to questions differ depending on the level of education received.[37] Predictably the further in the education system one has gone the more accurately one can answer questions on history. For Philippe Joutard and Jean Lecuir, commenting on a survey published in 2000 on the French and historical knowledge: "L'école reste un élément essentiel dans la transmission de la mémoire historique" (Schools remain an essential element in the transmission of historical memory).[38] According to the answers given in the interviews conducted for this book, the other significant source of information is the family. If information is gained from the family it can be very detailed, but there is a risk that on the Algerian War members of the family do not transmit information on the war—be they for example *appelés* (conscripts), *pieds-noirs* (settlers), *harkis* (Algerian soldiers who fought in the French army), or ex-FLN or MNA (former members of the FLN or MNA rival nationalist movements). The information is also subjective and partial (i.e., a lot of information on a limited number of issues) rather than the global objective view supposedly given through the class.

Other sources of information are available to young people and can be said to play a role in the transmission of memories, but their impact is perhaps limited due to the number of people who had received information from such vectors in the sample. It is possible for example that pupils have read books (novels rather than scholarly books) on the Algerian War. Quantitatively two or three pupils out of twelve had read novels, each of whom had read one or two books on the Algerian War, that is, there is relatively little impact from this source. Pupil 10 had read one book *Un Eté algérien* (An Algerian Summer) by Jean-Paul Nozière; Pupil 1 had read two books whose names she could not remember, one based in Oran the other on the struggle between the FLN and the OAS; Pupil 2 had possibly read novels but could not remember exactly. Teachers said that it was perhaps not even worth asking them to read books or watch films due to the lack of time, a point that supports what has already been said on the difference between classes in *terminale* and *seconde* and *première*.[39] Furthermore we must remember that pupils study *Géographie* (Geography) as well as *Histoire* (History). Also they have other subjects at the *baccalauréat*, with higher weightings. Pupil 3 said she could not read outside of lessons because: "J'ai déjà la philo, les lettres, je n'ai pas trop le temps" (I'm already doing philosophy and literature, I don't really have time) and those pupils who said they had read books often said it had been earlier in their life or during the holidays. It is also interesting to note that secondary schools have CDI's ("Centres de Documentation et d'Information:" information centers/libraries). I visited two of these and in both there was virtually nothing in terms of books on the Algerian War. The CDI's mainly stocked textbooks and the press and were places where pupils could work. However, the central public library in Lyon has a wide selection of sources on the Algerian War.

Pupils who have seen films on the Algerian War are rare but slightly less so than those who have read books on the conflict—five pupils had seen films on the Algerian conflict. Pupil 3 had seen one film but could not remember its name. She said it was a film with Roger Hanin and Gina Lolobrigida on television. Pupil 12 had seen three films though he could not give the names. Pupil 8 had seen *Chronique des années de braises* (Chronical of the Final Years) and Pupil 11 had seen Yves Courrière's documentary *La Guerre d'Algérie* (The Algerian War) on ARTE television channel and on satellite television a program on the role of women in the Algerian War. Pupil 2 had possibly seen films especially in Algeria. Pupil 10 commented on the impact of films by stating: "on dirait que ça a existé vraiment parce que quand on en parle comme ça ce n'est pas pareil que quand on regarde vraiment ce qui s'est passé à l'époque" (it makes it seem real because talking about it in an abstract way is not the same as visualizing what took place at the time). For Pupil 9: "ça marque bien" (it's memorable). Pupil 3 talked of the way in which a film gives the "ambiance de l'époque" (atmosphere of the time). Pupil 4 spoke of the difference between the lesson and a film. She had not seen a film on the Algerian War so spoke of a film on World

War Two. She mentioned the films *Il faut sauver le soldat Ryan* (Saving Private Ryan) and *La vie est belle* (Life is Beautiful). She said:

> J'ai vu des films sur la Seconde guerre mondiale avec le génocide et des choses comme ça, et je pense que même si c'est un peu . . . ça fait un peu roman parce qu'il y a une histoire derrière, je pense que c'est vraiment intéressant de voir comment ils ont vécu réellement et ça permet de mettre des images au cours qu'on a. Dans nos têtes, les images on les retient plus que des phrases. Donc ça choque plus. (I've seen films on the Second World War and genocide and things like that, and I think that even if it's a bit . . . it's a bit like a novel because there's a plot, I think it's really interesting to see how they actually lived and it allows us to put images to the notes we have. In our heads, we remember images more than phrases. So it's more memorable.)

We should also note that these two films are far more "mainstream" than anything that has been made on the Algerian War. Since the Second World War affected many countries, the number of sources on the war is logically greater and the "market" is also greater, in this example in terms of audience. We have also seen how World War Two can arguably more easily transmit values than the Algerian War. It is worth noting that no pupils could actually name a book or film that they knew existed but that they had not read or seen. Perhaps this shows that such films and books are not well known or mainstream. Most pupils also had difficulty remembering the name of books and films that they had read or seen. The findings from our small sample are supported by larger scale surveys into French historical memory. Generally this has led commentators to question whether there is "un appauvrissement du modèle d'histoire scolaire français" (a weakening of the French school history model), faced with an increasingly powerful "école parallèle" (parallel school), a key element of which is television as shown in "le succès des . . . films qui continuent à choisir leurs thèmes dans notre mythologie nationale" (the commercial success of . . . films that continue to draw on themes from our national mythology).[40] For Jean-Pierre Rioux, the two are better seen as complementary. Commenting on a survey conducted in 1996 on French historical memory he noted:

> On distingue désormais assez bien deux images du goût pour l'histoire: la première, visuelle et télévisuelle, privilégie la réception passive, la découverte de pure curiosité; la seconde, imprimée, mise sur une recherche permanente qui conforte la curiosité spontanée, sur une volonté d'approfondissement de connaissances déjà acquises, sur la valorisation culturelle. (We can now distinguish quite well between two images of interest in history: the first, visual and televisual, gives greater place to passive reception, and to discovery motivated by pure curiosity; the second, in print form, counts on a continual research that feeds spontaneous curiosity, on a desire to further deepen already acquired knowledge, and on enhancing cultural value.)[41]

A survey conducted in 1990 on French people's historical knowledge of the Second World War also showed both television and schools to be important, particularly for young people, thus highlighting the importance of distinguishing between different ages and ways of learning history. For eighteen to forty-four year olds, television was the top source of information on the Second World War. However, for students and pupils teachers were the main source of information.[42]

Reviews and magazines are another source of information. Given the age of pupils and the lack of time or need for reading, pupils who read reviews are not numerous but both Pupil 10 and Pupil 12 read L'Histoire. In fact such reviews have sold more and more in recent years, and have played a role in diffusing history and especially contemporary history. Information on the Algerian War is not really obtained from the television. There are possibly more programs with information on the war in Algeria on satellite television. Films on the Algerian conflict are highly rare at the cinema. Neither papers nor ceremonies would seem to influence young people on the Algerian War either. Regular reading Le Monde over a period of time shows how few articles there usually are in that paper on this colonial war. Of course, in this chapter we are going to focus on the period 2000-2001 when there were a significant number of articles on the French army's use of torture during the Algerian War. Larger scale surveys into French historical memory have indicated an increasing influence of the media on historical memory. In 1987, Rioux, commenting on a survey published in L'Histoire, noted that "l'actualité envahit la conscience historique" (current affairs are invading historical consciousness) since when asked "Si vous pouviez vous entretenir pendant une heure avec un personnage de l'histoire de France, lequel choisiriez-vous?" (If you could talk for an hour to a famous person from French history, whom would you choose?) five of the thirteen people chosen by those surveyed were contemporaries of the interviewees (e.g., Mitterrand) displacing the likes of Joan of Arc and Marie Curie. Nonetheless, Rioux remained circumspect when he stated "Laissons à d'autres le soin de dire si la France 's'emballe,' si ce présent devenu omniprésent pèse trop sur le passé ou si la mémoire collective est condamnée à n'être que médiatique un jour" (We'll leave it up to other people to conclude whether France "is getting carried away," whether this present that has become omnipresent crowds out the past too much or if collective memory is condemned to be purely media driven one day).[43] Nearly ten years later however, Rioux, again commenting on a survey published in L'Histoire spoke of "un présent envahissant, médiatisé, à temporalité élastique" (an all-encompassing present, mediatized, with elastic temporality) and the "irruption dans la trame historique d'une présence quotidienne du vécu et du télévisé" (irruption in the historical framework of a daily presence of the lived and the televised), reflecting what he called a "historisation accélérée" (accelerated historization).[44]

The last influence on pupils discussed in the interviews was the present. The present clearly influences lesson content as was seen in a previous chapter. In the interview Teacher 17 mentioned current affairs and the importance of a site of memory as aspects of the present that influenced her to spend more time on the harkis in class. Another teacher mentioned the demonstration that ended tragically at the metro station Charonne and current affairs: the way in which during the Papon trial[45] there had been a lot of media coverage of this event, leading her to cover it in more detail than other years. A third teacher mentioned recent books on the events of the night of 17 October 1961, leading him to want to spend more time on this subject in future. Theoretical work on memory highlights the link between the present and memory. In interviews with pupils, present concerns often came to the fore. They mentioned the present in terms of the war in Kosovo and the situation in Algeria (the group of Teacher 11's three pupils, and Pupil 11). They also talked of *lieux* (sites): for example Pupil 1 whose mother when passing through Lyon with her daughter pointed out that it was there that there had previously been the *bidonville* (shantytown) where a lot of *harkis* had lived. Pupil 10 also mentioned another *lieu* that had stimulated her memory of the Algerian War. It was a cemetery in which her father is buried (he died in 1998). Visiting the cemetery she had noticed the tombstones of young people who had died in the Algerian War.

We can therefore state that media coverage is likely to be important not only in transmitting memories directly to individuals but also indirectly by influencing the content of classes for young people. It may be unlikely that articles in *Le Monde* transmitted much historical memory directly to young people, but one would expect older people to be more avid readers of the paper.[46] Furthermore, *Le Monde*'s coverage itself led to documentaries and films that may have been seen by young people. Let us now turn then to test these initial ideas in our case study of the media's coverage in France in 2000-2001 of the French army's use of torture during the Algerian War.

Quantitative Study of Articles: Diachronic and Synchronic

Diachronic

One initial way to approach media analysis of *Le Monde*'s recent retrospective coverage of the Algerian War is quantitatively in a diachronic study.[47] Diachronically we look at the total number of articles on the Algerian War over the last three decades. In addition, we focus on themes (subjects) over time. These tables are presented in the appendices. This method allows us to gauge overall trends in the number of articles published.

In this chapter an examination of subjects and topics will be at the heart of most of what we do.[48] Teun van Dijk undertook a similar study concerning media coverage of ethnicity. Following van Dijk, we can think of a pyramid with headlines at the top, a handful of topics near the top and then much more information and detail at the bottom of the pyramid so that "only a few topics 'at the top' may summarize large amounts of information 'at the bottom.'"[49] Van Dijk refers to topics as "semantic macro-structures" or "summarizing macro-propositions."[50] They are important since they represent what journalists think the most important or relevant information in the article is. They are often used to formulate headlines—a point we will develop below. For van Dijk:

> They (topics) are also crucial in cognitive information processing, and allow readers to better organize, store and recall textual information in memory. Experimental research has repeatedly shown that topics are usually the best recalled information of a text.[51]

Topics tend to be paragraphs in news items. There can be a hierarchy of topics in an article. Subjects on the other hand tend to be bigger:

> A subject is a single concept, such as "crime" or "education," which stands for a large social or political domain or a complex issue about which the Press offers potentially an infinite number of specific news reports. Each news report has its own, unique, topics, which do not consist of a single concept but of a more complex structure of concepts[52]

The campaign launched by Le Monde in 2000-2001 was undoubtedly significant. The numerical significance of coverage in Le Monde is clearly shown by the fact that 109 and 168 news items were published in 2000 and 2001 respectively on the Algerian War, compared to twelve and thirty-eight in 1998 and 1999.[53] Since then, numbers of articles have returned to their more typical levels—the average for the 1990s being thirty-six per year. According to the Le Monde website there were eighty-six articles on "the Algerian War" in 2002 and a further twenty-four in the first five months of 2003. Consequently we can state that the media are important in representing historical events, but their inevitable focus on the present means that coverage cannot be sustained. The media are therefore a very specific vector of memory—very actual and temporary.

Over time we can note the importance of commemorations/anniversaries to media coverage. Anniversary years after the end of the war in 1962—1977 (Fifteenth), 1982 (Twentieth), 1987 (Twenty-Fifth), 1992 (Thirtieth), 1997 (Thirty-Fifth) and 2002 (Fortieth)—all stand out as years with more articles on the Algerian War. This is a clear specificity of this vector of memory. Similarly, during the year, certain key events linked to key dates also generate regular articles. Two examples suffice to illustrate this phenomenon: 17 October 1961 and the "putsch des généraux" (putsch by army generals). As we saw in the introduction to this book, according to Guy Pervillé, 1991 was the first year that the media covered in any depth the events of 17 October 1961 so in 1991 it "a réussi à percer le mur d'ignorance et d'indifférence des médias" (succeeded in breaking through the media's wall of ignorance and indifference).[54] In 2001, the fortieth anniversary of the events of 17 October 1961, dozens of articles were published in Le Monde—providing testimony of the events of that night (e.g., "Le témoignage sans égal d'Elie Kagan, un photographe au cœur de la bataille," The Standout Testimony of Elie Kagan, a Photographer at the Center of the Battle), editorial comment (e.g., "Mémoire et lucidité," Memory and Lucidity), coverage of historical debates (e.g., "Entre 30 et 200 morts: l'impossible bilan," Impossible to Know the Exact Number of Deaths: Between 30 and 200 Victims), and details of the commemoration of the massacre (e.g., "Les controverses politiques sur la guerre d'Algérie marquent la commémoration du 17 octobre 1961," Political Controversy about the Algerian War Surrounds the Commemoration of the Events of 17 October 1961).[55] Similarly, April 2001 saw three news items on the putsch—a bibliography of books on the topic, an article providing biographical information about the main participants in the putsch ("Quatre généraux et quelques colonels," Four Generals and a Few Colonels), and an article analyzing the putsch ("Le putsch manqué d'Alger," The failed Putsch in Algiers).[56] These key dates and key anniversaries all (periodically) generate articles on the Algerian War. This is one example of the media providing the "frames of memory" to, in this instance, readers.

If we further breakdown the topics over the years, we can see the ways in which at different stages "media events" or campaigns take place surrounding certain groups. Latterly the group has been the French army and the question of torture, with other groups including Algerians and French who resisted the Algerian War also assuming a large place in that coverage. Previously, *harkis* were clearly a group on which the media focused (in 1991). European settlers enjoyed extensive media coverage in 1977. For the *harkis*, it is very interesting to note that despite significant media coverage in 1991 their situation improved little. Debate then focused upon revolts by children of *harkis*. 1977 is also a very interesting year as there were 125 articles on the *rapatriés* (European settlers who "returned" to France). It is interesting to note that in each of these instances the media tend to focus on one group at a time. This phenomenon reflects the wider collective memory of the Algerian War, that we have identified as being made up of a series of often mutually hostile group memories that have yet to be overcome. There is little relation between these groups. If such a relation exists, to date, it is always adversarial.

We therefore begin to see the way in which the media are a site of contestation as various groups and events, directly or indirectly, consciously or not, vie for a place in the collective memory. Groups use the media. One example of this is torture. Torture had been discussed before. For instance, Jean-Marie Le Pen had been accused of torturing suspects in the 1980s. Indeed, Jacques Massu in *La Vraie bataille d'Alger* (The Real Battle of Algiers) published in the early 1970s, to which Jules Roy responded in *J'accuse le général Massu* (I Accuse General Massu), justified the French army's use of torture. We can remember Henri Alleg's *La Question*, published during the Algerian War and that was instrumental in informing French public opinion about the methods employed by the French army in Algeria to obtain "renseignements" (information) and terrorize. Pierre Vidal-Naquet has also played an important role, during and since the Algerian War in denouncing torture. In *Le Monde* (1984-1986) twenty-one articles were published on Le Pen and torture in 1985 after *Le Canard Enchaîné* and then *Libération* published articles accusing Le Pen of torturing suspects during the Algerian War, and were then sued by Le Pen.[57] Accusing Le Pen of torturing people during the war in Algeria reoccurred in 2002. Articles were written in particular by Florence Beaugé and then Le Pen sued the paper. This then needs to be understood as a case of repetition of unresolved issues. Furthermore, nothing was resolved in the last debate, so we cannot say that there has been any closure. In contemporary France, it is still impossible to obtain justice for crimes that were committed during the Algerian War. A series of amnesties were passed after the war. Stora in *La Gangrène et l'oubli* (The Gangrene and the Forgetting) rightly identifies amnesties as one important way that the memory of the Algerian War has been occluded. The difficulty of trying people in France for crimes committed during the Algerian War and obtaining justice will be developed further below.

Synchronic

Let us now consider our corpus synchronically. In the quantitative synchronic study of the articles, we continue to look at the number of articles over time but shorten the period to the years 2000/2001. We consider the respective total number of articles per month during this period and the number and type of themes per month. This information is provided in the appendices. We also expand our study to two other daily newspapers: *Libération* and *Le Figaro*.

In 2000/2001 the sheer number of articles meant that the Algerian War achieved a media presence it had never before achieved. Whereas previously there may have been a handful of articles, sporadically, during this period readers were quite regularly provided information on the Algerian War, often several articles at a time. This makes it more difficult for readers to miss or skip the issue. In December 2000 there were fifty articles on the Algerian War, ten in January 2001, six in April, twenty-three in June, and seventeen in November. Sustained coverage of the Algerian War is rare and significant. The media are usually predominantly focused on the present, unable to provide sustained coverage of issues or go into a great deal of depth on topics. In our case however, for once, the Algerian War remained in the press for an extended period. There were months where coverage was more or less extensive. This tended to follow a "life cycle" of the issue. At first Louisette Ighilahriz's testimony and reactions to this started the ball rolling, but it was only later when Ausarresses became involved that coverage intensified and then again only when he published his book that the issue was "relaunched." In between each peak in coverage there are frequent lulls.

If we then breakdown these months into themes per month in 2000/2001 we note that one common point in each of the months analyzed in detail is the preponderance of articles on torture. We can also note that the other issues examined tend to be negative aspects of the Algerian War. This would seem to be typical of the role of the media—whose role is largely to criticize. In other spheres—such as ethnic minorities and the media—it has been noted that the media can often convey and disseminate negative images. This was a charge particularly aimed at the media after the Presidential election shock in April

2001. For many observers, the media had focused far too much on insecurity in French towns and in its coverage linked law and order issues to immigrants and/or their children. This in turn had facilitated Le Pen's reaching the second round of the election. The media then are particularly suited, through investigative journalism, to forcing society to look at issues that it would rather forget. But this tends to mean that the representation of the historical event in question will be partial— orientated towards sensational aspects of history. This "work of memory" undoubtedly needs to be undertaken, but, in order to reconcile the groups involved in the Algerian War, perhaps the media could also cover less sensationalist issues and identify common elements from the war. Such editorial choices obviously cannot be "imposed" on the media, but if journalists really want to facilitate a "work of memory" on this topic, it is a point they should consider.

It would be unwise to focus solely on *Le Monde*. A number of national and local newspapers exist in France, although *Le Monde* traditionally has a reputation as "the national journal of record." A glance at the coverage of *Libération* and *Le Figaro* in June 2001 provides us with a useful comparative angle. This information is given in the table in the appendices. It is noteworthy that *Le Monde* and *Libération*, both left-leaning newspapers, have a large number of articles on the French army's conduct during the Algerian War, whereas *Le Figaro*, a more right-wing newspaper, has far fewer. *Le Figaro* only published seven articles on the Algerian War, whereas *Libération* published twenty-three that month. Furthermore, the articles that are published in *Le Figaro* give a preponderant place to interviews with those charged with torturing suspects during the Algerian War or "apologizing for war crimes." Consequently, both Aussaresses and Schmitt are interviewed. Schmitt is also given space to write his own article and Xavier de Bartillat—Aussaresses's editor—is also interviewed.

The articles in *Libération* are, perhaps unsurprisingly, quite different. The paper ran a series of articles entitled "Mémoires d'Algérie" (Memories of Algeria), with articles on "Torture: l'Express en première ligne" (Torture: l'Express Magazine under Pressure), "L'affaire Audin, un mensonge d'Etat" (The Audin Affair, a State Cover-Up), "Bollardière, le général qui a dit non"(Bollardière, the General Who Said No), "Le silence en héritage" (Silence as Heritage) and "Paroles cachées d'appelés" (Unspoken Experiences of Conscripts). The articles published in *Libération* are clearly much more focused on the "victims" of the Algerian War and the ordinary person. Coverage is more focused on ethnic minorities. Taken together then, the coverage of all three newspapers appears more plural and diverse than if we were solely to focus on *Le Monde*. A greater variety of viewpoints and perspectives are presented.

Qualitative Study of Articles: Themes, Styles, and Language

Themes

As mentioned above, we have differentiated between subjects and topics. We were interested in subjects in the previous section, in a quantitative perspective. This section focuses above all on how news item subjects (e.g., torture) are "topicalized." Torture is a subject. How it is topicalized is how it is approached. We can identify clusters of topics. A cluster is when there are several articles on the same topic. This kind of study gives us a general introduction to the contents of these stories. There is still a quantitative aspect to this study, but we begin to look at news items and articles qualitatively. The five-month study of articles indicates a number of subjects and topic clusters. Let us here focus on the one subject of torture and break down its topicalization.[58]

A number of factors can be noted in terms of the topics. Firstly, the broad issue of the French State's use of torture is reduced to the cases of a small number of key people: Generals Aussaresses, Schmitt, Massu, and Bigeard as perpetrators and Louisette Ighilahriz or Larbi Ben M'Hidi as victims allied with those who opposed the Algerian War or the French army's methods such as Paul Teitgen and General de Bollardière.[59] One important point to note when considering coverage of torture in *Le Monde* is the question of actors. Who are the perpetrators? Who are the victims? Who is named as an agent? One striking example of the personification of the (complex) issue of torture can be found in the following portrait of General Aussaresses:

> il part ensuite en Indochine où il sert sous les ordres du général Pâris de Bollardière, qu'il vénère. Serait-il resté auprès du plus célèbre des militants anti-torture que le cours de sa vie en aurait peut-être été changé. Mais c'est le général Massu qui l'appelle à ses côtés en 1957. (he then goes to Indo-China where he serves under the command of General Pâris de Bollardière, whom he reveres. If he had stayed under the most famous of anti-torture militants, perhaps his life would have taken a different course. But he's called to General Massu's side in 1957.)[60]

Not only do we have an example of a dichotomy tortured/resisted torture reduced to a few people, but the question of how it came to be that Aussaresses ended up as a torturer after being a "hero of the Free French" is resumed to whom he worked with. This replicates World War Two and Vichy whereby only a handful of perpetrators (e.g., Maurice Papon) were ever tried and in each case they tended to represent all of the perpetrators since with so few trials each trial inevitably becomes a show trial, even if they themselves are charged as individuals for their own crimes. Secondly, the negativity of the coverage is evident in the topics covered in the media: torture, rape, executions/massacres, and the shame surrounding the treatment of the *harkis*. There is a rather "sensationalist" coverage of this affair, probably associated with the medium (the media) and investigative journalism, as mentioned in the previous section. Issues that are hardest to discuss lend themselves most readily to investigative journalism. Thirdly, the question of torture clearly preoccupies.

Fourthly, if we look at the content of the articles, the extent to which this coverage constitutes a "debate" can be questioned. The print media struggle to avoid "imposing" their views through the newspaper. There is little scope for dialogue on issues. Readers have only limited opportunity to express their own opinions. The "work of memory" in this arena then has inherent limits. It amounts to media coverage and representation of issues that French society would rather not address. This does mean that readers will have to confront the issue and no doubt the coverage in the media will generate discussion (in coffee shops, associations, or amongst friends for example). However the editorial line or content of the paper cannot really be influenced a great deal by readers. Indeed, the positions and coverage of Le Monde are criticized in a number of readers' letters[61] and "Horizons-Débats" sections.[62] The latter are usually longer than letters and written by "more important people" such as a writer (René-Victor Pilhes), the former Ambassador to the Gabon (Pierre Dabezies) or Micislas Orlowski (President of the "Médaillés militaires"). Readers' letters are accompanied by a name but no title. The key theme in most of the letters is the alleged biased nature of the reporting that leads to a misrepresentation of the issue of torture resulting in an unjust representation of soldiers in the French army in particular. The letters also clearly show the strength of feeling that still exists on this topic. For Pilhes: "cette belle unanimité pour condamner les tortures me paraît louche, dangereuse, peu rassurante" (this fine unanimity to condemn torture seems dubious, dangerous, and worrying to me) and he questions "pourquoi si tard? Pourquoi toujours si peu d'opposants déclarés aux oppressions, aux violations des droits de l'homme, aux machineries racistes en tout genre, au temps où elles sévissent? Pourquoi tant de héros et sabres de bois si longtemps après" (why so late? Why are there always so few who declare their opposition to oppression, to human rights violations, and to expressions of racism in all its forms, at the time of the events? Why are there so many heroes and saber rattlers decades later?).[63] So for Pilhes it is much easier, and more comforting, to criticize conduct forty years after the event than to have stood out at the time. For Guy-Remi Vollauris: "Il serait souhaitable que Le Monde fasse état d'autres témoignages qui mettent en lumière d'autres attitudes plus conformes à la dignité des appelés du contingent" (Le Monde would do well to print other testimony that show other attitudes that better reflect the dignity of conscript soldiers).[64] Vollauris is clearly unhappy that the reputations of all conscripts are being tarnished through a limited representation of a very complex issue. Dabezies also criticizes journalists and intellectuals for their overly simplistic positions. For him (a veteran of the Algerian War, former Ambassador to Gabon and Emeritus Professor at the Sorbonne):

Vouloir donc mettre en exergue, si longtemps après, sous prétexte de "repentance," des excès—trop nombreux et incontestablement regrettables—, c'est, consciemment ou non, jeter l'oppobre d'une façon inacceptable sur l'ensemble de l'armée et chercher, une fois encore, à dénigrer la France. (To want to underline, so long after the events, under the pretext of "repentance," excesses—too numerous and indisputably regrettable—, amounts, consciously or not, to heap opprobrium on the whole army and attempt, once more, to denigrate France.)[65]

Orlowski, taking us back to the debates that took place during the Algerian War in which a "defeatist press" was criticized for damaging the morale of the army—criticizes "une certaine presse" (a certain press) since: "Il n'est pas possible de percevoir ce qu'est en fait la torture si on est installé dans le confort d'un salon ou d'une salle de rédaction" (It is impossible to know what torture is when in the comfort of one's own living room or at work in editorial offices).[66] Furet makes a similar point: "C'est à croire que tous ceux qui ont multiplié les articles sur ce thème depuis deux mois dans les pages *du Monde* ne savent pas ce qu'est la guerre: c'est un infâme creuset dans lequel les hommes qui y participent, en dehors de quelques êtres d'exception, sont moralement broyés, où toute éthique disparaît, où les perversités naissent ou se développent" (Anyone would think that all those people who have written so many articles on this theme over the last two months in *Le Monde* don't know what war is like: it is a vile test in which the men who participate, apart from a few exceptional human beings, are morally ground down, where all ethics disappear, where perversity is born and develops).[67] All of the readers therefore want to see a more nuanced approach to the French army's use of torture that better reflects the difficult situation that the conscripts found themselves in and the harsh realities of war. Given the depth of feeling on this issue that these letters reveal, and their criticism of the paper's coverage, it is difficult to see how *Le Monde*'s campaign can have been therapeutic. It is more likely that the coverage actually subsequently led to a shutting down of discussion, at least amongst conscripts, due to a rejection of much of what was written. It is nonetheless the case that this "work of memory" is—while incredibly difficult—necessary. Although the print media would seem to be unable to sustain a dialogue on the issue, other media—such as television talk shows—and other vectors of memory—such as associations—may have provided more room to debate these issues more widely and more fully.

Jean Pierre Meyer, a veteran of the Algerian War and retired secondary school German teacher, engages at length in whether and how French society should discuss the topic, and seeks to put forward his view of what happened in Algeria—"la torture était pratiquée systématiquement" (torture took place systematically), particularly by professional units (e.g., paratroopers) and DOP[68] but "les deux millions d'appelés et d'engagés de tous grades envoyés en Algérie n'ont pas tous été impliqués de la même façon" (the two million conscripts and volunteers of all ranks sent to Algeria were not all involved in the same way or to the same degree). Consequently:

> Le débat actuel sur ce thème est de ce fait ambigu et frustrant, dans la mesure où une repentance nationale impliquerait et culpabiliserait tous les anciens d'Algérie. En outre, la création d'une commission d'enquête parlementaire préconisée par certains ne serait pas exempte de visées partisanes. (The current debate on this theme is therefore ambiguous and frustrating, given that an act of national repentance would implicate all veterans of the Algerian War, causing

attendant feelings of guilt. In addition, a parliamentary commission that some would like to see created would inevitably be partisan.)[69]

Fifthly, a detailed study of the articles reveals that a limited number of core issues and questions crosses the majority of the articles. They are: Should Aussaresses be judged? (How) Should French society "discuss" this topic? Who is responsible for torture during the Algerian War? What took place in Algeria? The latter point is described below when we discuss in more depth how the articles show that the media are an important arena in which different versions of the past are contested. In doing so, different versions of the past can be presented by various actors. Similarly the question of whether and how French society—or the media at least—should discuss the French army's use of torture has been described at length above. The "core issue" of whether Aussaresses should be judged reminds us of French society's procrastination over whether to judge Vichy collaborators in the 1980s and 1990s. So let us deal here with the central core issue of the articles' attempts to establish responsibility for what took place in Algeria. To a large extent, this is to be expected given that much of the media coverage was generated by coverage of Aussaresses's trials. However, it is interesting to note that it has been impossible to "faire le procès de la torture" (try over torture), to use the words of one *Le Monde* journalist.[70] Aussaresses could only be tried for "apologies de crimes de guerre" (justifying or defending war crimes), whereas the content of many news items shows that the underlying issue in news coverage is who is/was responsible. Hence Aussaresses can be "Un soldat qui a fait son travail pour la France" (A Soldier Who Did His Duty for France), therefore merely a soldier following orders and acting in the national interest, given that "Au premier jour de son procès, Paul Aussaresses endosse tous les crimes qu'il a ordonnés" (On the First Day of his Trial, Paul Aussaresses Assumes all the Crimes he is Charged With) or alternatively "Même s'il s'en défend, le général Aussaresses cherche à mettre en cause le pouvoir politique de l'époque" (Even if he Denies it, General Aussaresses is Trying to Implicate the Political Authorities of the Time) since it was the political authorities that insisted on keeping Algeria French and fighting a war to achieve this end. Public opinion is also blamed in items such as "Une opinion informée mais largement indifférente" (An Informed but Largely Indifferent Public Opinion) and "Torture: Nous savions tous" (Torture: We All Knew).[71] Responsibility then becomes collective. Since amnesties were passed after the Algerian War, it is impossible to have an "official" legal ruling on who was responsible. Consequently we can expect such debates over responsibility over the French army's use of torture to continue in the future.

Importantly and interestingly, if we divide the articles up by type, we see that it is the letters from the public that are quite critical of the general editorial line of the newspaper—to pursue Aussaresses, support "l'appel des douze" etc. Many of the letters address the issue of who was responsible for the use of torture. Roger Monié, a veteran of the Algerian War and retired Reserves Lieutenant places the blame squarely on the shoulders of the leaders of the army and on politicians: "Si le gouvernement de la France ne voulait pas de la torture, il fallait qu'il l'exprime officiellement et clairement. Si l'armée, en l'absence de consignes claires, ne voulait pas de la torture, pour préserver son honneur ou celui de la France (pourquoi pas?), il fallait que ses chefs le disent de façon explicite" (If the French government was not in favor of torture, it should have declared so officially and clearly. If the army, in the absence of clear advice, did not favor the use of torture, in order to preserve its honor and that of France [why not?], its leaders should have explicitly said so).[72] For Boris Brehat Goiremberg: "L'armée comme la police ne sont que des instruments aveugles et brutaux; seul est en cause le pouvoir civil, aveugle et lâche" (The army, like the police, are but blind and brutal instruments, blind and cowardly civil authorities are the real culprits).[73] Again French politicians are blamed for what happened in Algeria. For another reader:

> Laissons les généraux avec leur conscience et interrogeons-nous plutôt pour savoir si notre pays peut, de bonne foi, prétendre effacer une page aussi sombre de son histoire en reportant sur les seuls exécutants le choix de moyens inhumains utilisés pour atteindre les objectifs impossibles d'une politique imbécile dans le droit-fil de celle que la France n'a cessé de mener en Algérie. (Let us leave the Generals with their conscience and focus rather on trying to establish whether our country can, in good faith, try and erase such a somber page from its history by dumping the responsibility for using inhumane methods solely on the shoulders of those who carried out the orders and who were trying to achieve impossible objectives, as part of the imbecilic policy that France continually followed in Algeria.)[74]

Sixthly, throughout the period studied, the media coverage can be seen to be an arena in which competing versions of the past are contested. The articles provide ample examples of the media as an arena in which "memory battles" are fought. For example, the cluster of articles that examine various groups' opposition to torture essentially amounts to contesting versions of the past. The articles on the attitude of the French Communist Party illustrate this point well. "Le PCF et l'Algérie Française" (The French Communist Party and French Algeria) and "Guerre d'Algérie: contes et légendes du PCF" (Algerian War: Tales and Legends of the French Communist Party) denounce the PCF. The latter criticizes "un comportement qui n'a pas été aussi idyllique qu'on veut bien nous le faire croire" (behavior that was not as idyllic as they would have us believe). Both pieces, a readers letter and a Horizons-Débats item, respond to Roland Rappaport's positions in "Guerre d'Algérie: des avocats contre l'aveuglement" (The Algerian War: Lawyers for Justice), a Horizons-Débats item that defends the PCF for its support of Algerians in their struggle for independence. He was a lawyer and a member of the French Communist Party during the Algerian War. The articles on the "Appel des douze" similarly allow this group to seek to impose their view of history by their clever use of the media. They contest the position of President Jacques Chirac (1995-) for whom "ces atrocités, indéniables, ont été le fait de minorités" (these atrocities, that undeniably took place, were carried out by a minority).[75] Their views obviously also clash with those of Jean-Marie Le Pen, hence the demonstrations that took place by the Extreme Right. In the article "Jean-Marie Le Pen et les 'interrogatoires musclés'" (Jean-Marie Le Pen and "Hard Interrogations") Le Pen challenges terminology by preferring the term "interrogatoires musclés" (hard interrogations) to torture, thus contesting what happened in Algeria.[76] The article "Mobilisation pour une prise de position officielle contre la torture" (Mobilization For an Official Stance Against Torture) also highlights contemporary political battles between the Left and the Right that draw on opposing versions of the past. Articles like "Ce ne fut pas si simple" (Things Weren't That Simple), written by an ex-colonel in the paratrooper regiment, challenges the belief that everybody tortured and explains how matters went astray in Algeria—by a triple lack in political power. He ends with a cutting criticism of communist positions:

> Chargée, par la démission du pouvoir en place, d'une mission "politique" qui la dépassait, une partie de l'armée, convaincue qu'elle ne pouvait pas faire autrement, s'est laissé aller, c'est vrai, à commettre des excès. On ne peut s'empêcher, pour autant, de sourire en voyant aujourd'hui la surenchère communiste . . . Quid de la repentance de ce parti qui, pendant des décennies, a couvert, voire approuvé à demi-mot, avec Staline et ses séides, les pire ignomies? (Politicians shirked their responsibilities and put the army in charge of a "political" mission that forced it out of its depth. A part of the army, convinced that there was no choice, let itself, it's true, go too far. That said, one can't help but smile when listening to communist sensationalism . . . And what of this party's repentance that, for decades, covered, even implicitly approved, with Stalin and his henchmen, the most disgraceful acts.)[77]

The whole Aussaresses "affair" emerged from testimony published in *Le Monde* of Louisette Ighilahriz that challenged dominant official discourses of the Algerian War. Bigeard flatly denied the allegations. Massu on the other hand changed his earlier position exposed in his 1971 book *La Vraie bataille d'Alger* (The Real Battle of Algiers). For editorialists at *Le Monde*:

> Le général Massu, à sa façon, ne veut pas tourner la page; il ne veut pas oublier; il participe au travail de mémoire. Pas par mode de la repentance. Mais pour adresser un message qui pèse lourd, venant de cet homme-là: *"Non la torture n'est pas indispensable en temps de guerre . . .* , dit-il. *Quand je repense à l'Algérie, on aurait pu faire les choses différement."* Ne serait-ce que pour entendre cette leçon, cette dernière phrase, il fallait revenir, en effet, sur la torture en Algérie. (General Massu, in his own way, does not want to move on; he does not want to forget; he is participating in the work of memory. Not in order to repent. Rather to address a message that has a lot of weight coming from him. For Massu: *"No, torture is not indispensable in wartime . . . When I think back to Algeria, we could have done things differently."* Just to hear this lesson, this last phrase, we think justifies investigating the issue of torture again.)[78]

Similar "memory battles" can be seen in the paper's coverage of the courtroom. The article "Au procès de Paul Aussaresses, le général Schmitt a justifié l'usage de la torture en Algérie" (At the Trial of Paul Aussaresses, General Schmitt Justified the Use of Torture in Algeria) the diametrically opposed positions—that were adopted during the Algerian War—of justifying/criticizing the use of torture are once again rehearsed. General Schmitt justifies the use of torture in his statement: "S'il faut se salir les mains ou accepter la mort d'innocents, je choisis de me salir les mains" (If it is a choice between getting one's hands dirty or accepting the death of innocent people, I choose to get my hands dirty), a position countered by Henri Alleg who invokes at length "l'horreur des sévices" (the horror of being tortured).[79]

Style

Thusfar we have paid considerable attention to subjects and topics—themes. For van Dijk: "not only the order and prominence of topics is highly relevant in telling ideologically biased news stories, but so also are the ways these topics become implemented at the 'local' level of the meanings of words and sentences, for instance by the addition of irrelevant details that can be interpreted in accordance with prevailing stereotypes and prejudices . . ."[80] While van Dijk is examining news items and ethnicity, we find parallels in the media coverage of the "Aussaresses affair."

Examples of irrelevant details can be found in Florence Beaugé's portrait article of Aussaresses: "Aussi surprenant que cela paraisse, le vieux général espérait, semble-t-il, attirer l'attention d'une femme qui le fascinait alors, Christine Deviers-Joncour" (As surprising as it may seem, the old General hoped, it would seem, to attract the attention of a woman whom he was fascinated by, Christine Deviers-Joncour).[81] Hence Aussaresses is ridiculed and an extremely tenuous explanation of his actions is given. In another article Aussaresses is referred to as a "drôle de général" (strange General) who is "sourd comme un pot" (deaf as a doorpost).[82] Elsewhere we can detect Aussaresses and his entourage portrayed in a universally negative light, whereas people who resisted the Algerian War are portrayed positively. An example can be found in coverage of a trial. Aussaresses is surrounded by a "quarteron de généraux en retraite" (small group of retired Generals), of course reminding the reader of de Gaulle's pejorative statements about the generals who revolted against him in the April 1961 putsch, who "ont une apparence: courbés, chenus, décorés, à moitié sourds, pleins de souvenirs et d'arthrite" (all look the same: stooped, hoary, decorated, half deaf, full of memories and arthritis) and calls upon a witness described by the journalist as a "copain restaurateur" (restaurant-owner mate), whereas Henry Alleg is described as "digne, profond, touchant" (dignified, deep, touching).[83] In another article Pierre Vidal-Naquet, another who resisted the Algerian War, is described positively as a "historien et infatigable militant contre la torture" (historian and untiring anti-torture activist).[84] While the brave actions of Alleg and

Vidal-Naquet certainly command respect, the style further contributes to the adversarial nature of the coverage that simply replicates and reinforces existing divisions.

In Florence Beaugé's piece entitled "Algérie: 'Ne pas créer d'événement qui pourrait raviver les plaies du passé'" (Avoid Anything that Reopens the Wounds of the Past) we can clearly detect criticism of Jacques Chirac's speech in the following comment: "Enfin, à ceux qui attendaient de lui une reconnaissance et une condamnation solenelles de la torture, M. Chirac réplique en bottant en touche: ce n'est pas aux historiens qu'il propose de faire leur travail, mais au temps. Autrement dit: laissons de l'eau couler sous les ponts" (Lastly, to those who were hoping to hear an official statement of recognition and condemnation of torture, Mr. Chirac replies by kicking that idea into touch: it is not historians who should do their work, rather time. In other words: let more water go under the bridge). [85]

Linguistic: A Case Study of Headlines

In their work on discourse analysis of national representations in the Australian and French press at the time of nuclear testing in the South Pacific in 1995, Christine Develotte and Elizabeth Rechniewski have argued convincingly that headlines are a particularly rich way to approach media analysis. For Van Dijk, headlines:

> formulate the most crucial words of such reports. Their position, semantic role, and cognitive consequences are such that they literally cannot be overlooked. They express the major topic of the report, as the newspaper sees it, and thereby at the same time summarize and evaluate a news event. In other words, they essentially define the situation. It is this definition that also plays a prominent role in the ways the readers understand and memorize news.[86]

In this section we examine the various functions of headlines (semantic, cognitive, ideological) quantitatively (lexical style and headline structure) and qualitatively. We focus on the articles in our corpus on torture.

This method reinforces a number of the points our other approaches to media analysis have already uncovered. The qualitative work, for example, highlights the frequency of legal terminology in the headlines—the extent of words like "procès" (trial), "juger" (to try), "crimes" (crimes), "amendes" (fines), "victimes" (victims) etc. The structure of the headlines similarly serves to identify agents. The predicates used highlight the accusatory framework: "contre" (against) and "accuser/porter plainte/mettre en cause" (accuse/sue/implicate). Examples of such headlines include:

> PROCES Dix mille francs d'amende requis contre le général Aussaresses et ses éditeurs. La notion d'"apologie de crimes" au cœur des débats (TRIAL Ten

thousand Franc Fine Requested Against General Aussaresses and his Editors. At the Core of the Debates the Notion of "Apology for Crimes.")[87]

Guerre d'Algérie: juger les tortionnaires? (Horizons Analyses) (The Algerian War: Try Torturers?)[88]

GUERRE D'ALGERIE: La FIDH a porté plainte contre le général Aussaresses pour "crimes contre l'humanité" (The Algerian War: the Human Rights Federation Sues General Aussaresses for "Crimes Against Humanity.")[89]

Tortures en Algérie: une ancienne combattante du FLN met en cause le général Maurice Schmitt. L'ancien chef d'état-major des armées entre 1987 et 1991 dénonce "le témoignage d'une terroriste" (Torture in Algeria: a Veteran of the FLN Implicates General Maurice Schmitt. The Former Head of the Armed Forces Between 1987 and 1991 Rejects "the Testimony of a Terrorist.")[90]

GUERRE D'ALGERIE La famille Ben M'hidi dépose à son tour une plainte contre "Paul Aussaresses et tous autres" (ALGERIAN WAR The Family of Ben M'hidi Sues "Paul Aussaresses and all the Others.")[91]

The lexical style further draws out how the complex issue of the French army's use of torture is reduced to a few key actors (particularly Aussaresses). This point was developed at length above.

Theory: Explaining and Accounting for this Treatment

As Jürgen Habermas has argued the media do play an important role in constituting a "public sphere" for collective memory. Yet, our case study of media coverage of the French army's use of torture during the Algerian War—when analyzed in terms of the representations it creates—has been shown to be problematic in a number of respects. In explaining and accounting for this treatment, this chapter continues to defend a theoretical approach to memory that draws on several schools of thought concerning collective memory. Three schools of thought have been retained as particularly useful. The approach taken in this chapter, as throughout this book, consists of defending a *bricolage* of theories. It is felt that drawing on as many theories as possible gives the richest understanding of collective memory. I argue that this "media event" can only be understood through reference to all three models. All three are true to some extent, but none suffices on its own to explain it.

The event cannot simply be seen as a therapeutic working through of problematic memories in a Freudian perspective. This process needs to be seen as but one step in a long and arduous process of coming to terms with this past. We should neither overemphasize nor underestimate its importance. The subject is clearly still hugely divisive, and I see little if any evidence of "passions and tensions . . . receding."[92] For example the trials that were launched against Aussaresses in them selves prove that nothing has been resolved and are tangible evidence of the amount of unresolved feelings remaining. They too have failed once more, running up against the amnesties granted after the Algerian War and that have been a central element of occlusion of the war (understood to mean state hiding of the truth).[93] Inevitably trials focus on a few individuals—as the judicial system seeks to establish the innocence or guilt or individuals on specific (limited) charges. Also we have seen that as the coverage unfolded, the terms of the debate became much less clear.

The methods used would not seem to indicate "the emergence of a 'new history'"[94] since very quickly the episode turned to judicial proceedings that were wholly unsuccessful. Examples of judicial proceedings include the "Fédération Internationale des Droits de l'Homme" (FIDH: International Federation of the Rights of Man) attempting to sue Aussaresses for "crimes contre l'humanité" (crimes against humanity) but the judge declaring no trial could take place since those crimes did not relate to the Algerian War. Harkis also attempted to sue for "crimes against humanity" with the same outcome. Aussaresses and his editor were sued for "apologie de crimes de guerre." Lawyers, following revelations made in Aussaresses's book Services Spéciaux, endeavored to have a trial reopened, that of the massacre of El Hali for which several people were found guilty during the Algerian War. The family of Ben M'Hidi also attempted to sue Aussaresses for "crimes contre l'humanité."[95] In the case of the Algerian War, only the trial for "apologie de crimes de guerre" was "successful" since editors were fined—although many have criticized this judicial outcome. It is unlikely that more will be debated on the Algerian War when editors risk being sued for publishing this material. It is clearly the case that occlusion is still taking place since the amnesties passed after the Algerian War still officially prohibit perpetrators of crime from being punished.

Another problem with the Freudian model emerged when the "debates" on torture tended to very quickly focalize on an accusation/denial framework—Bigeard and Schmitt denying torturing suspects, their victims claiming they were tortured. Philippe Bernard summarized the situation well when he described it as: "Parole contre parole, mémoire contre mémoire, dans l'ombre protectrice des lois d'amnéstie" (One person's word against another's, one memory against another, in the protective shadow of legal amnesties).[96] The media are a site in which this battle takes place. Furthermore, we have seen how elitist the debate was. Just as in a previous chapter we were able to get a sense of the whole continuum of practices from the State to the pupil, so with readers' letters do we get a sense of how the representations in the media have impacted upon the readers. It is true that in a Halbwachsian perspective memories are constructed collectively, and in a sense the debate did evolve and give a voice to readers, particularly in December 2000. Yet it would seem that, judging by readers letters, ordinary soldiers' memories correspond little to representations of the French army as portrayed by Le Monde.

Individual activists are easily identified and are often those who campaigned against the war at the time. For example "l'appel des douze" (Petition by Twelve

Intellectuals) was instigated by intellectuals such as Pierre Vidal-Naquet and Henri Alleg who were key anti-torture activists during the Algerian War. Maître Halimi defended those found guilty of the El Halia massacre at the time of the Algerian War. Also interesting is the generational and family angle. One is struck by the role of family members in these judicial proceedings—such as the families of Ben M'Hidi, Maurice Audin, and *harkis*. Other activism is evident in the role of the MRAP and FIDH in this episode. The work of Nora supports these findings, since he has shown how currently memory is often actually re-constructive recovery of history that official history previously omitted. Groups who are being incorporated into national history are reconstructing these tradi-tions, especially through the "memory work" of descendants of the groups.[97] All of this evidence points towards and can be understood through reference to the activism/pluralism model of collective memory. So, it would be more accurate to see this "debate," rather than solely a step towards a more serene discussion of the Algerian War, as another stage in "memory battles," representing a change in power in French society. Yet the old status quo just held out still. One can hy-pothesize that it will be the generation after President Chirac—who fought in Algeria as a conscript—that makes greater strides in discussing more serenely what took place during the Algerian War.

Journalists should also be seen as another group of "memory activists" in this affair, making the news, and not just reporting it. The relationship between contemporary history and journalism is crucial. Stora notes that: "Sur la 'pre-mière' guerre d'Algérie, les enquêtes récentes de journalistes ont été en avance sur les travaux d'historiens, elles ont plus bousculé les choses" (On the "first" Algerian War, recent investigations by journalists were ahead of the work of historians and they rocked the boat more).[98] The media are an important site of contestation, as is the education system. Yet the education system is State-run and dominated in France by Republican ideology. Following a pluralistic view of collective memory, groups can compete and vie for a place in the collective memory; achieving representation in the media is one tool to achieve this goal. The media and the education system have different professional codes. Yet con-temporary history—*l'histoire des temps présents*—and journalism are not neces-sarily radically opposed, as François Bédarida reminds us. In France at least, a "tournant hisioriographique" (historiographical turning point) occurred in the 1970s with the (re)development of contemporary history that radically modified the scope, approach, and status of historians. This broke the previous division past/history present/journalism of the 1800s and earlier 1900s with its "division du travail communément admise: à l'historien l'investigation savante, patiente et en profondeur sur le passé, au journaliste le champ de connaissance ondoyant de l'immédiateté" (commonly accepted division of work: scholarly research for the historian, a patient and in depth study of the past, work on the variable current affairs for the journalist).[99]

Reference to the work of Maurice Halbwachs can also help us understand this "media event." A key tenant of Halbwachs's theorization of collective mem-ory is that there are social frames of memory—time, language, and space. Time and language certainly seem particularly important in shaping media discourse—language in terms of names (e.g., Aussaresses) and time in terms of dates (e.g., commemorations). For Halbwachs "the past is a social construction mainly, if not wholly, shaped by the concerns of the present" since "it is in society that people normally acquire their memories. It is also in society that they recall, recognize, and localize their memories."[100] In our case study "investigative journalism" has forced the issue of torture into the public domain, and it is clear from readers' letters that their own recollections are shaped by this public debate. Consequently, for Halbwachs "the past is not preserved but is reconstructed on the basis of the present" and "Every collective memory requires the support of a group delimited in space and time."[101] We have seen various groups' involvement in the media—"l'Appel des douze," *harkis*, soldiers, and settlers at various times since the 1970s. We have clearly identified many ways in which "memory battles" are taking place in the present over a contested past, as various groups vie for a place in contemporary France. We further see that is the concerns of the present—justice in the present—that shape the discussion of the past.

Conclusion

What role do the media play in the construction of collective memory? The media inform and shape public consciousness and participate in the construction of a shared past in several important ways. Our case study has provided one instance where the media were able to provide sustained coverage of history, although even in this most rare of cases—essentially due to the stakes involved and the passions generated by such a debate in France—that sustainability was limited. In most cases, this is not possible. The media, like the education system, contribute to the creation of a shared "memory culture" by bringing together "diverse stories," but it does so in quite different ways. We have seen that the media are a site of contestation (in a pluralist perspective). Journalists, in their (partial) control of diffusion of information, make important choices about how to represent the past. Other groups use the media to contest or defend various versions of the past. The media do constitute a public sphere, spurring us to remember, particularly with *Le Monde*'s strength in investigative journalism—enabling some, inherently limited, debate (supporting Habermas's concept of the "public sphere") of the past and contest over how it should be interpreted, and providing a frame of memory for readers (in a Halbwachsian perspective). This "debate" provides little scope for ordinary people to have their story told. This debate is firmly grounded in the present, with much still at stake in contemporary France in discussing this issue. The various papers' coverage would appear to be influenced by their own history during the Algerian War. The extent to which they cover the issue now, as well as how, is influenced by such concerns.

We have seen that the media are a site of contestation (in a pluralist perspective) in the sense that journalists—in terms of the choices they make about what to print—are agents themselves. The coverage was inherently limited—in terms

of the issues it raised, the portrayal of the war it defended etc. Essentially it followed an "investigative journalism" model, with sensationalist coverage of an
"affair." Yet the media are also a place where other agents play out memory battles. In our case study, the issue has been torture—with underlying issues of responsibility, etc.—and the agents have been the perpetrators of crimes during the
Algerian War and their victims. In many ways the same issues as at the time of
the Algerian War seem once more to have been rehearsed, with little "new" material. Furthermore, the State has not facilitated this work of memory in its decla-
rations on the Algerian War—via Messrs. Jospin and Chirac—or the maintaining
of amnesties that inhibit any justice being achieved.

At the beginning of this chapter we asked how the media, in a Halbwachsian
perspective, provide a "social frame" for group and individual memories. The
media themselves would seem to be influenced by a wider "social frame" of language, time, and space in so far as what they print is heavily influenced by internal and external constraints (e.g., the judicial framing of the issue). The language
the media use, that itself sets the terms of reference for a debate (torture, responsibility), the dates on which articles are published—particularly surrounding
commemorations—come from society. As we saw with readers' letters—a particularly useful way of judging "reader reception"—readers are clearly respond-
ing to this public debate so the media also provide the "social frames of memory." And the debate has a life, evolves. A plurality of perspectives appears to
emerge if one varies the media consulted.

We also asked earlier if, in our case study, the media coverage allowed repressed memories to be worked through in a Freudian (updated by Haber-
mas/Ricœur) perspective. This is clearly a difficult question. It is not convincing
that the debate helped veterans, but it probably has been more helpful to victims
of the French army's use of torture. It is much more likely, as shown in readers'
letters, that the coverage led to a further rejection of debate. Similarly, the amnesties passed since the Algerian War have once again prevented any "closure"
on this issue. One is struck by the repetitive nature of this debate. Therefore, we
have argued that the event needs to be seen more as a "return of repressed
memories" rather than as a therapeutic working through of problematic memories in a Freudian perspective. Nonetheless this "work of memory" is important
in forcing French society to address issues that it would rather forget. If the media want to contribute further to this work, more sustained coverage will be
needed and other issues, that are less divisive, less adversarial, or cross groups,
could be covered.

We have seen that media coverage is likely to be important not only in
transmitting memories directly to individuals but also indirectly by influencing
the content of classes for young people. It may be unlikely that articles in *Le
Monde* directly transmitted much historical memory to young people, but one
would expect older people to be more avid readers of the paper. Furthermore, *Le
Monde*'s coverage itself led to documentaries, films, and other cultural production that may have been seen by young people. This chapter has also shown that
in contemporary France, while "minorities" can be seen to be challenging domi-

nant discourses on the Algerian War, the balance of power still remains with the State. This supports the conclusions of the second chapter—where we saw that despite the family background of many children in France's schools today little is taught about the Algerian War—and was also apparent in the previous chapter on the family and transmission of memory, in so far as while there is some evidence of activism—for example in literature—the sheer weight of forgetting and occlusion acts as a significant break on the potential of this kind of memory work.

Notes

1. Rousso defines a vector of memory (or carrier) as "any source that proposes a deliberate reconstruction of an event for a social purpose. The collective memory of an event is shaped by all representations of that event, whether conscious or unconscious, explicit or implicit" in Henry Rousso, *The Vichy Syndrome. History and Memory in France since 1944* (Cambridge, MA: Harvard University Press, 1991), 219.

2. Philippe Joutard, "L'enseignment de l'histoire," in *L'histoire et le métier d'historien en France 1945-1995*, ed. François Bedarida (Paris: Editions de la Maison des sciences de l'homme, 1995), 54.

3. Defined as "An increasingly rapid slippage of the present into a historical past that is gone for good, a general perception that anything and everything may disappear" in Pierre Nora, "Between Memory and History," *Representations* no. 26 (Spring 1989): 7.

4. Pierre Nora (ed.), *Les Lieux de mémoire*, volume three *Les France*, book three *De l'archive à l'emblème* (Paris: Gallimard, 1992), 984 and 985. Nora goes on to state that "Ce n'est plus à l'école, instrument central du dispositif traditionnel, sur les places publiques, dans le rituel de moins en moins vivant des 11 Novembre, 14 Juillet et autres 1er Mai que s'affirme l'identité collective et que s'exprime l'esprit de la commémoration, mais à la télévision, dans les musées, au Mémorial de Caen et à l'Historial de Péronne, dans les milliers d'associations créées à cet effet, dans le déluge de représentations théatrales et musicales et d'animations folkloriques" (It is no longer in schools, the central instrument of the traditional model, in public squares, in the more and more stale rituals of 11 November, 14 July, and other days like 1 May that collective identity is affirmed and the spirit of commemoration is expressed, rather on TV, in museums, at the memorial in Caen and the Péronne History Museum, in thousands of associations created to remember, in the deluge of theatrical, musical, and folkloric representations), 985.

5. Nora, "Between Memory and History:" 7-8.

6. Pierre Bourdieu, *On Television and Journalism* (London: Pluto Press, 1998), 1 and 2.

7. Konrad H. Jarausch, "Living with Broken Memories: Some Narratological Comments," in *The Divided Past: Reuniting Post-War Germany*, ed. Christoph Klessmann (Oxford: Berg, 2001), 184-85.

8. Béatrice Fleury-Vilatte, *La mémoire télévisuelle de la guerre d'Algérie 1962-1992* (Paris: L'Harmattan, 2000), 24.

9. Jill Forbes and Michael Kelly, eds., *French Cultural Studies* (Oxford: Oxford University Press, 1995), 233 and 146.

10. In 1961, frustrated with General de Gaulle's moves towards granting Algerian independence, several Generals and professional units instigated a putsch. De Gaulle used

the medium of transistor radios to address soldiers in the French army directly. His radio and television broadcasts stiffened the reluctance of conscripts who might have followed officers and professional soldiers in the putsch.

11. *Le Monde*, 13 March 1957. Oradour is a French village whose inhabitants were massacred by the German army.

12. Benjamin Stora, *La Gangrène et l'oubli* (Paris: La Découverte, 1992), 73.

13. Quoted in Stora, *La Gangrène et l'oubli*, 71.

14. Philip Dine, "(Still) *A la recherche de l'Algérie perdue*: French Fiction and Film, 1992-2001," in *Historical Reflections* no. 2 (vol. 28, summer 2002): 263.

15. Didier Daeninckx, *Meurtres pour mémoire* (Paris: Gallimard, 1984), 38.

16. See Nancy Wood, *Vectors of Memory: Legacies of Trauma in Postwar Europe* (Oxford and New York: Berg, 1999) especially Chapter 2 "Public Memory and Postconventional Identity."

17. Jürgen Habermas, *A Berlin Republic: Writings on Germany*, transl. Steven Rendall (Cambridge: Polity Press, 1998), 19.

18. Wood, *Vectors*, 40.

19. "Le remords d'un général," editorial, *Le Monde*, 22 June 2000, 16.

20. Paul Ricœur, *La mémoire, l'histoire, l'oubli* (Paris: Le Seuil, 2000). Subsequently translated by Kathleen Blamey and David Pellauer as *Memory, History, Forgetting* (Chicago and London: University of Chicago Press, 2004). For a summary of the book's impact and arguments, see François Dosse, "Le moment Ricœur," in *Vingtième Siècle* (January-March 2001): 137.

21. Paula Hamilton, "The Knife Edge: Debates about Memory and History," in *Memory and History in Twentieth Century Australia*, ed. Paula Hamilton and Kate Darian-Smith (Melbourne: Oxford University Press, 1994), 9-32.

22. *Le Monde*, 1 January 2001, 19.

23. Andrew Jakubowicz et al., *Racism, Ethnicity and the Media* (St Leonards, NSW: Allen & Unwin, 1994).

24. For the most comprehensive scholarly examination of torture see Raphaëlle Branche, *La Torture et l'armée pendant la guerre d'Algérie 1954-1962* (Paris: Gallimard, 2001). She states that torture became tolerated by the State (355). The book also briefly examines the period before the war of decolonization and other decolonizations (notably elucidating the link between the war in Indochina and the Algerian conflict yet also referring to other Empires such as British and Dutch). The author uses a wide range of sources: from archives inaccessible until recently to testimony and secondary sources. The extent of civil and public knowledge is clearly demonstrated. Torture is shown to be more than simply obtaining information and/or secrecy, although this was a central concern particularly during the Battle of Algiers. It is influenced by the fact that officially there was no war in Algeria, colonial mentalities, group dynamics, the ineffectiveness of the justice system, and so on. Above all it represented a "counterterror" in a conflict characterized by total warfare.

25. Jack Lang, French Education Minister, in a speech given in August 2001, accessed at www.education.gouv.fr/discours/2001/algeriejl.htm.

26. "Torturée par l'armée française en Algérie, 'Lila' recherche l'homme qui l'a sauvée," *Le Monde*, 10 March 2000, 11.

27. General Schmitt was the French Chief of Staff of the Army during the Gulf War under President François Mitterrand.

28. See Isabelle Lambert, "Vingt ans après," in *La Guerre d'Algérie et les Français*, ed. Jean-Pierre Rioux (Paris: Fayard, 1990), 553-59; and Béatrice Fleury-Vilatte, *La mémoire télévisuelle de la guerre d'Algérie 1962-1992* (Paris: L'Harmattan, 2000).

29. Neil MacMaster, "The Torture Controversy (1998-2002): Towards a 'New History' of the Algerian War?" *Modern and Contemporary France* 10, no. 4 (2002): 449-59.

30. Les 12 are: Henri Alleg, Josette Audin, Simone de Bollardière, Nicole Dreyfus, Noel Favrelière, Gisèle Halimi, Alban Liechti, Madeleine Rébérioux, Laurent Schwartz, Germaine Tillion, Jean-Pierre Vernant, and Pierre-Vidal Naquet. Their petition, first published in the communist newspaper *L'Humanité*, subsequently signed by thousands of people, requested that President Jacques Chirac and Prime Minister Lionel Jospin condemn the use of torture during the Algerian War in a public declaration.

31. "Les signataires de 'l'appel des douze' invitent Jacques Chirac à se manifester et Lionel Jospin à aller plus loin," *Le Monde* 7 December 2000, 11.

32. Paul Thibault, "La torture en Algérie. L'avenir en panne," *Le Monde*, 14 December 2000, 17.

33. *Le Monde* was founded in 1944 by Hubert Beuve-Méry. It is sometimes referred to as the "journal de référence" (national journal of record) in France. Its editorial line can perhaps best be described as center left. For a history of the newspaper see Patrick Eveno, *Le Monde 1944-1995* (Paris: Le Monde Editions, 1996).

34. *Libération* and *Le Figaro* are both daily broadsheets. *Libération* was founded in 1973, although it originated in resistance publications during World War Two. In 1973 Jean-Paul Sartre and the current editor, Serge July, were amongst its founders. It is usually viewed as left-leaning. *Le Figaro* was founded in 1826. It is usually viewed as right-leaning.

35. Alain Coulon, *Connaissance de la guerre d'Algérie. Trente ans après: enquête auprès des jeunes Français de 17 à 30 ans* (Paris: Université de Paris VIII, 1993), 23.

36. The *baccalauréat* is the examination sat by pupils at the end of high school in France and is of crucial personal and communal significance there. Eight interviews were conducted in Lyon, France, in 1999 with twelve pupils studying history in *terminale*. Questions were asked about classes (such as "When and how long was the Algerian War studied?"), the content of class (such as "Have you studied the origins of the war?" "What can you tell me about the origins of the war?"), and sources of information for pupils (such as "Have you seen films about the Algerian War?"). Both open and closed questions were asked. Eighteen teachers in Lyon and two historians in Paris were also interviewed. This book also draws on written sources such as textbooks and examination questions in its study of the teaching of the Algerian War. Interviewees' names are withheld for ethical reasons—we refer to Teacher 1 or Pupil 1—but a broad description of each interviewee is included in the appendices.

37. Such opinion polls are well surveyed and analyzed in Philippe Joutard, "L'enseignement de l'histoire," in *L'histoire et le métier de l'historien en France 1945-1995*, ed. François Bédarida (Paris: Editions de la Maison des sciences de l'homme, 1995), 45-55.

38. Philippe Joutard and Jean Lecuir, "Le palmarès de la mémoire nationale," *L'Histoire* no. 242 (April 2000): 38.

39. *Terminale* is the final year of high school in France, *première* the penultimate year, and *seconde* the year before that.

40. Joutard, "L'enseignement de l'histoire," 53-54.

41. Jean-Pierre Rioux, "Aux grands hommes, les Français reconnaissants," *L'Histoire*, no. 202, (September 1996): 17.

42. Philippe Bernard, "Les gardiens de la mémoire," *Le Monde*, 14 June 1990, 18.

43. Jean-Pierre Rioux, "Les Français et leur histoire," *L'Histoire*, no. 100 (May 1987): 74 and 75 respectively.

44. Rioux, "Aux grands hommes," 15.

45. In 1997 Maurice Papon was tried in France for "crimes against humanity" relating to his activities during the Second World War as a civil servant in Bordeaux in the Vichy regime. He was also the head of police ("préfet de police") in Paris in the early 1960s, after having pursued his career in the colonies. He was therefore implicated in the massacre in Paris of 17 October 1961, when dozens of French Algerians were killed by French police during a demonstration.

46. Circulation in 2002 was 389 000. Source: en.wikipedia.org /wiki/Le_Monde.

47. Various sources and methods allow us to ascertain and compare the numbers of articles over time, each leading to slightly different numbers/results. One approach is to use the *Index analytique du Monde* (a printed index of all the articles in *Le Monde* published annually). *Le Monde* groups all of the articles published under various headings, that we will call keywords (e.g., "la guerre d'Algérie"). Another approach is to use the *Le Monde* CD-ROM. It contains all articles since 1987 and has a search tool. Lastly, we can do keyword searches in the paper's archives on their website. For the purposes of this study, the *Index* has been consulted for the period 1997, 1981-1982, 1984-1986, 1991, 1996, 1998-2001. The CD-ROM was consulted for the period 1987-2002. Using the CD-ROM, printouts of articles published in the months of December 2000 and January, April, June, and November 2001 were also obtained.

48. In our quantitative analysis we will be more interested in subjects (e.g., torture); whereas in the qualitative analysis we will look at themes that equate to topics and topicalization (i.e., how torture is broken down).

49. Teun A. van Dijk, *Racism and the Press* (London and New York: Routledge, 1991), 72.

50. Van Dijk, *Racism and the Press*, 72.

51. Van Dijk, *Racism and the Press*, 73.

52. Van Dijk, *Racism and the Press*, 78.

53. Based on keywords in the *Index analytique du Monde*. The figures are 200 in 2000 and 300 in 2001 using the keyword "guerre d'Algérie" and the CD-ROM.

54. Guy Pervillé, "Bibliographie critique sur la guerre d'Algérie," *l'Annuaire de l'Afrique du Nord*, 1992: 1179.

55. All published in *Le Monde*, 15-17 October 2001.

56. All published in *Le Monde*, 23 April 2001, 12.

57. *Le Canard Enchaîné* is a satirical newspaper published weekly in France. It was founded in 1915 and is particularly well-known for investigative journalism.

58. The various topics for torture and the French army are: Aussaresses (what he did/who he is; Trial(s): coverage; opinion/comment on both of the above), the French army's use of torture, various groups' opposition to torture (PCF, Christians, l'Appel des 12, Porteurs de valise), Le Pen and torture, Schmitt, Torture and public opinion.

59. Aussaresses was in the special services of the army during the Battle of Algiers in 1957. Massu headed the Paratrooper regiment at that time and Bigeard was another well-known soldier of the time, and subsequently minister. Ighilahriz supported the Algerian nationalist movement and was raped and tortured by French soldiers. Ben M'Hidi was a leader in the Algerian nationalist movement who was murdered by Aussaresses. Teitgen was Head of the Police in Algiers and resigned in 1957 due to the number of disappearances in Algiers. Bollardière was a General in the French army who also refused to torture and resigned.

60. Florence Beaugé, "Le général Aussaresses jugé pour 'complicité d'apologie de crimes de guerre'—Portrait," *Le Monde*, 27 November 2001, 10.

61. For example B Furet, "Il n'y a pas de guerre propre," (letter) *Le Monde*, 4 January 2001, 15; Guy Remi Vollauris, "Crapahuts et dignité," *Le Monde*, 11 December 2000, 13; Alexandre Cortez, "Hypocrisie," (letter) *Le Monde*, 11 December 2000, 13.

62. For example René-Victor Pilhes, "La torture en Algérie. Souvenirs, souvenirs," (Horizons-Débats) *Le Monde*, 14 December 2000, 17; Roger Monié, "La torture en Algérie. La joie et l'agacement," (Horizons-Débats) *Le Monde*, 14 December 2000, 17; Pierre Dabezies, "Ce ne fut pas si simple," (Horizons Débats), *Le Monde*, 1 December 2000, 16; Jean Pierre Meyer, "Algérie: la torture et ses exceptions," (Horizons-Débats) *Le Monde*, 1 December 2000, 16; Pierre Merlin, "Torture: nous savions tous," (Horizons-Débats) *Le Monde*, 26 June 2001, 21.

63. Pilhes, "La torture en Algérie," 17.

64. Vollauris, "Crapahuts et dignité," 13.

65. Dabezies, "Ce ne fut pas si simple," 16.

66. "La torture, enfant naturel de la guerre," *Le Monde*, 29 December 2000, 14.

67. Furet, "Il n'y a pas de guerre propre," 15.

68. DOP ("détachement opérationnel de protection:" Protective Operational Unit) were specialist units of the army whose mission was to dismantle FLN networks.

69. Meyer, "Algérie: la torture et ses exceptions," 16.

70. See "Du général Aussaresses à Jean-Marie Le Pen, l'impossible procès de la torture," *Le Monde*, 27 November 2001, 10.

71. Articles published in *Le Monde* 27 November 2001, 10; 28 November 2001, 12; 28 November 2001, 12; 4 December 2000, 13; and 26 June 2001, 21, respectively.

72. Monié, "La torture en Algérie. La joie et l'agacement," 17.

73. Boris Brehat Goiremberg, "Question d'honneur," (lettter) *Le Monde*, 11 December 2000, 13.

74. Jean Pierre Mettas, "Mémoire commune," (letter) *Le Monde*, 11 December 2000, 13.

75. "Mobilisation pour une prise de position officielle contre la torture," *Le Monde*, 30 January 2001, 10.

76. Similar to his stances on World War Two, such as his statement that Nazi gas chambers were a mere detail of the war. Terminology has been important concerning remembering the Algerian War in particular given the amount of euphemisms used to describe what was for many years "the war without a name."

77. Dabezies, "Ce ne fut pas si simple," 16.

78. "Le remords d'un général," editorial , *Le Monde*, 22 June 2000, 16.

79. "Au procès de Paul Aussaresses, le général Schmitt a justifié l'usage de la torture en Algérie," *Le Monde*, 29 November 2001, 14.

80. Van Dijk, *Racism and the Press*, 78.

81. Beaugé, "Le général Aussaresses jugé," 10.

82. Johannes Franck, "100,000 francs d'amende requis contre le général et ses éditeurs," *Le Monde*, 30 November 2001, 14.

83. Johannes Franck, "Au procès de Paul Aussaresses, le général Schmitt a justifié l'usage de la torture en Algérie," *Le Monde*, 29 November 2001, 14.

84. Johannes Franck, "Au premier jour de son procès, Paul Aussaresses endosse tous les crimes qu'il a ordonnés," *Le Monde*, 28 November 2001, 12.

85. *Le Monde*, 16 December 2000, 11.

86. Van Dijk, *Racism and the Press*, 69.

87. *Le Monde*, 30 November 2001, 14.

88. *Le Monde*, 2 December 2000, 1.

89. *Le Monde*, 1 June 2001, 11.

90. *Le Monde*, 15 June 2001, 40.

91. *Le Monde*, 29 June 2001, 8.

92. Macmaster, "The Torture controversy," 449.

93. See Philippe Bernard, "Du général Massu à Jean-Marie Le Pen, l'impossible procès de la torture," *Le Monde*, 27 November 2001, 10; and Stora, *La Gangrène*, 214-16.

94. Macmaster, "The Torture controversy," 454.

95. See *Le Monde*, 29 June 2001 for a list.

96. Philippe Bernard, "De nouveaux témoignages accusent le général Schmitt de torture," *Le Monde*, 29 June 2001, 8.

97. Nora, *Les Lieux de mémoire*, 997.

98. *Le Monde*, 24 April 2001, 16.

99. François Bédarida, "Le temps présent et l'historiographie contemporaine," *Vingtième Siècle*, 69, Jan-March 2001: 153.

100. Maurice Halbwachs, *On Collective Memory*, translated by Lewis A. Coser (Chicago and London: University of Chicago Press, 1992), 25 and 38.

101. Halbwachs, *On Collective Memory*, 84.

Chapter Five

Conclusion: Teaching, Reporting, and Discussing the Algerian War in Contemporary France

Collective memory and the resulting representations of the past are a major pre-occupation in many societies around the world today. The Truth and Reconciliation Commission in South Africa, the tensions caused by Japanese history textbooks in China and Korea, the "history wars" in Australia and Europe's difficulties representing and remembering the Holocaust are but a few contemporary examples of contested arenas of collective remembrance. The need to create collective understandings of the past is crucial to the building of a coherent community and national identity. At no other time in history has this process of coming to terms with the past been so important—rapid globalization, enhanced communication, extensive migration, and "the acceleration of history" (Nora) have all ensured that the dramatic ruptures of war, holocaust, and apartheid are important. This new unique confluence of events has created a pressing need among individuals and governments for deeper understandings of past trauma in order to build cohesive societies.

France has a particularly fractious history, hence Michel Winock's choice of *La Fièvre hexagonale* (Hexagonal Fever) as title for his 1986 study of political crises in France since 1871. May 1958 was of course one of these crises. The dramatic return to power of de Gaulle and the collapse of the Fourth Republic were both a direct result of the Algerian War. France also developed, and over the last century has drawn considerably on, an "exceptional" model of nation building, that relied heavily on history and memory to create a unified national identity from the varied regional identities and group divisions that existed within the borders of what we now understand as France. That national, unitary, Republican model is currently under extreme strain, seemingly no longer able to effectively draw together the various histories and memories within France, with contemporary French society consequently split by a "fracture sociale" (social fracture) that operates largely along ethnic and generational lines—large numbers of youth of immigrant parents who are excluded from full participation in French society—and a number of commentators evoking the decline of France or "le désarroi français" (French disarray).[1]

One element of this breakdown is the Algerian War and its legacy. Over forty years after the conflict ended, the Algerian War continues to be highly relevant to an understanding of contemporary French society due to its difficult legacy, yet its significance remains underestimated by many. The war finished merely forty-five years ago. Millions of people now in France fought in or lived through the conflict, that lasted seven years and was a tremendously fiercely fought campaign that caused huge division in French society. The war brought down the Fourth Republic and caused immense division in France and Algeria as different communities emerged: such as conscripts, professional soldiers, OAS members, gaullists, *porteurs de valise* (French who supported Algerian nationalists), *harkis* (Algerians who fought for the French army), and *pieds-noirs* (settlers). These communities are still very evident in French society today, often having formed associations and communities that tend to be very hostile to other groups. The conclusion of the war effectively heralded the end of over one hundred and thirty years of French presence in Algeria and dealt the decisive deathblow to the French Empire. Memories of the Algerian War regularly (re)emerge directly in numerous polemical developments and debates in contemporary France around, for example, the issue of the use of torture during the war "discussed" in hundreds of articles in 2000/2001.

Its significance can also be seen in many crucial issues in contemporary France, notably those concerning the place of ethnic minorities in the French Republic. Migration patterns to France post-Second World War have largely mirrored the territory and the borders of the old French Empire, literally reversing previous flows from the *métropole* (mother country) to the colonies. By the early 1980s Algerians were the largest foreign nationality group in France, numbering some eight hundred thousand persons. Nearly one million European settlers left Algeria in 1962. We have seen how both teachers (in my sample *pieds-noirs*) and pupils (in my sample pupils of Algerian origin) can be concerned by the Algerian War and how they bring memories to class. Indeed, it is in important ways their history. This history is linked to identity: the identity of pupils, teachers, and ultimately the French in general.

A key contention of this book is that the question of transmission of memories is central to these issues of dealing with the past in the present. The conflict affected so many people—with Benjamin Stora in his book *Le Transfert d'une mémoire* (Memory Transfer) estimating there to be four or five million people in France who have "une mémoire à vif" (vivid memories) of the war—and was repressed and occluded for so long that "the work of memory," to use Paul Ricœur's concept, needs to accelerate and last much longer if the divisions and wounds of the war are to be overcome. Whereas a lot of effort has been invested in Franco-German reconciliation and overcoming the legacy of the Second World War in recent decades, there has been no comparable investment by French society in working through or overcoming the legacy of the Algerian

War or colonial history more broadly, yet it is precisely here where reconciliation needs to occur most urgently. The "work of memory" includes discussing the war in families, teaching its history in schools, and representing the conflict in the media, despite the difficulties involved. If there were greater discussion of this period, French views of Algeria (and Algerians and their descendants) would be significantly different—more aware of the long and complex history linking France and Algeria, more knowledgeable about the tremendous contribution of Algerians to French society—and French of Algerian descent might then be able to better find a home in France since they would be viewed less as outsiders, discriminated against less, and more integrated into the dominant national history.

The trauma and bitterness of the colonial era and its bloody end, while appearing to belong to a far off period, are in reality unresolved and highly actual as both Stora and Kristen Ross have shown. The divisive memories and attitudes inherited from the colonial period have not yet been overcome. French perceptions of minority ethnic groups reflect this: Algerians are regularly cited as the worst integrated group by the French.[2] In a 1990 poll, only three out of ten respondents saw second-generation Maghrebis as French. In a 1984 survey Algerians came last in a list of sixteen minority groups in terms of perceptions of integration: 21 percent of respondents stated Algerians were well integrated, 70 percent that they were badly integrated. West Europeans were at the top of the list, Central and East Europeans in the middle, and Africans at the bottom with Moroccans and Tunisians above Algerians. The riots throughout many French cities in late 2005 showed the extent to which exclusion functions along ethnic lines in France and the sheer scale of the problem. For several weeks pitched battles pitted young people living in the underprivileged outer suburbs (*banlieues*) against the police. While such disturbances have been a regular occurrence in a handful of particularly deprived suburbs since the early 1990s, such as Vénissieux on the outskirts of Lyon, for the first time these severe riots engulfed towns and cities throughout France with a previously unseen intensity and duration. President Chirac may have campaigned in the 1995 Presidential campaign on a platform aimed at combating the "fracture sociale" (social fracture), however over ten years later these issues have clearly been exacerbated rather than addressed.

For some people an "Algerian syndrome" has replaced the "Vichy syndrome." The Algerian War contributed to present day phenomena in France such as the French National Front, anti-Arab racism, and difficult Franco-Algerian international relations; without forgetting the legacy of a civil war situation in Algeria. Indeed many commentators link the electorate and the organization of the French National Front to people very clearly involved in the Algerian War. The central argument of Stora's *Le Transfert d'une mémoire* (Memory Transfer) is that memories of the Algerian War feed into contemporary racism. The National Front burst onto the national political scene in the early 1980s. The party can regularly poll 15 percent of the vote, even more at local or Presidential elections. When surveyed, 20 to 25 percent of the French population state that they "share the values" of the party.[3] It campaigns on a resolutely anti-immigrant stance. Key figures in the French National Front participated in the Algerian War, most notably of course its leader Jean-Marie Le Pen. In the 2002 Presidential election Le Pen eliminated the incumbent Prime Minister Lionel Jospin to make it through to the second round of the Presidential election against Jacques Chirac. Le Pen was in Algeria for three months between January and March 1957. He volunteered to serve and was a Lieutenant in the First Regiment of Paratroopers. Jean-Jacques Susini, formerly a key figure in the OAS, stood for the National Front in the 1997 legislative elections in Marseilles. The National Front is strongest in the South-East of France (Provence-Alpes-Côte d'Azur: PACA), an area where most of the *pieds noirs* who left Algeria settled, due to the similarities in geography and climate between the south of France and North Africa.

The data discussed in the preceding chapters of this book demonstrates the lack of transmission of memories of the Algerian War in contemporary France in three crucial vectors of memory—the teaching of school history, discussion in the family, and reporting in the media—clearly showing the way the conflict continues to be difficult to work through in present-day France in these arenas. These three areas are amongst the most important for young people in particular in learning about history. This book has studied transmission of memories of the Algerian War. The question of generation is crucial concerning the war in Algeria because it is precisely "the Algerian generation" who are currently in power in France, most clearly represented by President Chirac. Chirac was twenty-three when he arrived in Algeria to lead thirty-two men between April 1956 and June 1957. He then returned to Algeria between July 1959 and March 1960 as a functionary. Yet their sons and daughters and even their grandchildren now have been affected by the legacy of the conflict. While we focused largely on young people, the transmission of memories often involves people who directly participated in the Algerian War, since it is often they who transmit memories or who are the subject of the memories transmitted. In addition, these vectors of memory are important since we established very early on that memory is inherently social. Remembering is a social activity. All three of our chosen vectors of memory are resolutely social. They have also allowed us to analyze individual memories as well as group memories and the wider memory culture in France. Previous work in this area threw up conflicting claims surrounding the extent of transmission of memories of the Algerian War in France: for some commentators it was taught sufficiently, for others it was not discussed enough in the classroom; for certain scholars family transmission of memory was taking place, while for others what was taking place in most families was silence on this taboo subject; and for some, recent media coverage was to be understood as an important "working through" of the past in a Freudian perspective, while others argued, again drawing on Freud, that the coverage was simply another example of repressed memories "returning." More generally there has long been confusion about whether France can be said to have "turned the page" on the Algerian episode, was (perhaps) undertaking the work of memory or grieving, or the amnesia was over. This book argues that these episodes need to be seen as stepping stones in a long and arduous, never complete, working though of the past. There is a tendency to view each "development"—such as a spate of films on the topic, an extended period of media coverage, or a commemoration—as an "overcoming" of the occlusion of the topic. Each event does represent a stage in the working through of the topic, but none is sufficient to fully, immediately overcome such a great deal of trauma and bitterness caused by the war, that has been hidden for so long. We need to recognize that the "work of memory" is a multifaceted and long-term undertaking.

Furthermore, given the weaknesses and inherent limits of the three vectors of memory examined, there is a convincing argument that new forums are needed to discuss the past. France has experienced such rapid change over recent decades that the old national model forged in the Third Republic is increasingly strained and challenged in a multicultural, globalizing, transnational era. That model presented a unitary history and mobilized history to integrate various disparate groups and forge a common national identity. For Nora: "Il y avait donc autrefois *une* histoire nationale et *des* mémoires particulières; il y a aujourd'hui *une* mémoire nationale, mais dont l'unité est faite d'une revendication patrimoniale divisée, en permanence démultiplication et recherche de cohésion" (There used to be *a* national history and *various* particular memories; today there is *a* national memory, but whose unity is made up of divided patrimonial claims, that is constantly reduced in a search for cohesion).[4] For Hobsbawm and Ranger, this involved the "invention of tradition" whereby nearly one hundred years after the French Revolution a number of symbolic elements of the revolution were resurrected—such as the Marseillaise, the tricolor, and the Republican motto to name but a few. The divisions to be overcome were the separation of Church and State (secular versus Catholic France), class divisions (right wing monarchists and left wing anarcho-syndicalists), and Paris/province (the centralization of France and the overcoming of regional identity). While some point to the decline of France, or the end of French exceptionalism, it is perhaps more accurate to talk of tremendous changes occurring in French society and an old Republican model struggling to deal with these changes. That model tends to override cultural, ethnic, religious, and generational differences and favors a clear, French, and territorially (ie. "hexagonale") grounded, Republican identity. Yet the 2005 riots show the limits of the Republican model of integration, as do the "affaires du foulard" (Islamic veil affairs). The 2006 demonstrations against the "Contrat de Première Embauche" (First Job Contract) illustrate that exclusion does not solely operate along ethnic lines. Other "fracture lines" exist in French society and have become deeper over the last thirty years. Yet even here we see a division between the "included" and the "excluded" within the group of young people, operating between students campaigning against the CPE and the "casseurs" (vandals) from the *banlieues* (suburbs).

This book contends that the way the Algerian War is taught is typical of a narrative that minimizes the importance of the colonial era; and that the fact that transmission of memories takes place so little—including in schools—partly explains French reactions to "revelations" about the use of torture during the Algerian War and continuing phenomena such as strained race relations. The way that the Algerian War is taught in France is an excellent example of the narrative identified by Ross in her book *Fast Cars, Clean Bodies: Decolonization and the Reordering of French Culture* that sees modernization and decolonization as separate. Teachers said that for pupils the Algerian War was "ancient history." This narrative involves what is effectively a denial of the colonial period since it portrays this period as "archaic" and "exterior," when in fact this epoch and its dramatic end involved many people now living in France and are therefore a very important part of contemporary French identity. As Ross explains:

> Keeping the stories apart is usually another name for forgetting one of the stories or for relegating it to a different time frame. This is in fact what has occurred. For, from this perspective (a prevalent one in France today), France's colonial history was nothing more than an "exterior" experience that somehow came to an abrupt end, cleanly, in 1962 . . . colonialism itself was made to seem like a dusty archaism, as though it had not transpired in the twentieth century and in the personal histories of many people living today, as though it played only a tiny role in France's national history, and no role at all in its modern identity.[5]

Education continues to participate in very important ways to imagining the contemporary French nation. What is taught in schools is perhaps one of the last widely shared cultures in what is an increasingly fragmented society. This has been shown in this book to be particularly important concerning the Republic. Jean-Pierre Rioux said in the interview conducted by this author: "Le problème de l'enseignement en France comme ailleurs est toujours: que dire à tout le monde?" (The difficulty for the education system in France, as elsewhere, is to know what to say to everyone). It is clear that history classes still play an important role in constructing a collective memory in France. This can be seen through the numerous statements of participants in and commentators on education given throughout this book. As Antoine Prost wrote in the review *L'Histoire*: "La démission de la société charge l'école d'une fonction très lourde de socialisation des élèves" (Society has retreated, leaving schools with a very onerous task of socializing pupils).[6]

The link between education and imagining the French nation is particularly relevant to the "integration" of children of foreign descent, since all French pupils should be taught the same broad French history. For Jean Peyrot, former President of the APHG, the history program essentially aims to "transmettre une mémoire collective revue et corrigée à chaque génération" (transmit a collective memory that is reviewed and corrected each generation) since "L'histoire et la géographie sont aussi instruments de cohésion sociale, mémoire d'un groupe qui prend conscience d'un destin commun sur un territoire commun" (History and Geography are also instruments of social cohesion, the memory of a group that becomes conscious of a common destiny on a common territory).[7] We pointed out how closely this last phrase corresponds to Ernest Renan's ideas on the nature of nationhood:

> A nation is a soul, a spiritual principle. Two things, which in truth are but one, constitute this soul or spiritual principle. One lies in the past, one in the present. One is the possession in common of a rich legacy of memories; the other is present-day consent, the desire to live together, the will to perpetuate the value of the heritage that one has received in an undivided form.[8]

Winock, discussing immigration to France in the review *l'Histoire*, has argued that second and third generation descendants of immigrants receive "French memories." Making direct reference to the ideas of Renan he said: "La question (de la possession en commun d'un riche legs de souvenirs), il est vrai, s'effaçait avec la deuxième et la troisième générations: les enfants issus de l'immigration, nés en France n'ont que des souvenirs français" (The question (of the common possession of a rich legacy of memories), it is true, was no longer relevant for the second or the third generation: children of immigrant descent, born in France, only have French memories).[9] This process takes place to a large extent in schools including in history classes and on the subject of the Algerian War. One fascinating example of this process and such issues can be found in an interview published in the French review *Hommes et Migrations*. In it, the eighteen-year-old son of a man thrown into the Seine in Paris on 17 October 1961 (and who was a witness at the 1997 trial in which Maurice Papon brought proceedings against the journalist Jean-Luc Einaudi for slander) spoke of how he had learned of these events. This was not at school, but more through his father. Throughout the interview, when talking of the French and the Algerian War, despite being born in France, he switched between various pronouns: "on" (we), "ils" (they) and "eux" (them). The person who conducted the interview pinpointed what she called his "difficile identification" (difficult identification) with France. In her view:

> Cette difficile identification se révèle dans le vocabulaire utilisé par Slim. Quand il dit "*On* a eu les Juifs en 1945," il s'assimile à la France. "Mais quand même, en 1961, *ils* ont été capable de recommencer:" *ils* désigne la France quand il s'en distancie et se dit Algérien. Cette double identité se manifeste à un autre moment de l'entretien: "En France, *on* a dénoncé les Allemands, mais *ils* ne dénoncent pas ce que, *eux*, *ils* ont fait avec les Algériens. (This difficult identification reveals itself in the vocabulary used by Slim. When he says "*We* had the Jews in 1945," he is assimilating a French perspective. "But however, in 1961 *they* were capable of starting over:" they denotes France from which he distances himself by stating he is Algerian. The double identity appears at another point in the interview: "In France, *we* denounced the Germans, but *they* do not denounce what they have done to Algerians.)[10]

Here memory can clearly be seen to be linked to concerns in the present and to identity. In this example, it is repression and denial in wider society that have led to what the interviewer called the interviewee's difficult identification with France and the French. While on the one hand some argue that the Algerian War must be forgotten to avoid aggravating memories, others argue that this forgetting is very negative, particularly for children of Algerian origin. Claude Liauzu has argued in this way that:

> Pour ce qui concerne l'Algérie, un tiers de siècle après, l'amnésie officielle reste lourde de conséquences. Elle laisse le champ libre aux mémoires opposées, elle a couvert des violations graves des valeurs républicaines dans une société française qui s'est déchargée du fardeau algérien. Elle laisse dans un désarroi identitaire les jeunes issus de l'immigration, les interdit d'histoire, leur interdit l'histoire nationale. Cela ne peut que favoriser les tensions ethniques. (Concerning Algeria, thirty years later, the official amnesty has serious consequences. It leaves the field open to rival memories, it has covered grave violations of Republican values in a French society that abandoned the Algerian burden. It leaves young people of immigrant descent with an unclear identity, takes history from them, banishes them from national history. That can only encourage ethnic tensions.)[11]

These are all important and valid points. The marginalization of the Algerian War in the education system, largely due to the divisive nature of the conflict and the secular and Republican principles guiding the school system, does encourage ethnic tensions by leaving the field open to rival memories and by not providing a segment of the school population with significant elements of its identity. Not all pupils can identify with the history taught. Since the war is highly divisive French school authorities' policy is not to focus much on this subject. Yet teachers and pupils can take more interest in the topic. However their margin for maneuver is very limited given the place of the war in the program, textbooks, and examination questions set at the *baccalauréat*. Teachers and pupils insisted on the lack of time, the size of the program, and the importance of the end of year examination in dictating what could or could not be done. Only a few hours can be spent on the topic, and even then it is very much within the framework of wider topics such as Decolonization, the French Fourth or Fifth Republics, or de Gaulle's presidency. The average time spent on the Algerian War decreased from two and a half hours to one and a half hours from 1997 to 1999. The average number of words on the Algerian War in textbooks also decreased between 1995 and 1998: from 1500 words (about two and a half pages) to 950 words (about one and a half pages). Nonetheless some teachers were able to do more on the Algerian War—in our small sample particularly teachers whose family came from Algeria (settlers), usually to the detriment of other topics—and pupils are able to shape what is done in class by asking questions—in our sample highlighting the importance of family background (Maghrebian). These findings highlight the extent that memory is socially constructed and fluid or varied. Rioux in the interview also mentioned how teachers and pupils can work outside of class on this subject. He gave an example of a teacher in the Jura who had organized a significant oral survey capped by a meeting between pupils and different participants in the war. He said:

> Je n'observe pas moi de regain ou de développement d'un enseignement de la
> guerre d'Algérie en classe, par contre on observe aux alentours de la classe pas
> mal de manifestations, d'enquêtes, d'entretiens. (I haven't personally observed
> any renewal or development in class of teaching on the Algerian War, on the
> other hand we see outside of class quite a lot of activities, surveys, interviews,
> etc.; Rioux 2000.)

Hence pupils only have quite a partial and superficial knowledge of the war.
Given the importance attributed by historians and school authorities to the teaching of history—explicitly mentioned in statements that link history, memory, and
(national) identity—it is fair to say that the school system is failing to meet some
of the objectives it has set itself. In some ways the education system, given its
essential role in supporting the French Republican model of society, cannot be
an arena for greater discussion of the Algerian War. The composition of French
society has changed tremendously over the last thirty years—particularly the
increasingly multicultural makeup of the student body. The history program, in
the words of its designers, is supposed to "procurer aux jeunes Français ces éléments d'une mémoire nationale qui forge leur identité" (to provide French youth
with these elements of a national memory that forge their identity),[12] consequently with so little taught on the Algerian War the education system is not able
to meet this aim. As Rioux mentioned in the interview, there is no "volontarisme
de mémoire" (desire to foster memory) of the Algerian War in the education
system at present in France.

   While Rioux said that there is no "volontarisme de mémoire" (desire to foster memory) concerning the Algerian War in the history *terminale* program, he
also insisted that there is no "volonté d'occultation" (attempt to occlude memories) either. He said that it is "peu enseigné en termes de volume" (taught little in
terms of volume) but that what is said is correct: "On dit peu mais ce que l'on dit
est intéressant et surtout assez sûr, il n'y a pas d'enseignement partial de la
guerre d'Algérie" (We say little but what we say is interesting and above all
quite sure, there is no partial teaching of the Algerian War). He spoke of "le
minimum vital en connaissance" (vital minimum amount of knowledge) although he accepted that this is not necessarily enough. Findings from interviews
I conducted with pupils in Lyon clearly show the way memories of the Algerian
War are still present in the classroom, a point that Rioux referred to in the interview. We should also note how they can be highly divisive in so far as some
pupils referred to *harkis* as traitors. Pupil 2, who is of Algerian origin, speaking
of *harkis* said: "j'en ai entendu parler" (I've heard about them) and used the
word "collaborateurs" (collaborators). This information would not have come
from class. In her family she had described the division between her mother's
and father's sides relating to actions in the Algerian War. This division was between France and Algeria as her father's family were in France whereas her
mother's family were in Algeria. Another group also spoke of *harkis*. Pupil 9

said: "c'est ceux qui ont trahi l'Algérie" (they betrayed Algeria) and Pupil 8 used
the word "traîtres" (traitors). Pupil 11 spoke in the interview of her grandfather's
"hantise de l'Etat français" (obsessive fear of the French State). One pupil also
gave details of an argument she (the daughter of an FLN member) had had with
the son of a *pied-noir*. There is a convincing argument that it is time for a much
more ambitious "volontarisme de mémoire" (desire to foster memory) on the
Algerian War that enables more time to be spent in class on this important subject so that divisive memories can be countered with history and so that the history taught does allow pupils whose families are from North Africa to learn more
about their history. Given that Algeria was part of France for over one hundred
and thirty years, all French children need to learn more about this topic. The significant and growing problems in French society surrounding racism and exclusion along ethnic lines indicate that the colonial period needs to be given much
more prominence in the public sphere, including in schools.

Very little has yet been discussed or resolved; there has been no reconciliation, evidence of which is also found in family transmission of memory and the
way the Algerian War has been represented in the French media recently. We
looked in detail at the French daily newspaper *Le Monde*'s coverage in 2000-
2001 of the French army's use of torture during the Algerian War. Hundreds of
articles were published during this period, beginning with the paper's publication
of testimony from an Algerian woman, Louisette Ighilahriz, who claimed she
had been tortured in 1957. The "affair" of whether or not Generals Massu and
Bigeard had been present while Ighilahriz was tortured later dramatically esca-
lated into the "Aussaresses affair." We have seen that the media could be a
source of information for pupils in learning about the war in Algeria, and we
discovered that French historians were acutely aware of the fierce competition
from this vector of memory (what Joutard called a "parallel schooling"), and its
arguably significant impact on historical consciousness (Rioux and Nora). Various theories of collective memory were seen to be relevant to understanding collective memory and the media. A pluralistic model of collective memory that
highlights the role of "memory activists"—individuals and groups including
journalists, intellectuals, associations, and participants in the war—helps explain
how this "media event" came to be. In our case study activists included intellectuals (for example those who signed the "Appel des douze"), journalists, and
editors (through their "investigative journalism"), but also to a very limited extent readers through their letters to the paper. Consequently the media are a site
of contestation where memory battles take place. We saw many examples of
contested versions of the past: concerning, for instance, the role of the French
Communist Party during the Algerian War, the extent of the French army's use
of torture, or where the responsibility for the use of torture lay.

Yet the media also seemed to be an arena—a "public sphere"—where the
past could be "worked through" by "discussion." The media are an area where
diverse stories are brought together and a "memory culture" is created. The media also provide the "frames of memory" for individuals and groups. As
Halbwachs reminds us, we need other people to spur us to remember or to con-

firm our memories. In this way, there are similarities between the educative vector of memory and the media—both are "public spheres" where diverse individual and group memories are made collective. Both provide a frame on to which
individual perspectives can be attached. Both set the terms of reference for debates by providing broad discourses into which individual stories need to (or
should) fit. Obviously a central problem in representing the Algerian War in contemporary France is the fact that many individual stories do not fit into these
dominant narratives, consequently shaping the nature of inclusion and exclusion
in French society. In a Halbwachsian perspective, naming and dating the past is
particularly important. Both the education system and the media largely provide
the words and the timing for our remembering. Readers are made to think about
the Algerian War by the articles published in the paper. They respond to this
debate. While it was beyond the scope of this project to conduct detailed analysis
of reader reception, it is likely that articles in the paper would have generated
discussion in, for example, families, the classroom, coffee shops, or associations.
We can obtain some idea of reader reception by the readers' letters to the paper
that contributed to the "debate."

Judging by the criticism leveled at the paper in many of the letters, it is not
at all clear that the discussion has been therapeutic. It is likely that veterans often
resented so much discussion of the issue of torture and the way the French army
was portrayed. Many readers' letters complained that veterans' reputations were
being unjustly tarnished. We identified a gulf between the editorial and journalistic positions of the paper and those of the readers who fought in Algeria. There
was also a significant difference between the positions expressed in the readers'
letters and those in the "Horizons-Débats" pieces. More direct lines of communication than the print media are needed between anybody debating the Algerian
War if a genuine "debate" is to take place. It is also likely that although the victims of torture may have taken some satisfaction from the recognition of their
plight, "closure" is still impossible due to the absence of any possible justice
through the court system. The amnesties passed after the Algerian War still prohibit justice being rendered. Nobody who fought in the Algerian War can be
tried for war crimes or crimes against humanity due to these amnesties. The actual Evian Peace Agreement signed in 1962 and a series of subsequent amnesties
passed by the French parliament created this situation. This effectively closes
down discussion and reconciliatory efforts. Arguably even worse, the inability to
try Aussaresses (and others) for their crimes committed in Algeria led to other
judicial efforts that took the form of trials for "apologies de crimes de guerre"
(justifying war crimes), that is a crime in France. However this further closes
down the ability to discuss the Algerian War. As Paul Thibaud asked: "Une juste
sanction envers un homme qui ne regrette rien? Ou une menace contre la liberté
d'expression?" (Is this a fair penalty for a man who regrets nothing, or a threat to
freedom of speech?).[13] Slama goes further when he declares:

> On voit mal en revanche comment, quarante-cinq ans après les événements
> rappportés, alors que la lente ouverture des archives commence seulement à li-

vrer quelques vérités, un magistrat peut apprécier si la froide relation des faits
rapportés par l'ancien chef des services spéciaux entre 1955 et 1957 doit être
considérée comme une provocation ou comme un témoignage. En se déclarant
competent en la matière, le juge sacrifie un des principes fondateurs de la démocratie: la liberté d'expression. (It is difficult to see however, forty-five years after the events, while the archives are only slowly beginning to reveal some
truths, how a judge can decide whether the facts described by the former head of
the Special Services between 1955 and 1957 should be considered as provoca-
tive or as testimony. By claiming to be capable of doing this, the judge sacrifices
a fundamental democratic principle: freedom of speech.)[14]

Consequently, the issue of torture will periodically reappear since it cannot yet
be overcome. The role of the media in the construction of collective memory is
heavily determined by this fact—we saw that the representation by the media
depended largely on what was being reported (in our example torture, trials).
The media is a very specific vector of memory—in our case study heavily focused on key actors, ephemeral and generally unable to provide sustained discussion, quite "sensationalist," and with limited opportunity for readers to participate in any "debate." Similarly, the educative vector of memory was also
seen to be inherently limited—aimed at teaching "global history" therefore unable to go into much detail on a topic like the Algerian War, suspicious of memory, and very teacher-orientated and "magistral" (whereby the teacher talks and
pupils take notes) with limited opportunity for pupils or teachers to maneuver.

Having looked at two key "public sphere" arenas, we also considered the
"private sphere" of the family concerning transmission of memories. Due to the
nature of the Algerian War—specifically the way that the French State used conscription of soldiers to wage the war—almost all French families were affected
by the conflict: a whole generation of husbands, sons, brothers, and fathers were
sent to war. Everybody in Algeria was also affected by the conflict and many of
those people—namely *harkis*, *pieds noirs*, and other Algerians and their descendants. Young people depend to a large degree on their families—parents and
grandparents—to understand their family history. These narratives of belonging
gain particular saliency when one's "natural place" is called into question or
unclear, such as when French society does not view Algerians or their descendants as truly French. Migrants to France, and their descendants, are still engaged in a process of making France home. Beyond the family, we can also note,
amongst the teachers in my sample, the very high number of people known by
them who participated in the war that shows the importance of the shock wave
on French society caused by the Algerian War. Of those asked, they all knew
somebody closely involved in the war in Algeria (usually a conscript but sometimes a *pied-noir*): such as a cousin, a colleague, in-laws, an uncle, or the boy-
friend of a sister. One of the older teachers had been a student during the war
(Teacher 4), while others had been children at the time and mentioned memories
(notably Teacher 2, Teacher 8, and Teacher 16).

My work on family transmission of memory shows the way that family
transmission of memory is very difficult in all groups who lived through or par-

ticipated in the Algerian War—conscripts, *pieds noirs*, professional soldiers, *harkis*, or FLN supporters. The different theories of collective memory that we have referred to throughout this book can all help to explain this fact— particularly Freud's work on repression and occlusion of traumatic memories and Halbwachs's work on the role of memory in providing "the framework for family memory, which it tries to preserve intact, and which, so to speak, is the traditional armor of the family."[15] Particular attention was given to *beurs* and to children of *harkis* because it was felt that the silence of the parents was particularly prevalent in these groups. The lack of transmission of memories in these two groups was shown to be considerable. While the Lyon-based case study showed that some of the pupils had received very detailed memories from their parents or grandparents, this was not the case for all. Pupil 8, Pupil 9, and Pupil 12 said that they did not talk much with their grandparents. Nonetheless, the fact that relatively speaking so many children of Algerian descent volunteered for an interview probably indicates greater interest in this topic from this group, perhaps reflecting a disappointment in what has been able to be found out from other sources (e.g., the family or history class). We also saw that family history affected teachers, since the teachers who were of *pied noir* background covered the Algerian War in far more detail in class than did other teachers. Three of the teachers interviewed were *pied-noir* or *pied-noir* origin: Teacher 6, Teacher 13, and Teacher 17. The two *pied-noir* teachers were close to retirement and had been on the forum in Algiers to listen to de Gaulle and had lived through the exodus from Algeria at the end of the war. All three *pied noir* teachers taught more on the Algerian War than their colleagues, sometimes spending up to six hours on the topic when the average was two or three hours.

If memories are transmitted in families they were seen to be far more detailed than information given in class. On the question of torture, relatively little had been covered in class, whereas two pupils had received a significant amount of detailed information from their family. Whereas their answers to other questions in the interviews were usually brief, they were able to talk at length about this subject by drawing on material they had been told about from family members. Wider reading however shows that in the vast majority of cases there is very little discussion of the Algerian War in families whose parents or grandparents come from Algeria. This was variously described as "ce fossé entre les vieux migrants et les jeunes beurs où la communication ne passe pas" (this divide between aged migrants and young *beurs* where communication fails),[16] "les banlieues de l'antimémoire" (antimemory suburbs),[17] or "le silence des pères" (the silence of the fathers).[18] Yet, silence can lead to activism, and increasingly it would seem literature and cinema are tactics of intervention in the cultural field that enable previously marginalized groups to achieve recognition and representation. For, as Abrial correctly points out, recognition of one's history and culture is crucial to a sense of belonging, and the case of the *harkis* clearly shows that formal nationality is not enough to feel French or be accepted as French. *Harkis* have held French nationality since the Algerian War but they have been excluded from French society in many ways. Again we return to the ideas of

Renan, and the importance of memory and history to fostering a sense of (national) identity in the present.

The discovery that lack of family transmission of memories can in some cases lead to "memory activism" also allows us to assess the extent to which previously marginal memories can be said to be challenging more dominant narratives of the Algerian War. The conclusion we draw is that such challenges do exist, are increasingly influential, but faced with the overwhelming weight of forgetting and occlusion of memory—and the competition of the dominant discourses of the education system and the media—are inherently limited in their impact. As we saw, it is largely through literature and cultural production that dominant narratives of the war are challenged and memories transmitted and contested. There would, for example, seem to be a substantive shift in tactics from socioeconomic approaches to the inclusion of the *harkis* and violent tactics of intervention, toward a focus on memory, representing the *harkis*, and achieving voice in recent years.[19] We identified an emerging corpus of writing by children of *harkis*. For example, Hadjila Kemoum's *Mohand le harki* (Mohand the *Harki*), Dalila Kerchouche's *Mon père ce harki* (My Father the *Harki*) and Zahia Rahmani's *Moze* were all published in 2003. All are French women, children of *harkis*, living in France at present. We can hypothesize that such "tactics of intervention" will be increasingly successful due to the way "inclusion" functions in France—namely the tremendous importance of history and memory to Identity. Memory functions in the novels in different ways. Writing can be seen as healing trauma (in a Freudian perspective), as an example of agency in collective memory (in a pluralist perspective) and as constructing memories that provide group cohesion in the present (in a Halbwachsian perspective). It constitutes a vector of memory and on a personal level aids in the working through of difficult memories resulting from a traumatic past. Literature, and history—"historical fiction"—also function(s) as a discourse. The writing of children of *harkis* sets out to challenge dominant discourses. Each of the three understandings of memory is therefore relevant, and each functions on different levels—from personal to group, and from national to international. As Géraldine Enjelvin shows, in recent years there has been a passage from "maux aux mots" (suffering to words) with concomitant "encrage" and "ancrage" (anchoring) in a more ambitious memorial policy concerning the Algerian War (commemorations, plaques, speeches), and our brief study of literature by children of *harkis* provided a further important example of this shift.[20]

So where is France up to in "coming to terms" with the Algerian War? In absolute terms memories are not significantly transmitted on the Algerian War in *terminale* history classes, the media, or families in France. Transmission of memories has been shown to be very difficult in each of these areas, and we have seen that each vector of memory has its own strengths and weaknesses. This has important consequences for the wider collective memory of the war, notably across the change in generation. We can argue that the main changes in the collective memory of the Algerian War have come about due to the change in generation. The change in memory has occurred over the change in generation, but this is achieved on the whole through marginalizing and avoiding the subject rather than confronting it. The subject is still potentially divisive, principally amongst its actors. In reality young people do not receive much information on the Algerian War and for them therefore it is not as divisive a subject as it (probably) was for their teachers or elders in their families. Beyond actors in the war it is a little known period and one that is underestimated in its importance and rarely referred to in private or public life in France. Yet this also means that young people are frustrated by a lack of information on this topic.

The stakes of the (memory of the) Algerian War are still very high. Many polemical disputes in recent years have demonstrated this fact. The "Algerian generation" is still in power, mostly notably represented by President Chirac. A very interesting argument concerning Chirac's relationship to the memory of the Algerian War was formulated in an article in *Le Monde*, in comment on Chirac's inauguration of a monument in Paris in 1996 in memory of the victims of the war in Algeria. The editorialist argued that: "Il reviendra peut-être au successeur de Jacques Chirac, issu de la génération suivante, de faire la clarté sur les responsabilités des uns et des autres" (It will perhaps be left to Jacques Chirac's successor, from a different generation, to clearly establish various people's responsibilities).[21] This seems to be logical as we have seen the way Chirac, notably in a speech on 16 July 1995, took a groundbreaking stance on the memory of Vichy when he stated that the French State was clearly responsible during the Vichy regime for deporting Jews. This was the most explicit declaration of French collective liability during Vichy (and much more explicit than Mitterrand had, or had not, formulated). It was perhaps only possible since it was "une querelle qui n'était pas celle de sa génération, mais celle de la génération précédente, dont l'itinéraire personnel de François Mitterrand symbolisait les divisions et les ambiguïtés" (a quarrel that was not that of his generation, rather that of the previous generation, whose ambiguities and divisions were symbolized by the personal life history of François Mitterrand).[22] Indeed Mitterrand would seem to have tried to delay the trial of Maurice Papon in order to avoid opening old wounds. Other politicians currently very evident on the national stage and involved in the Algerian War include Lionel Jospin, who was a student at the time and opposed the war; Michel Rocard; Bernard Stasi; Pierre Joxe; Jean-Pierre Chevènement; and Jean-Marie Le Pen. If French society is to move beyond the current situation regarding remembering the war in Algeria (mutually hostile group memories, periodic flare ups in memory in the public sphere, repression and occlusion of the war), the State needs to assume its responsibility in the conduct of the Algerian War. We saw in our detailed analysis of media coverage of the French army's use of torture that soldiers often put the blame squarely on the civil power of the time. If the State had not decided to fight a war in Algeria and to win at all costs many, if not all, the tragedies of the conflict would not have occurred. Until it is possible for the French State to admit this fact, the various groups will continue to focus on their respective divisions and no common elements can be found. What unites all of the actors in the Algerian War is their suffering during the war.

One can also state that there has been little "change" in the memory of the Algerian War in so far as there is still no national memory of this colonial war. Actual memories of actors have evolved little, although recent developments suggest changes, and logically (following the model of other conflicts) actors will gradually open up about the war. This was the case with World War Two. In general as people age, especially toward the end of their lives, they consent more to remembering painful pasts since if they say nothing and die that past will be lost forever. Memory is something that is in constant evolution so recent changes were to be expected and the future should see many more. Another key period in the evolution of the French collective memory of the Algerian War may be around 2007 which will be the forty-fifth anniversary of the end of the war. We have seen the importance of anniversaries to encouraging remembering the Algerian War.

In the Introduction to this book a number of new developments in recent years were described. All contribute to the formation of a national memory and a richer memory culture. Progress is being made on the memory of the Algerian War in so far as the subject is becoming less taboo. This can be seen in changes in street names, stamps (paying homage to *pieds-noirs* and the *contingent*), monuments, official developments (notably naming the war and a French judge in court admitting a massacre in Paris on 17 October 1961), historiography, and films. Many of these however concern groups; groups which as of yet are not significantly communicating. The memory of the Algerian War is still limited to competing groups. We can still talk of memories (plural). Developments have taken place in terms of recognition of groups/actors rather than transmission, yet . . . These conditions are perhaps a *sine qua non* for transmission and debate outside of groups. More progress is needed within these groups before discussion between groups takes place and then greater transmission of memories occurs.

A much stronger "will" and effort are needed at present if this subject is to cease to be the protected domain of competing groups and more widely discussed. French elites need to recognize the clear link between unresolved memories of the Algerian War and current exclusion along ethnic lines in French society. Much more time and effort needs to be invested in this "work of memory" in order to reconcile different parts of French society, just as there has been a considerable amount of investment in Franco-German reconciliation. Other factors (such as the impact on memory of *beurs* in search of their origins) may also lead to significant change in the memory of the Algerian War. Ultimately the collective memory of the Algerian War reflects the characteristics of the wider French collective memory in general as described by Nora: fragmented, no longer unitary. Nora describes commemoration and concludes that: "En vérité, le modèle traditionnel a éclaté" (In truth, the traditional model of commemoration has broken up).[23] For Nora the traditional model of commemoration has been destroyed and replaced by a more varied model that is "un système éclaté, fait de langages commémoratifs disparates, qui suppose avec le passé un rapport différent, plus électif qu'impératif, ouvert, plastique, vivant, en perpétuelle élaboration" (a splintered system, made up of disparate commemorative languages, that assumes

a different relationship to the past, more elective than imperative, open, ma-
niable, alive, continually being reconstructed).[24] French collective memory in
general is therefore more fragmented than it was previously. This is due to, and
can be seen in, the proliferation of memories and identities. Hence the title of the
third volume of *Les Lieux de mémoire*: *Les France* (plural). This may mean that
no national memory of the Algerian War may exist at least for a long time. Until
the stakes of the war significantly decrease it is unlikely that the Algerian War
will become more visible in the "public sphere," except in periodic polemical
irruptions, unless a greater "will to remember" can be summoned. One argument
in favor of such moves would consist of recalling that while Renan indicated that
forgetting is necessary, he also indicated that painful memories and loss are potentially the most powerful: "suffering in common unifies more than joy does.
Where national memories are concerned, griefs are of more value than triumphs,
for they impose duties, and require a common effort."[25] The "work of memory"
then also needs to focus on commonalities—an acknowledgement of common
suffering on all sides in an unjust war where human rights abuses were perpetrated by both sides perhaps being a possible initial step in this direction. French
society does need a stronger national identity. Given the age of participants in
the Algerian War, this task is urgent. French society could also find new forums,
beyond the old Republican unitary model, in which the past could be discussed.
Such forums could perhaps focus on intergenerational communication, and certainly aim to go beyond existing groups (associations). For example, new places
where existing groups could meet and interact would be useful. Just as there are
history centers on resistance and deportation, there need to be more history centers on the Algerian War and colonial history, and these need to be designed so
that they are interactive and can be sites where different individuals and groups
can come to exchange perspectives on the Algerian War. Existing forums, such
as schools, museums, commemorations, and historiography, to name but a few,
could also try and adapt to the new makeup of French society by being more
inclusive. There is an increasing amount of scholarship written on the Algerian
War that needs to be much more widely disseminated and discussed in French
society. Films and literature on the topic also exist in significant numbers, they
too need to be more widely read and discussed. The "work of memory" needs to
take place in all of these vectors of memory. Only then can the deep "fracture
lines" that are increasingly evident in French society be healed, and a society
closer to the ideals of the French Republic actually exist in the present.

Notes

1. See Alain Duhamel, *Le Désarroi français* (Paris: Plon, 2003), Jacques Julliard, *Le
Malheur français* (Paris: Flammarion, 2005) and Nicolas Baverez, *La France qui tombe*
(Paris: Tempus, 2003).
2. See Alec Hargreaves, *Immigration, "Race" and Ethnicity in Contemporary
France* (London and New York: Routledge, 1995), 152-60.

3. Jérôme Jaffré, "L'éclatement du FN est révélateur des difficultés de sa mutation," *Le Monde*, 24 February 1999.

4 . Pierre Nora, ed., *Les Lieux de mémoire*, volume three *Les France*, book three *De l'archive à l'emblème* (Paris: Gallimard, 1992), 1010.

5. Kristen Ross, *Fast Cars, Clean Bodies: Decolonization and the Reordering of French Culture* (Cambridge, MA: the MIT Press, 1995), 9.

6. Antoine Prost, "La fin des professeurs," *L'Histoire*, no. 158 (September 1992): 79.

7. Jean Peyrot, "A quoi sert l'enseignement de l'histoire et de la géographie?" *Historiens et Géographes*, no. 297 (December 1983): 285 and 286 respectively.

8. Ernest Renan, "What is a nation?" *Nation and Narration*, ed. Homi Bhabha (London: Routledge, 1990), 19.

9. Michel Winock, "L'intégration fonctionne-t-elle encore?" *L'Histoire* (February 1999): 59.

10. Camille Marchaut, "Cela me fait mal au cœur qu'on oublie ça," *Hommes et Migrations*, no. 1219 (May-June 1999): 62.

11. Claude Liauzu, "Le 17 octobre 1961: guerres de mémoires, archives réservées, et questions d'histoire," *Cahiers d'histoire immediate*, no. 15 (spring 1999): 24.

12. Serge Berstein and Dominique Borne, "L'enseignement de l'histoire au lycée," *Vingtième Siècle*, no. 49 (January-March 1996): 141-42.

13. Alain-Gérard Slama, "La tyrannie du droit," *L'Histoire*, no. 252 (September 2001): 32.

14. Slama, "La tyrannie du droit," 32.

15. Maurice Halbwachs, *On Collective Memory*, edited and translated by Lewis A. Coser (Chicago and London: University of Chicago Press, 1992), 59.

16. "ADATE: hommage aux pères," in *Villes, patrimoines, mémoires—Actions culturelles et patrimoines urbains en Rhône-Alpes* (Lyon: Editions La Passe du Vent, 2000), 63.

17. Ahmed Boubeker, *Familles de l'intégration* (Paris: Stock, 1999).

18. Abrial, *Les enfants de harkis*, 200. See also Michel Roux, "Le poids de l'Histoire," *Hommes et Migrations*, no. 1135 (September 1990): 21-27.

19. Dramatic revolts by children of *harkis* took place in Narbonne during the summer of 1991, but there were also important revolts in 1974 (hunger strikes at the Madeleine church), 1975 (revolts by children of *harkis* in Bias, Saint-Maurice l'Ardoise and Logis d'Anne) and 1997 (more hunger strikes) amongst others.

20. Géraldine Enjelvin, "Entrée des Harkis dans l'histoire de France?" *French Cultural Studies*, vol. 15, no. 1 (February 2004): 61-62.

21. "La Mémoire de la guerre d'Algérie," editorial in *Le Monde*, 12 November 1996, 18.

22. "La Mémoire de la guerre d'Algérie," 18.

23. Nora, *Les Lieux de mémoire*, 985.

24. Nora, *Les Lieux de mémoire*, 983/84.

25. Renan, "What is a nation?" 19.

Appendix A

Teacher Interview A Questions

Les Cours (The Lessons)

Combien de groupes avez-vous en terminale? Combien d'élèves y-a-t-il dans chaque groupe? Dans quelles séries? (How many classes do you teach in *terminale*? How many pupils are there in each class? What *série* are they in?)

Combien de cours par an passez-vous sur la guerre d'Algérie (sont-ils les CM ou les TD/TP)? Passez-vous plus ou moins de temps sur la guerre d'Algérie que sur d'autres parties du programme? Selon vous, est-ce assez? (How many classes per year do you spend on the Algerian War (are they lectures or tutorials)? Do you spend more or less time on the Algerian War than on other parts of the program? In your opinion, is this enough?)

A quel moment de l'année examinez-vous la guerre d'Algérie? [Quelles parties du programme se trouvent avant et après celle de la guerre d'Algérie?] (When in the year do you examine the Algerian War? [What part of the program is before and after this?])

Comment est-ce qu'on décide du contenu des cours? Qui décide? Selon quels critères? [Le programme d'histoire, les instructions officielles, les questions au brevet et au baccalauréat ou d'autres facteurs?] (How does one decide on what to teach? Who decides? What criteria are used? [the history program, Official Instructions, examination questions, or other factors?])

Quel est le contenu des cours sur la guerre d'Algérie? Quels aspects de la guerre d'Algérie examinez-vous? Dans quel contexte situez-vous la guerre? Dans le cadre de la quatrième République, la cinquième République ou la décolonisation? (What is the content of the classes on the Algerian War? Which aspects of the Algerian War do you examine? In what context is the war situated? In the Fourth Republic, the Fifth Republic, or Decolonization?)

Comment se déroulent les cours? (How do classes operate?)
- La prise des notes (note-taking)
- Le travail en groupe (group work)
- La discussion au niveau de la classe (discussion at class level)
- Le travail sur les documents etc. (work on historical sources etc.)

Comment les élèves sont-ils notés? Est-ce qu'il y a de contrôle continu? Quelle forme peut prendre ce contrôle continu? Quel est le poids relatif de l'examen par rapport au contrôle continu? (How are the pupils marked? Is there continuous assessment? How is this structured? What is the relative weight of continuous assessment and final examination?)

Cette année, est-ce que vous avez pu travailler sur le procès de Maurice Papon à l'égard de la guerre d'Algérie et surtout le 17 octobre 1961? (This year, have you been able to work on the Papon trial relating to the Algerian War and especially the events of 17 October 1961?)

Est-ce qu'un ancien combattant est venu à un moment donné parler aux élèves? Quand? Qui? De quelle guerre était-il un ancien combattant (la Première guerre mondiale, la Deuxième guerre mondiale, les guerres d'Indochine ou d'AFN)? Qui l'a invité? Comment cela s'est-il passé? (Has a veteran ever come to talk to the pupils? When? Who? A veteran of which war (First World War, Second World War, Indo-China, or North Africa)? Who invited him? How was it?)

Les Elèves (The Pupils)

Comment qualifieriez-vous la réaction des élèves aux cours sur la guerre d'Algérie? [Est-ce qu'ils participent plus ou moins que d'habitude? Quelles opinions expriment-ils? Quelles questions posent-ils? Est-ce que les élèves ont des difficultés particulières à étudier la guerre d'Algérie?] (How would you describe the reaction of pupils to the class on the Algerian War? [Do they participate more or less than usual? What are their opinions on the subject? What sort of questions do they ask? Do the pupils have any particular difficulty studying the Algerian War?])

Si vous êtes professeur depuis le début des années 1980, est-ce que vous avez remarqué des changements d'attitude des élèves depuis quinze ans sur ce sujet? Si c'est le cas, quels changements se sont produits et comment expliquez-vous de tels changements? (If you have been teaching since the early 1980s, have you noticed any changes in the attitudes of the pupils on this topic over the last fifteen years? If so, what sort of changes have you noticed and how do you account for them?)

Est-ce qu'il me serait possible de rencontrer les élèves et éventuellement de leur donner un petit questionnaire? (Would it be possible for me to meet some pupils and perhaps give them a short survey?)

Les Professeurs (The Teachers)

Quel âge avez-vous? (How old are you?)
• moins de 30 ans (less than 30)

- 30-40
- 40-50
- plus de 50 ans (over 50)

Etes-vous certifié (CAPES), agrégé (agrégation) ou maître auxiliaire etc.? Est-ce que vous avez étudié la guerre d'Algérie quand vous avez passé le CAPES ou l'agrégation? [Si c'est le cas, quelle forme cela a-t-elle prise: un cours sur la guerre, une question d'examen etc.] Est-ce que vous avez étudié la guerre d'Algérie à d'autres moments de votre formation? (Have you passed the CAPES or the *agrégation*? Did you study the Algerian War when you studied towards these professional qualifications? [If so, what form did this take: a class on the war, an examination question etc.] Have you studied the Algerian War at other points in your training?)

Depuis que vous êtes professeur, est-ce que la guerre d'Algérie est un sujet qui vous intéresse partculièrement? Si oui, comment cet intérêt se manifeste-il? (Since becoming a teacher, is the Algerian War a topic that interests you in particular? If so, how so?)

Est-ce que vous êtes abonné à un journal, une périodique, une revue historique etc.? Lequel/laquelle? (Do you have subscriptions to newspapers, periodicals, history reviews etc.? Which?)

Pendant votre carrière avez-vous eu des collègues qui ont fait la guerre d'Algérie/qui sont des rapatriés? En dehors du travail, connaissez-vous des personnes qui ont fait la guerre d'Algérie ou qui sont des rapatriés? (During your career, have you worked with people who fought in Algeria or were repatriated from Algeria? Outside of work, do you know people who fought in Algeria or were repatriated from Algeria?)

Trouvez-vous que la guerre d'Algérie est un sujet qui est difficile à enseigner? [Si c'est le cas, dites pourquoi] (Do you find that the Algerian War is a difficult subject to teach? [If so, why?])

Les Manuels scolaires (Textbooks)

Quels manuels conseillez-vous aux élèves? (What textbooks do you recommend to the pupils?)

Qui est-ce qui décide des manuels à conseiller? Comment est-ce qu'on juge les manuels, c'est-à-dire selon quels critères? (Who decides which textbooks to recommend? How are textbooks appraised, what criteria are used?)

Est-ce qu'il y a eu des changements de manuels employés sur les quinze derniè-res années? Si c'est le cas, précisez quand et pour quelles raisons. (Have the textbooks that you use changed over the last fifteen years? Is so, when and why?)

A quoi servent les manuels scolaires lorsqu'on enseigne la guerre d'Algérie? Est-ce qu'ils font partie du cours? (How are textbooks used when teaching the Algerian War? Are they used in class?)

Etes-vous satisfait(e) de la qualité des manuels scolaires? Avez-vous remarqué des améliorations depuis quinze ans/depuis que vous êtes professeur? (Are you happy with the quality of textbooks? Have you noticed any improvements over the last fifteen years/since you have been teaching?)

Au delà des manuels scolaires, est-ce que vous employez d'autres sources d'information? Lesquelles? Est-ce qu'il y a un Centre de Documentation à l'école? Est-ce qu'on y trouve des ouvrages sur la guerre d'Algérie? Me serait-il possible d'avoir une liste des livres qu'on a mis dans le Centre de Documenta-tion? (Beyond textbooks, do you use other sources of information in class? Which? Is there a library at the school? Are there any books on the Algerian War? Could I have a list of such books?)

Dans l'exercice de votre métier, avez-vous conseillé aux élèves des livres d'histoire/romans sur la guerre d'Algérie? Avez-vous conseillé ou fait visionner aux élèves un film sur la guerre d'Algérie? (While teaching, have you recom-mended any books or novels about the Algerian War to the pupils? Have you recommended or shown pupils any films on the Algerian War?)

Programme/examens (Program/Examinations)

Quelles remarques aimeriez-vous faire sur ce/le programme? (What comments would you like to make about this program?)

Pensez-vous que ce programme puisse être enseigné avec objectivité? Quelle que soit votre réponse, dites pourquoi (Do you think that this program can be taught objectively? Justify your response)

Appendix B

Teacher Interview B Questions

Combien de groupes avez-vous en terminale? Combien d'élèves y-a-t-il dans chaque groupe? Dans quelles séries? (How many classes do you teach in *terminale*? How many pupils are there in each class? What *série* are they in?)

Les Cours (The Lessons)

Combien de cours cette année passerez-vous sur la guerre d'Algérie? Passez-vous plus ou moins de temps sur la guerre d'Algérie que sur d'autres parties du programme? Selon vous, est-ce assez? Avez-vous passé autant de temps cette année sur la guerre d'Algérie que l'année dernière? (How many classes this year have you spent on the Algerian War? Do you spend more or less time on the Algerian War than on other parts of the program? In your opinion, is this enough? Have you spent as much time on the Algerian War this year as last year?)

A quel moments de l'année avez-vous examiné la guerre d'Algérie? [Quelles parties du programme se trouvent avant et après celle de la guerre d'Algérie?] Examinez-vous la guerre d'Algérie surtout dans le cadre de la décolonisation, de la quatrième République ou de la cinquième République? (When in the year do you examine the Algerian War? [What part of the program is before and after this?] Do you examine the Algerian War above all in the context of Decolonization, the Fourth Republic, or the Fifth Republic)

Comment est-ce qu'on décide du contenu des cours? Qui décide? Selon quels critères? [Le programme d'histoire, les instructions officielles, les questions au baccalauréat ou d'autres facteurs?] (How does one decide on what to teach? Who decides? What criteria are used? [the history program, Official Instructions, examination questions or other factors?])

Comment se déroulent les cours? [la prise de notes, la discussion etc.] (What is the format of the classes? [note-taking, discussion etc.]

Est-ce qu'un ancien combattant est venu à un moment donné parler aux élèves? Quand? Qui? De quelle guerre était-il un ancien combattant (la Première Guerre mondiale, la Seconde Guerre mondiale, les guerres d'Indochine ou d'AFN)? Qui l'a invité? Comment cela s'est-il passé? (Has a veteran ever come to talk to the pupils? When? Who? A veteran of which war (First World War, Second World War, Indo-China, or North Africa)? Who invited him? How did it go?)

Les interviewés (Interviewees)

Quel âge avez-vous? (How old are you?)
- moins de 30 ans (less than 30)
- 30-40
- 40-50
- plus de 50 ans (above 50)

Etes-vous certifié (CAPES), agrégé (agrégation) ou maître auxiliaire etc.? (Have you passed the CAPES, the *agrégation* or are you on fixed contract?)

Le contenu des cours (Class Content)

[Est-ce que vous examinez les origines de la guerre d'Algérie en classe? Oui ou non?] Quand vous expliquez les origines de la guerre d'Algérie aux élèves, examinez-vous (et si oui, comment?) [Do you examine the origins of the Algerian War in class?] When you explain the origins of the war to the pupils, do you examine (and if so, how):
- les différentes formes du nationalisme algérien (different forms of Algerian nationalism)
- la société algérienne—économie, populations etc. (Algerian society—the economy, demography etc.)
- Sétif le 8 mai 1945/la repression (the repression in Sétif on 8 May 1945)
- la réforme de 1947 (the 1947 reform)
- la deuxième guerre mondiale/l'ONU (the Second World War, the United Nations)
- d'autres mouvements de décolonisation? (other decolonization movements)

Presentez-vous l'insurrection du 1er novembre 1954 aux élèves? Si oui, comment? (Do you examined the uprising on 1 November 1954? If so, how?)

Par rapport au nombre total d'heures que vous passez sur la guerre d'Algérie, quelle proportion de temps passez-vous sur mai 1958? Comment traitez-vous le 13 mai en cours? (In relation to overall time spent on the Algerian War, what proportion of time is spent on May 1958?) How do you cover May 1958 in class?)

Qu'examinez-vous après le retour de De Gaulle? Examinez-vous (et si oui, comment?) (What do you examine after the return to power of de Gaulle? Do you examine (and if so, how?):
- le putsch (the putsch)
- Charonne (events at metro Charonne)
- l'exode (the exodus)

- la semaine des barricades (the week of barricades)
- l'OAS (the OAS)
- les accords d'Evian (the Evian peace agreement)
- la politique de De Gaulle (the policy of de Gaulle)
- la rue d'Isly (events at Isly Street)
- la résistance française à la guerre d'Algérie (French resistance to the Algerian War)
- les luttes internes au sein du FLN (power struggles within the FLN)

Comment abordez-vous en classe la question de la torture? (How do you deal with the question of torture in class?)

Examinez-vous les événements suivants? Si oui, comment? (Do you examine the following events? If so, how?)
- l'arrestation de Ben Bella (the arrest of Ben Bella)
- Sakiet Sidi Youssef (the bombing of Sakiet Sidi Youssef)
- le 17 octobre 1961 (17 October 1961)
- les harkis (*harkis*)
- la censure (censorship)

Que dites-vous en cours sur l'armée et le contingent? (What do you say in class about the army and the conscripts?)

Est-ce que vous examinez le côté militaire de la guerre? (Do you examine the military side of the war?)

Donnez-vous un bilan de la guerre en cours? Si oui, lequel? (Do you give an overall toll of the war in class? If so, which?)

Le programme (Program)

Quelles remarques aimeriez-vous faire sur ce/le programme? Qu'en pensez-vous par rapport au dernier programme? (What comments would you like to make about this program? How do you think it compares to the previous program)

Qu'est-ce qui change cette année par rapport à l'année dernière? (What has changed in relation to last year?)

Est-il possible de traiter des parties de cette programme en détail? Qu'en est-il pour la guerre d'Algérie? (Is it possible to go into detail on aspects of this program? What about the Algerian War?)
- avant la réforme 1998 (donc septembre 1989-juin 1998) (before the 1998 reform, so September 1989 to June 1998)

- après la réforme 1998 (after the 1998 reform)
- pendant les années 1980 (si la personne était professeur pendant cette période) (during the 1980s, if applicable)

Appendix C

Pupil Interview Questions

Les Cours (The Lessons)

Combien de cours cette année avez-vous passé sur la guerre d'Algérie? Avez-vous (peut-être l'impression d'avoir) passé plus ou moins de temps sur la guerre d'Algérie que sur d'autres parties du programme? (How many classes have you spent on the Algerian War this year? Have you (perhaps a sense of having) spent more or less time on the Algerian War compared to other parts of the program?)

A quel moment de l'année avez-vous fait la guerre d'Algérie? (When in the year did you cover the Algerian War?)

Comment se déroulent les cours? [la prise de notes, la discussion etc.] (What is the format of the classes? [note taking, discussion etc.])

Est-ce que vous avez fait partie d'une classe d'histoire où on a invité un ancien combattant venir parler en cours? Si oui, quand? Qui? Un ancien de quelle guerre? Où? Comment cela s'est il passé? Quelles impressions en avez-vous gardées? (Have you been in a class when a veteran came to talk? If yes, when? Who? A veteran of which war? Where? How was it? What memories do you have of it?)

Le Contenu (The Content of Classes)

Quelles sont les origines de la guerre d'Algérie? (What are the origins of the Algerian War?)

Quand et comment s'est déclenchée la guerre d'Algérie? Combien d'années la guerre d'Algérie a-t-elle duré? (When and how did the war begin? How long did the Algerian War last?)

Combien de temps avez-vous passé en cours cette année sur mai 1958? (How much time did you spend in class on May 1958?)

Qu'avez vous fait en cours après mai 1958/le retour de De Gaulle? Connaissez-vous ce que signifient les termes suivants (si oui, me les expliquez)? (What did you do in class on the period after 1958/the return to power of de Gaulle? Do you know what the following terms mean (if yes, please explain them to me)?):

- le putsch (the putsch)
- Charonne (Charonne)
- l'exode (the exodus)
- la semaine des barricades (the week of barricades)
- l'OAS (the OAS)
- les accords d'Evian (the Evian peace agreements)
- la politique de De Gaulle (the policy of de Gaulle)
- la rue d'Isly (Isly Street)
- la résistance française à la guerre d'Algérie (French resistance to the Algerian War)
- les luttes internes au sein du FLN (in-fighting within the FLN)

Qu'est-ce que vous avez appris cette année sur l'utilisation de la torture pendant la guerre d'Algérie? (What have you learnt this year on the use of torture during the Algerian War?)

Avez-vous examiné les événements suivants en cours? Si oui, qu'en pouvez-vous me dire? (Have you studied the following events in class? If yes, what can you tell me about them?)
- l'arrestation de Ben Bella (the arrest of Ben Bella)
- Sakiet Sidi Youssef (the bombing of Sakiet Sidi Youssef)
- le 17 octobre 1961 (17 October 1961)
- les harkis (the *harkis*)
- la censure (censorship)

Que vous a-t-on dit en cours sur l'armée et le contingent? Est-ce que vous examiné le côté militaire de la guerre? Combien de Français ont fait la guerre d'Algérie? (What were you told in class about the army and conscripts? Have you studied the military aspects of the war? How many French soldiers participated in the Algerian War?)

Pouvez-vous me donner un bilan (économique/humain) de la guerre? (Can you provide an (economic/human) assessment of the war?)

Est-ce qu'il y a d'autres choses que vous vous rappelez d'avoir vu en cours qui ne sont pas dans la liste ci-dessus? (Are there other things that you've done in class that are not on the above list?)

Les Interviewés (Interviewees)

Quel est votre nom? Quel âge avez-vous? Redoublez-vous? Qui est votre professeur d'histoire? Dans quelle série êtes-vous? (What is your name? How old are you? Are you resitting this year? Who is your history teacher? What stream are you doing in *terminale* (i.e., general, scientific, etc.)?

Les manuels, le baccalauréat et le programme (Textbooks, the Examination, and the Program)

Avez-vous un manuel? Si oui, lequel? S'en servez-vous souvent, parfois, jamais? Si oui, quand et comment/pourquoi/avec quel but? Qu'en pensez-vous/Comment trouvez-vous ce manuel? (Do you have a textbook? If yes, which? Do you use it a lot, sometimes, or never? If yes, when and how/why/to what end? What do you think of it?)

Parmi les moyens suivants, quels sont les moyens les plus utiles pour vous d'apprendre plus sur la guerre d'Algérie pour préparer le bac? Pour chaque moyen que je propose, veuillez me dire si c'est un moyen utile (ou non) et comment (From the following list, please choose those that are most useful in helping you prepare for the *baccalauréat*. For each means, please tell me whether it is useful (or not) and how so):
—les cours (classes)
—les manuels scolaires (textbooks)
—les livres parascolaires (i.d. Tous qu'il faut savoir . . .) (extracurricular books)
—les livres d'histoire (history books)
—la literature (literature)
—les films (films)
—les medias (the media)
—autres (other):

Cette année, pour préparer le baccalauréat, allez-vous réviser la guerre d'Algérie? Si, oui, pourquoi? Si non, pourquoi pas? (As you prepare for the *baccalauréat* examination this year, will you revise the Algerian War? If so, why? If not, why not?)

Est-ce que vous avez vu un film ou documentaire sur la guerre d'Algérie ? Si oui, lequel/lesquels et quand? (Have you ever seen a film or a documentary on the Algerian War? If so, which and when?)

Avez-vous lu un livre/roman sur la guerre d'Algérie? Si oui, lequel/lesquels et quand? (Have you read a book/novel on the war in Algeria? If so, which and when?)

Pouvez-vous citer quelques films et livres/romans qui parlent de la guerre d'Algérie (même si vous ne les avez pas lus/vus)? (Can you cite any films and books/novels that refer to the Algerian War (even if you haven't seen/read them)?)

Comment trouvez-vous le programme d'histoire en terminale? Avez-vous l'impression de pouvoir examiner en suffissament de détail les différentes parties du programme? (What is your opinion of the. *terminale* history program? Do you think you can examine in sufficient detail the different parts of the program?)

Comment avez-vous le plus appris sur la guerre d'Algérie? Pour chaque moyen que je propose, veuillez me dire si c'est un moyen utile (ou non) et comment (How have you learnt the most about the Algerian War? For each method that I propose, please tell me if it is a useful method [or not] and how):
—par vos professeurs (by your teachers)
—par votre famille (by your family):

> —par vos parents (parents)
>
> —par vos grands-parents (grandparents)
>
> —autres membres de la famille (other family members)

—par la famille de vos amis/vos amis/amis de votre famille (by your friends' families/your friends/friends of the family)
—par les médias (by the media):

> —par les journaux (newspapers)
>
> —par les magazines (magazines)
>
> —par la télévision (television)
>
> —par la radio (radio)

—par le cinema (cinema)
—par les livres (books)

> —romans (novels)
>
> —livres/revues d'histoire (books/history journals)
>
> —manuels scolaires (textbooks)

—par les cérémonies/associations (ceremonies/associations)
—autres (others):

Que comprennez-vous par le terme "la mémoire de la guerre d'Algérie"? Comment percevez-vous la mémoire de la guerre d'Algérie? Quelles impressions en avez vous? Entendez-vous souvent parler de la guerre d'Algérie? Assez? (What do you understand by the term "memory of the Algerian War"? How do you view this memory? What are your impressions of it? Do you often hear about the Algerian War? Enough?)

Connaissez-vous les noms de quelques associations d'anciens combattants/rapatriés? (Do you know the names of any veterans' or settlers' associations?)

Appendix D

List of Interviewees

Pupil Interviewees

Pupil 1 (a pupil of Teacher 7 in série L) is of Algerian origin: her grandfather was the son of a settler who left Algeria before the war. There is therefore a link to Algeria but much less than for certain others. Her family had no direct involvement in the war. She had received some information from her grandmother, but the information transmitted had come originally from another source (a neighbor). However her mother had also talked of *harkis* to her when they passed in front of what used to be a *bidonville* (shantytown). She is a pupil in a *lycée* in Décines on the outskirts of Lyon. A teacher in this school said that 20 percent of the pupils in the school were of Maghrebian descent.

Pupil 2 (a pupil of Teacher 1 in série S) is of Algerian origin: she has family who still live in Algeria. These are especially her mother's uncles and her grandparents. She spends time in Algeria. Members of her family had been tortured. She talked of her uncle "collaborating" but her grandfather "resisting." She had received a lot of information from the family especially in Algeria, since half of her family (on her mother's side, most of whom live in Algeria) talk about the war a lot whereas the other half (father's side in France) do not talk about the Algerian War. In France she had learnt nothing from her family. In Algeria she had learnt a lot, including, as discussed in the interview, about torture and forced relocation of populations to stop villagers helping Algerian nationalist fighters. She is a pupil in the same school as Pupil 1.

Pupil 3 (a pupil of Teacher 7 in série L) has no family links to Algeria. She is in the same school as Pupil 1 and Pupil 2.

Pupil 4 (a pupil of Teacher 1 in série S) has no family links to Algeria. Her grandfather interestingly had served in Indo-China. He did not talk much about this war. She is a pupil in the same school as the above pupils.

Pupil 5 (a pupil of Teacher 11 in série L; interviewed with Pupils 6 and 7) is of Algerian origin: her parents are from Algeria. She too has family who still live in Algeria. Her core family did not seem directly concerned by the Algerian War, given what she said in the interview, but she seemed interested by the subject since she stated that it was her country. Her father came to France as a manual worker, perhaps in the 1970s. She had not received much information from her family at all. This equated to sometimes looking at photographs with her mother and remembering people. She seemed quite interested in the interview, perhaps due to frustration at not getting information from other sources. She is a pupil in a school in Villeurbanne, near Lyon. The school was a fairly typical school with quite a lot of Maghrebian children. Teacher 9 works in this school and spoke of an "intérêt visible des élèves d'origine maghrébine" (visible interest from pupils of Maghrebian descent) in the subject of the Algerian War.

Pupil 6 (a pupil of Teacher 11 in série L; interviewed with Pupils 5 and 7) has an uncle who was in the *contingent*. She said that the Algerian War was a bad experience that he does not like to talk about. She has no other family links to Algeria. She is a pupil in the school in Villeurbanne.

Pupil 7 (a pupil of Teacher 11 in série L; interviewed with Pupils 5 and 6) has no family links to Algeria. She is a pupil in the school in Villeurbanne.

Pupil 8 (a pupil of Teacher 3 in série ES; interviewed with Pupils 9 and 12) is of Algerian origin: she did not give much detail of her family biography but has close contacts with Algeria and is of Algerian origin. She did not talk in the family about the war. She seemed however to talk about the present civil war situation in Algeria. She mentioned that her family would like to move back to Algeria but that this was difficult. She is a pupil in the school in Villeurbanne.

Pupil 9 (a pupil of Teacher 3 in série ES; interviewed with Pupils 8 and 12) is of Algerian origin: she did not mention much about her family history but has close contacts with Algeria and is of Algerian origin. She did not talk in her family about the war. She seemed however to talk about the present civil war situation in Algeria. In this respect she is therefore a lot like Pupil 8. She is a pupil in the school in Villeurbanne.

Pupil 10 (a pupil of Teacher 11 in série L) is the daughter of a man who did national military service. He died in 1998. She said he was involved in repatriation at the end of the Algerian War (although she was very unsure of dates). Apparently he had spoken to her about this. She mentioned a *lieu de mémoire*: a cemetery, since while visiting the grave of her father she had noticed graves of people, who had died during the Algerian War. She had no other family links to the war. Again, even though she is not of Algerian origin, her coming forward for the interview would seem to be motivated by a desire to know more about her family history (in the face of her father's death?). She is a pupil in the school in Villeurbanne.

Pupil 11 (a pupil of Teacher 7 in série L) is of Algerian origin: her grandparents were concerned by the war in Algeria, especially her grandfather with whom she talks about the Algerian War in France. This is therefore the only person to have gained significant information from the family in France (as opposed to Algeria). He lost members of his family including his brother during the war. She described him as being an Algerian resistance hero. He had been traumatized by the Algerian War. This pupil is also the only pupil to have seen a testimony given in class (in *troisième*) on the Algerian War, given by a *pied-noir* conscript. She is a pupil in the school in Décines.

Pupil 12 (a pupil of Teacher 3 in série ES; interviewed with Pupils 8 and 9) is of Algerian origin: his uncle, great uncle and grandparents were all directly concerned by the Algerian War. His great uncle had served five years of prison during the Algerian War and did not talk about it since it was too difficult. So this pupil talked a little with his father who was not involved in the war. This pupil was the only boy to be interviewed. He attends the school in Villeurbanne.

Teacher Interviewees

A Sample

Teacher 1 40-50, *agrégé*. He has cousins who fought in Algeria, but relatively few acquaintances involved in the Algerian War. He works in a school in the suburbs of Lyon in which 20 percent of the pupils are of Maghrebian descent. He arranged for me to interview some of his pupils.

Teacher 2 40-50, *agrégé*. He was thirteen years old when the Algerian War ended so has some memories of the war. In the interview he mentioned a *pied-noir* colleague (Teacher 17) who never talks of the Algerian War but was on the forum in Algiers for de Gaulle's speech "Je vous ai compris" (I have understood you). He also has a cousin who served in Algeria. This teacher previously worked in a school in which there were a lot of Maghrebian children which he said modified his approach to the Algerian War in class. He now works in a fairly typical *lycée* with quite a good reputation, but in which there are fewer Maghrebian children. Teacher 16, Teacher 17, and Teacher 18 also work in this school.

Teacher 3 30-40, *agrégé*. He has *pieds-noirs* friends. One of these friends was born in Algeria in 1948, whose mother he describes as still a defender of "Algérie française" ideas and who continues to believe de Gaulle betrayed them. He also has colleagues who were involved in the war, one of whom he mentions in particular. The person was a student at Aix-en-Provence who had described problems at the time with nationalist students. Apart from that he had no link to the Algerian War. He arranged for me to interview some of his pupils.

Teacher 4 over-50, *agrégé*. He was a student at the time of the war. He knows lots of people who were involved in the war. He was one of the two teachers who had invited a veteran of the Algerian War to class. He works in a prestigious school.

Teacher 5 40-50, *agrégé*. This teacher spoke of two colleagues of his. One of these was a woman who was *pied-noir* (Teacher 6) and another was a man who had been a student at the time of the Algerian War. He qualified their reactions on the subject of the Algerian War as "réactions épidermiques ou passionnelles" (gut or passionate reactions). He described his own family, in mainland France, as very "Algérie française." He works in a prestigious school (the same school as Teacher 4 and Teacher 6) in which he says the pupils are not concerned in their family history by the Algerian War.

Teacher 6 40-50, CAPES. She lived in Mostaganem in Algeria. She claimed that her uncle had been killed on 1 November 1954, and was therefore amongst the first victims of the war. Her father had also been killed by the FLN in 1957. Her family lived in Algeria until Algerian independence in 1962, where they had a vineyard. They then fled Algeria. She spent significantly more time than her colleagues in class on the Algerian War.

Teacher 7 30-40, CAPES. She said that her father-in-law had been a conscript in Algeria and that this was "un sujet dont il ne parlait pas énormement" (a subject he did not talk about much). During the interview she mentioned interest in the Algerian War in class of pupils from *pied-noir* and *maghrebi* families. She works in the same school as Teacher 1 and said that there was "une communauté maghrébine assez importante" (fairly large Maghrebian community). She arranged for me to interview some of her pupils.

Teacher 8 40-50, CAPES. She was young at the time of the war and remembers friends of her elder sister going to fight in Algeria.

Teacher 9 30-40, CAPES. He spoke of an "intérêt visible des élèves d'origine maghrébine" (visible interest from students of Maghrebian descent) concerning the Algerian war in class. In his private life he has an uncle who fought in Algeria and now supports the French National Front (the FN). He works in the same school as Teacher 3, Teacher 10, and Teacher 11.

Teacher 10 40-50, CAPES. He said that he knew people at work and in his private life who had links to the Algerian War but said: "c'est des gens qui généralement n'en parlent pas" (it's people who generally don't talk about it). He linked a "communauté maghrébine" (Maghrebian community) to "classes demandeures" (classes that want more) on the subject of the Algerian War. This teacher talked me through a chronology from *Le Monde*.

B Sample

Teacher 11 40-50, CAPES. She did not mention anybody in her life closely linked to the war in Algeria. She insisted on the fact that the Algerian War was a very distant event for her pupils. This teacher arranged for me to interview some of her pupils.

Teacher 12 40-50, CAPES. She works in the same prestigious school as Teacher 14. She did little on the Algerian War.

Teacher 13 30-40, CAPES. This teacher's family were involved in the Algerian War: his mother was a *pied-noir*; his grandfather was a pilot in Air Africa. Two of his uncles were in the OAS. He gave a presentation at university in the early 1980s on Alleg's *La Question* (The Question) that had led to strong reactions from other students. He was one of the three teachers of *pied-noir* origin to devote a lot of time to the Algerian War in class.

Teacher 14 30-40, *agrégé*. He had been at the IEP in Lyon when a lecturer there, who had served in Algeria, had worked on the Algerian War using a film. He had also taught Didier Daeninckx's *Meurtres pour mémoire* (Murders for Memory) in French classes in the north of France (before moving to Lyon and teaching history). He devoted little time in history to the Algerian War.

Teacher 15 40-50, *agrégée*. She had been in "coopération" in Algeria with her husband. Due to her age she said "je l'ai connue" (I lived through it) concerning the Algerian War. She described how she had had a "mauvaise conscience" (guilty conscience) at the time. Although she is not of *pied-noir* origin, she did a lot on the Algerian War, perhaps reflecting her experience and her beliefs and interests.

Teacher 16 over-50, CAPES. She mentioned nothing on her family or acquaintances.

Teacher 17 over-50, CAPES. She was born in Algeria in the Oranie region. She also lived in Algiers, in Bab-El-Oued, so experienced first-hand the "semaine des barricades" (week of barricades). Talking of May 1958 in Algeria she said "j'y étais!" (I was there!) She came to France in 1962, first to Nice then to Lyon. In the year 1998-1999 she did significantly more than others because, despite the change in program, she had not reduced the amount of time she spent on the Algerian War.

Teacher 18 over-50, CAPES. One of the two teachers who had invited a veteran of the Algerian War to class.

Appendix E

Media Appendices

CDROM

Using CDROM, keyword "guerre d'Algérie," (Algerian War) search conducted in Bordeaux in 2002.

Approximate number of articles/year on the Algerian War 1987-2002 in *Le Monde*

1987	28
1988	18
1989	18
1990	22
1991	40
1992	58
1993	17
1994	48
1995	24
1996	24
1997	50
1998	30
1999	50
2000	200
2001	300
2002	100 (until June)

INDEX ANALYTIQUE DU MONDE

Using the *Index Analytique* du Monde, keywords "guerre d'Algérie" (Algerian War), "Aussaresses," "rapatriés" (repatriated settlers), "harkis," search conducted in Paris and in Lyon in 2003.

Approximate number of articles/year on the Algerian War 1977-2001 in *Le Monde*

1977	143 = 18 (guerre d'Algérie) + 125 (rapatriés)
1981	62 = 11 (guerre d'Algérie) + 16 (Commémoration) + 35 (rapatriés)
1982	129 = 112 (guerre d'Algérie) + 17 (rapatriés)
1984	85 (guerre d'Algérie) + 20 (rapatriés)
1985	49 (guerre d'Algérie) + 20 (rapatriés)
1986	53 = 24 (guerre d'Algérie) + 29 (rapatriés)
1991	105 = 12 (guerre d'Algérie) + 84 (harki) + 9 (rapatriés)
1996	17 = 15 (guerre d'Algérie) + 3 (rapatriés)
1998	12 = 9 (guerre d'Algérie) + 3 (rapatriés)
1999	38 = 11 (guerre d'Algérie) + 1 (rapatriés) + 16 (Papon) + 6 (manifestation d'algériens Paris) + 4 (harkis)

2000   109 = 90 (guerre d'Algérie) + 13 (harki) + 4 (Papon) + 1(rapatriés)
2001   168 = 21 (harki) + 1 (rapatriés) + 71 (guerre d'Algérie) + 75 (Aussaresses)

Themes (subjects) per month in *Le Monde*:

Month	Total number articles	Number articles on torture	Other topics covered
December 2000	50	27	Harkis: 3 Rape: 2 Archives: 4 Algeria: 3 Memory: 12 17-10-61: 1 Literature: 1 Obituaries: 3
January 2001	10	5	Archives: 2 Memory: 2 TV: 1
April 2001	6	0	Putsch: 3 Memory: 1 Historians: 1 Other: 2
June 2001	23	17	Harkis: 3 Memory: 2 TV: 2 Theatre: 2 Historians: 1
November 2001	17	10	Harkis: 1 Rape: 3 Archives: 2 Cinema: 1

Synchronic *Le Monde*, *Libération*, *Le Figaro*: June 2001

Newspaper	Total number articles	Number articles on torture	Other topics covered
Le Monde	23	17	Harkis: 3 Memory: 2 TV: 2 Theatre: 2 Historians: 1
Le Figaro	7	4	Harkis: 1 Rapatriés: 1
Libération	19	13	17-10-61: 1 Harkis: 1 Memory: 2 Veterans: 1

Bibliography and Filmography

Books/Scholarship

Abbas, Ferhat. *Autopsie d'une guerre—L'Aurore*. Paris: Garnier, 1980.

Abrial, Stéphanie. *Les enfants de harkis*. Paris: L'Harmattan, 2001.

Ageron, Charles-Robert., ed. *La Guerre d'Algérie et les Algériens 1954-1962*. Paris: Armand Colin, 1997.

Alleg, Henri. *La Question*. Paris: Les Editions de Minuit, 1961.

Amato, Alain. *Monuments en Exil*. Paris: Editions de l'Atlanthrope, 1979.

Anderson, Benedict. *Imagined Communities*. London, New York: Verso, 1991.

Aussaresses, Paul. *Services Spéciaux Algérie 1955-1957*. Paris: Perrin, 2001.

Azzedine, Commander. *On nous appelait fellaghas*. Paris: Stock, 1976.

———.*Et Alger ne brûla pas*. Paris: Stock, 1980.

Baverez, Nicolas. *La France qui tombe*. Paris: Tempus, 2003.

Benguigui, Yamina. *Mémoires d'immigrés, l'héritage maghrébin*. Paris: Albin Michel, 1997.

Bhabha, Homi. *Nation and Narration*. London: Routledge, 1990.

Billig, Michael. *Freudian Repression*. Cambridge: Cambridge University Press, 1999.

Boubeker, Ahmed. *Familles de l'intégration*. Paris: Stock, 1999.

Bourdieu, Pierre. *On Television and Journalism*. London: Pluto Press, 1998.

Branche, Raphaëlle. *La torture et l'armée pendant la guerre d'Algérie*. Paris: Gallimard, 2001.

Coulon, Alain. *Connaissance de la guerre d'Algérie. Trente ans après: enquête auprès des jeunes Français de 17 à 30 ans*. Paris: Université de Paris VIII, 1993.

Courrière, Yves. *La Guerre d'Algérie*. Paris: Robert Laffont, 1990.

Cros, Vitalis. *Le temps de la violence*. Paris: Ed. Presses de la Cité, 1971.

Czechowski, Nicole, and Claudie Danzinger., eds. *Deuils. Vivre c'est perdre*. Paris: Editions Autrement, 1992.

De Gaulle, Charles. *Mémoires d'espoir: Le renouveau*. Paris: Plon, 1970.

Descombes, Vincent. *Le Même et l'autre. 45 ans de philosophie française (1933-1978)*. Paris: Les Editions de Minuit, 1979.

Dine, Philip. *Images of the Algerian War: French Fiction and Film, 1954-1962*. Oxford: Clarendon Press/OUP, 1994.

Djazairinfos no. 3, February-March 2003.

Droz, Bernard, and Evelyne Lever. *Histoire de la guerre d'Algérie 1954-1962*. Paris: Le Seuil, 1982.

Duhamel, Alain. *Le Désarroi français*. Paris: Plon, 2003.

Einaudi, Jean-Luc. *La Bataille de Paris*. Paris: Seuil, 1991.

Eveno, Patrick. *Le Monde 1944-1995*. Paris: Le Monde Editions, 1996.

Fleury-Vilatte, Béatrice. *La mémoire télévisuelle de la guerre d'Algérie 1962-1992*. Paris: L'Harmattan, 2000.

Forbes, Jill, and Michael Kelly., eds. *French Cultural Studies*. Oxford: Oxford University Press, 1995.

Fouchet, Christian. *Au service du général de Gaulle*. Paris: Plon, 1971.

Freedman, Jane, and Carrie Tarr., eds. *Women, Immigration and Identities in France*. Oxford and New York: Berg, 2000.

Goffman, Erving. *Stigma: Notes on the Management of Spoiled Identity*. Englewood Cliffs, NJ: Prentice-Hall, 1963.

Habermas, Jürgen. *A Berlin Republic: Writings on Germany*, translated by Steven Rendall. Cambridge: Polity Press, 1998.

Halbwachs, Maurice. *La Mémoire collective*. Paris: Presses Universitaires de France, 1950.

———.*Les Cadres sociaux de la mémoire*. Paris and The Hague: Mouton, 1976. Republished Paris: Albin Michel, 1994.

———.*On Collective Memory*, edited and translated by Lewis A Coser. Chicago and London: University of Chicago Press, 1992.

Harbi, Mohammed. *Le FLN Mirage et Réalité, des origines à la prise du pouvoir (1945-1962)*. Paris: Jeune Afrique, 1980.

———.*Les Archives de la Révolution algérienne*. Paris: Jeune Afrique, 1981.

Hargreaves, Alec G. *Immigration, "Race" and Ethnicity in Contemporary France*. London and New York: Routledge, 1995.

———.*Immigration and Identity in Beur Fiction*. Oxford: Berg, 1997.

Hargreaves, Alec G., and Mark McKinney., eds. *Post-Colonial Cultures in France*. London and New York: Routledge, 1997.

Haroun, Ali. *La 7e wilaya, la guerre du FLN en France 1954-1962*. Paris: Seuil, 1986.

Hobsbawm, Eric, and Terence Ranger., eds. *The Invention of Tradition*. Cambridge: Cambridge University Press, 1992.

Horne, Alistair. *A Savage War of Peace: Algeria, 1954-1962*. London: Macmillan, 1977.

Jakubowicz, Andrew et al., *Racism, Ethnicity and the Media*. St Leonards, NSW: Allen & Unwin, 1994.

Jauffret, Jean-Charles, ed. *La Guerre d'Algérie par les documents 1, L'Avertissement, 1943-46*. Vincennes: SHAT, 1990.

———.*La Guerre d'Algérie par les documents 2, les portes de la guerre: des occasions manquées à l'insurrection, 10 mars 1946-31 décembre 1954*. Vincennes: SHAT, 1998.

Jordi, Jean-Jacques, and Mohand Hamoumou. *Les harkis, une mémoire enfouie*. Paris: Autrement, 1999.

Julliard, Jacques. *Le Malheur français*. Paris: Flammarion, 2005.

Kara, Mohamed. *Les tentations du repli communautaire*. Paris: L'Harmattan, 1997.

La Guerre d'Algérie dans l'enseignement en France et en Algérie. Paris: CNDP, 1993.

Le Monde, 2000-2001.

Lowenthal, David. *Our Past Before Us: Why Do We Save It?*, London: Temple Smith, 1981.

Massu, Jacques. *La vraie bataille d'Alger*. Paris: Plon, 1971.

Mauss-Copeaux, Claire. *Les Appelés en Algérie: la parole confisquée*. Paris: Hachette, 1999.

Mémoire et enseignement de la guerre d'Algérie: actes du colloque, 13-14 mars 1992, tenu à Paris. Paris: Institut du Monde arabe/Ligue de l'enseignement, 1993.

Middleton, Derek, and David Edwards. *Collective Remembering*. London: Sage, 1990.

Mitterrand, François. *Le Coup d'Etat permanent*. Paris: Plon, 1964.

Muller, Laurent. *Le silence des harkis*. Paris: L'Harmattan, 1999.

Nora, Pierre., ed. *Les Lieux de mémoire*. 3 vols, Paris: Gallimard, 1984-1992.

———.*Realms of Memory*. Edited by Lawrence D. Krizman and translated by Arthur Goldhammer. New York: Columbia University Press, 1996-1998.

Ricœur, Paul. *La mémoire, l'histoire, l'oubli*. Paris: Le Seuil, 2000. Subsequently translated by Kathleen Blamey and David Pellauer as *Memory, History, Forgetting*. Chicago and London: University of Chicago Press, 2004.

Rioux, Jean-Pierre, ed. *La Guerre d'Algérie et les Français*. Paris: Fayard, 1990.

Rioux, Jean-Pierre, and Jean-François Sirinelli., eds. *La Guerre d'Algérie et les intellectuels français*. Brussels: Editions Complexe, 1991.

Ross, Kristen. *Fast Cars, Clean Bodies: Decolonization and the Reordering of French Culture*. Cambridge Massachusetts and London: the MIT Press, 1995.

Rousso, Henry. *Le Syndrome de Vichy*. Paris: Seuil, 1987.

———.*The Vichy Syndrome. History and Memory in France since 1944*. Cambridge, MA; London, England: Harvard University Press, 1991.

Roy, Jules. *J'accuse le général Massu*. Paris: Le Seuil, 1972.

Salan, Raoul. *Mémoires: fin d'un empire*. Paris: Presses de la Cité, 1972-1974.

Simon, Pierre-Henri. *Contre la torture*. Paris: Editions du Seuil, 1957.

Smith, Tony. *The French Stake in Algeria*. Ithaca: Cornell University Press, 1978.

Stora, Benjamin. *La Gangrène et l'oubli*. Paris: La Découverte, 1991.

———.*Histoire de l'Algérie coloniale*. Paris: La Découverte, 1991.

———.*Ils venaient d'Algérie*. Paris: Fayard, 1992.

———.*Histoire de la guerre d'Algérie*. Paris: La Découverte, 1992.

———.*Dictionnaire des livres de la guerre d'Algérie*. Paris: L'Harmattan, 1996.

———.*Le Transfert d'une mémoire*. Paris: La Découverte, 1999.

Stora, Benjamin, and Mohammed Harbi, eds. *La Guerre d'Algérie 1954-2004: la fin de l'amnésie*. Paris: Robert Laffont, 2004.

Talbott, John. *The War Without a Name: France in Algeria, 1954-62*. London: Faber and Faber, 1981.

Thénault, Sylvie. *Une drôle de justice, les magistrats dans la guerre d'Algérie*. Paris: La Découverte, 2001.

Tribalat, Michèle. *Faire France: Une enquête sur les immigrés et leurs enfants*. Paris: La Découverte, 1995.

Tristan, Anne. *Le Silence du fleuve*. Bezons: Au nom de la mémoire, 1991.

Van Dijk, Teun A. *Racism and the Press*. London and New York: Routledge, 1991.

Winter, Jay, and Emmanuel Sivan, eds. *War and Remembrance in the Twentieth Century*. Cambridge: Cambridge University Press, 1999.

Winock, Michel. *La Fièvre hexagonale*. Paris: Calmann-Lévy, 1986.

Wood, Nancy. *Vectors of Memory: Legacies of Trauma in Postwar Europe*. Oxford and New York: Berg, 1999.

Articles/Book Chapters

Abdallah, Mogniss, H. "Le 17 octobre et les médias. De la couverture de l'Histoire immédiate au 'travail de mémoire.'" *Hommes et Migrations*, no. 1228, (November-December 2000): 125-33.

"ADATE: hommage aux pères." Pp. 62-63 in *Villes, patrimoines, mémoires—Actions culturelles et patrimoines urbains en Rhône-Alpes*. Lyon: Editions La Passe du Vent, 2000.

Ageron, Charles-Robert. "Une histoire de la guerre d'Algérie est-elle possible en 1992?" Pp. 155-58 in *La Guerre d'Algérie dans l'enseignement en France et en Algérie*. Paris: CNDP, 1993.

———."'Drame des harkis' mémoire ou histoire?" *Vingtième Siècle*, no. 68 (October-December 2000): 3-15.

Aïchoune, Farid. "On leur a volé leur histoire." *Le Nouvel Observateur*, 1-7 November 2001, 22.

Amrane-Minne, Danièle Djamila. "La guerre d'Algérie à travers les manuels français et
    algériens de classes terminales." Pp. 372-75 in *Mémoire et enseignement de la
    guerre d'Algérie: actes du colloque, 13-14 mars 1992, Paris*. Paris: Institut du
    Monde arabe/Ligue de l'enseignement, 1993.
Assoun, Paul-Laurent. "Le sujet de l'oubli selon Freud." *Communications*, no. 49 (1989):
    97-111.
Beaugé, Florence. "Le général Massu exprime ses regrets pour la torture en Algérie." *Le
    Monde*, 22 June 2000, 6.
Bédarida, François. "Le temps présent et l'historiographie contemporaine," *Vingtième
    Siècle*, 69, Jan-March 2001: 153-60.
Begag, Azouz. "Les relations France-Algérie vues de la diaspora algérienne." *Modern
    and Contemporary France* 10, no. 4 (2002): 475-82.
Bencharif, Lela, and Virginie Milliot. "Les zones d'ombre du patrimoine." Pp. 66-67 in
    *Villes, patrimoines, mémoiresActions culturelles et patrimoines urbains en Rhône-
    Alpes*. Lyon: Editions La Passe du Vent, 2000.
Benguigui, Yamina. "L'héritage de l'exil." *Qantara*, no. 30, Winter 1998-99, 32-33.
Berchadsky, Alexis. "La question de la torture à travers les manuels français de classes
    terminales." Pp. 386-94 in *Mémoire et enseignement de la guerre d'Algérie: actes du
    colloque, 13-14 mars 1992, Paris*. Paris: Institut du Monde arabe/Ligue de
    l'enseignement, 1993.
Bernard, Philippe. "Mémoire d'Algérie, mémoire d'en France." *Le Monde*, 19 March
    2002.
———."Du match France-Algérie au 17 octobre 1961." *Le Monde*, 26 October 2001, 16.
———."Immigrés et harkis face à face." *Le Monde*, 30 June-1 July 2002, 18.
———."L'Algérie de la deuxième mémoire IV. Un seul pays, deux histoires." *Le Monde*,
    20 March 1992, 5.
———."Les gardiens de la mémoire," *Le Monde*, 14 June 1990, 18.
Berstein, Serge, and Dominique Borne. "L'enseignement de l'histoire au lycée."
    Vingtième Siècle, no. 49 (January-March 1996): 122-42.
Billig, Michael, and David Edwards. "La construction sociale de la mémoire." *La
    Recherche* vol. 25, no. 267 (July-August 1994): 742-45.
Borne, Dominique. "L'Histoire du vingtième siècle au lycée. Le nouveau programme de
    terminale." *Vingtième Siècle*, no. 21 (January-March 1989):101-10.
Borne, Dominique, and Jean-Paul Delahaye. "La laïcité dans l'enseignement: problémati-
    que et enjeux." *Regards sur l'actualité*, no. 298, (February 2004): 25-32.
Borrel, Catherine. "Près de cinq millions d'immigrés à la mi-2004." *Insee première* no.
    1098, August 2006.
Bourdieu, Pierre. "Dévoiler et divulguer le refoulé." Pp. 21-27 in *Algérie-France-Islam*,
    edited by Joseph Jurt. Paris: L'Harmattan, 1997.
Cornette, Joël, and Jean-Noël Luc. "Bac-Génération 84. L'Enseignement du temps
    présent en terminale." *Vingtième Siècle*, no. 6 (April-June 1985): 103-30.
Derderian, Richard L. "Algeria as a *lieu de mémoire*: Ethnic Minority Memory and
    National Identity in Contemporary France." *Radical History Review*, no. 83, (spring
    2002), 28-43.
Develotte, Christine, and Elizabeth Rechniewski. "Discourse Analysis of Newspaper
    Headlines: a Methodological Framework for Research into National Representa-
    tions," *Web Journal of French Media Studies* (November 2001) consulted online at
    wjfms.ncl.ac.uk/.
Dine, Philip. "(Still) *A la recherche de l'Algérie perdue*: French Fiction and Film, 1992-
    2001." *Historical Reflections*, no. 2 (vol. 28, summer 2002): 255-75.

"D'Octobre 1961 à la Double peine." *Quo Vadis* (autumn-winter 1993): 77-79.

Dosse, François. "Le moment Ricœur." *Vingtième Siècle* (January-March 2001): 137-52.

Droz, Bernard. "Le cas très singulier de la guerre d'Algérie." *Vingtième Siècle. Revue d'histoire* no. 5, (January-March 1985): 81-90.

Dufay, François. "L'Octobre noir de Maurice Papon." *Le Point*, no. 1311 (November 1, 1997): 54.

Durmelat, Sylvie. "Yamina Benguigui as 'Memory Entrepreneur'." Pp. 171-88 in *Women, Immigration and Identities in France*, edited by Jane Freedman and Carrie Tarr. Oxford & New York: Berg, 2000.

Enjelvin, Géraldine. "Entrée des Harkis dans l'histoire de France?" *French Cultural Studies*, vol. 15, no. 1 (February 2004): 61-75.

Fournier, Paul. "La guerre d'Algérie dans les manuels scolaires de Terminale." *Historiens et Géographes*, no. 308 (March 1986): 897-98.

Frank, Robert. "Les troubles de la mémoire française." Pp. 603-8 in *La Guerre d'Algérie et les Français*, edited by Jean-Pierre Rioux. Paris: Fayard, 1990.

Frodon, Jean-Michel. "Bourlem Guerdjou, messager de justice." *Le Monde*, 3 March 1999, 34.

Gedi, Noa, and Yigal Elam. "Collective Memory—What Is It?" *History and Memory* 8, no. 1 (1996): 30-50.

Gibelin, Henri. "Pour en finir avec la querelle des manuels," *Les Cahiers Pédagogiques*, no. 369 (December 1998):13.

Guyon, Madeleine et al. "Trente ans après: la guerre d'Algérie à travers les manuels d'histoire des classes terminales." Pp. 438-42 in *Mémoire et enseignement de la guerre d'Algérie: actes du colloque, 13-14 mars 1992, Paris*. Paris: Institut du Monde arabe/Ligue de l'enseignement, 1993.

Guyvarc'h, Didier. "La Mémoire Collective, de la recherche à l'enseignement." *Cahiers d'Histoire Immédiate* no. 22 (Fall 2002): 101-19.

Hamilton, Paula. "The Knife Edge: Debates about Memory and History." Pp. 9-32 in *Memory and History in Twentieth Century Australia*, edited by Paula Hamilton and Kate Darian-Smith. Melbourne: Oxford University Press, 1994.

Hargreaves, Alec G. "Resistance and Identity in *Beur* Narratives." *Modern Fiction Studies* 35, no. 1 (spring 1989): 87-102.

———."France and Algeria 1962-2002: Turning the Page?" *Modern and Contemporary France* 10, no. 4 (2002): 445-47.

———."Generating Migrant Memories." In *Memory, Identity and Nostalgia*, edited by Patricia ME Lorcin. Syracuse, NY: Syracuse Press, forthcoming.

"Jacques Chirac demande une journée d'hommage aux harkis." *Le Monde hébdomadaire*, 17 February 2001, 10.

Jaffré, Jérôme. "L'éclatement du FN est révélateur des difficultés de sa mutation." *Le Monde*, 24 February 1999.

Jarausch, Konrad H. "Living with Broken Memories: Some Narratological Comments." Pp. 171-98 in *The Divided Past: Reuniting Post-War Germany*, edited by Christoph Klessmann. Oxford: Berg, 2001.

Joutard, Philippe. "L'enseignent de l'histoire." Pp. 45-55 in *L'histoire et le métier d'historien en France 1945-95*, edited by François Bedarida. Paris: Editions de la Maison des sciences de l'homme, 1995.

Joutard, Philippe, and Jean Lecuir. "Le palmarès de la mémoire nationale." *L'Histoire* no. 242 (April 2000): 31-39.

Kajman, Michel. "L'Algérie de la deuxième mémoire: Des historiens encombrés." *Le Monde*, 17 March 1992, 15.

Kerleroux, Pierre, and Herbert Tisson. "Entretien avec Serge Berstein et Gilbert Gaudin sur les programmes d'histoire et de géographie," *Historiens et Géographes*, no. 348 (May-June 1995): 41-50.

Lambert, Isabelle. "Vingt ans après." Pp. 553-59 *La Guerre d'Algérie et les Français*, edited by Jean-Pierre Rioux. Paris: Fayard, 1990.

"La Mémoire de la guerre d'Algérie." *Le Monde*, 12 November 1996, 18.

"La mémoire enfouie de la guerre d'Algérie." *Le Monde*, 5 February 1999, 1 and 9.

Lavabre, Marie-Claire. "Usages du passé, usages de la mémoire." *Revue française de science politique* no. 3 (1994): 480-93.

La Voix du Combattant, no. 1644 (April 1999), 6-7.

Liauzu, Claude. "Voyage à travers la mémoire et l'amnésie: le 17 octobre 1961." *Hommes et Migrations*, no. 1219 (May-June 1999): 56-61.

———."Le 17 octobre 1961: guerres de mémoires, archives réservées, et questions d'histoire," *Cahiers d'histoire immediate*, no. 15 (spring 1999): 11-24.

———."Mémoires souffrantes de la guerre d'Algérie." *L'Histoire*, no. 260 (December 2001): 32-33.

MacMaster, Neil. "The Torture Controversy (1998-2002): Towards a 'New History' of the Algerian War?" *Modern and Contemporary France* 10, no. 4 (2002): 449-59.

Marchaut, Camille. "Cela me fait mal au cœur qu'on oublie ça." *Hommes et Migrations*, no. 1219 (May-June 1999): 62-64.

Mekki, Ali. "Opening Remarks." *Zaàma*, special issue, 2002: 5-8.

———."Introduction." *Zaàma*, special issue, 2002, 3-4.

Namer, Gérard. "Quand la société batît son passé." *Sciences Humaines* no. 43 (October 1994): 28-33.

Nora, Pierre. "Between Memory and History: Les Lieux de Mémoire." *Representations*, no. 26 (Spring 1989): 7-25.

"Notre mémoire algérienne," *Le Monde*, 5 February 1999, 14.

"Où vont les beurs?" *Le Nouvel Observateur*, no. 1930, 2 November 2001.

Pastor, Geneviève. "L'enseignement de la guerre d'Algérie en classe de terminale. Instructions officielles et sujets au baccalauréat en France." Pp. 418-25 in *Mémoire et enseignement de la guerre d'Algérie: actes du colloque, 13-14 mars 1992, Paris*. Paris: Institut du Monde arabe/Ligue de l'enseignement, 1993.

Pervillé, Guy. "Bibliographie critique sur la guerre d'Algérie." *l'Annuaire de l'Afrique du Nord*, 1976: 1337-63.

———."Bibliographie critique sur la guerre d'Algérie." *l'Annuaire de l'Afrique du Nord*, 1982: 937-44.

———."Le point sur la guerre d'Algérie." *Historiens et Géographes*, no. 293 (February 1983): 635-52.

———."Les Agoras Méditerranéennes." *Historiens et Géographes*, no. 308 (March 1986).

———."La guerre d'Algérie dans les manuels scolaires de Terminale." *Historiens et Géographes*, no. 308 (March 1986): 893-97.

———."Bibliographie critique sur la guerre d'Algérie." *l'Annuaire de l'Afrique du Nord*, 1992: 1169-86.

Pervillé, Guy, and Paul Fournier. "La guerre d'Algérie dans les manuels scolaires de Terminale." *Historiens et Géographes*, no. 308 (March 1986): 893-97.

Peyrot, Jean. "A quoi sert l'enseignement de l'histoire et de la géographie?" *Historiens et Géographes*, no. 297 (December 1983): 285-86.

———."Aux chocs de la vie." *Historiens et Géographes*, no. 328 (July-August 1990): 9-15.

———."L'enseignement de l'Histoire et la démocratie." *Historiens et Géographes*, no. 353 (June-July 1996): 11-13.

Prost, Antoine. "La fin des professeurs." *L'Histoire*, no. 158 (September 1992), 78-81.

Remaoun, Hassan. "Un seul héros, le peuple" and "L'Histoire confisquée." *Télérama hors série*, 1995: 90-93.

Renan, Ernest. "What is a Nation?" Pp. 8-22 in *Nation and Narration*, edited by Homi Bhabha. London: Routledge, 1990.

Rioux, Jean-Pierre. "Les Français et leur histoire," *L'Histoire*, no. 100 (May 1987): 70-80.

———."La flamme et les bûchers." Pp. 497-508 in *La Guerre d'Algérie et les Français*, edited by Jean-Pierre Rioux. Paris: Fayard, 1990.

———."Preface." In *La Guerre d'Algérie dans l'enseignement en France et en Algérie* Paris: CNDP, 1993.

———."Trous de mémoire." *Télérama* (1995), 90-92.

———."A quoi servent les cours d'histoire?" *L'Histoire*, no. 202 (September 1996): 49-50.

———."Aux grands hommes, les Français reconnaissants." *L'Histoire*, no. 202, (September 1996): 15-17.

Rouyard, Frédéric. "La bataille du 19 mars." Pp. 545-552 in *La Guerre d'Algérie et les Français*, edited by Jean-Pierre Rioux. Paris: Fayard, 1990.

Roux, Michel. "Le Poids de l'Histoire." *Hommes et Migrations*, no. 1135 (September 1990): 24/25.

Slama, Alain-Gérard. "La cicatrice ouverte." *Le Point*, no. 899, (11 December 1989), 18.

———."La tyrannie du droit." *L'Histoire*, no. 252 (September 2001): 32.

Stora, Benjamin. "1999-2003, guerre d'Algérie, les accélérations de la mémoire." Pp. 501-14 in *La Guerre d'Algérie: 1954-2004, la fin de l'amnésie*, edited by Mohammed Harbi and Benjamin Stora. Paris: Robert Laffont, 2004.

———."Quelques réflexions sur les images de la guerre d'Algérie." Pp. 333-40 in *La Guerre d'Algérie et les Algériens 1954-62*, edited by Charles-Robert Ageron. Paris: Armand Colin, 1997.

———."Indochine, Algérie, autorisations de retour." *Libération*, 30 April-1 May 1992, 5.

———."Cicatriser l'Algérie." Pp. 227-43 in *Oublier nos crimes: l'amnésie nationale, une spécificité française?* No. 144, edited by Dimitri Nicolaidis. Paris: Editions Autrement, Série Mutations, 1994.

———."La mémoire retrouvée de la guerre d'Algérie?" *Le Monde*, 19 March 2002.

———."Les jeunes de l'immigration algérienne et les représentations de la guerre d'Algérie." *Historiens et Géographes*, no. 384 (October-November 2003): 363-71.

———."Jeunes de l'immigration algérienne. Mémoires de guerre." *Peuples Méditerranéens*, no. 70-71 (January-June 1995): 293-308.

Thelen, David. "Memory and American History." *The Journal of American History*, vol. 75, no. 4, (March 1989): 1117-29.

Thibault, Paul. "La torture en Algérie. L'avenir en panne." *Le Monde*, 14 December 2000, 17.

Thompson, Paul. "Believe it or not: rethinking the historical interpretation of memory." www3.baylor.edu/Oral_History/Thompson.pdf.

Vattimo, Gianni. "L'impossible oubli." Pp.77-89 in *Usages de l'oubli*, Yosef H. Yerushalmi, Nicole Loraux et al. Paris: Le Seuil, 1988.

Vidal-Naquet, Pierre. "Algérie, du témoignage à l'histoire." *Le Monde*, 14 September 2001.

Wihtol de Wenden, Catherine. "La Vie associative des harkis." *Migrations Société* 1, no. 5-6 (October-December 1989): 9-26.

———."La Génération suivante entre intégration républicaine et clientélisme ethnique." *Modern and Contemporary France* 8, no. 2 (May 2000): 234-39.

Wieviorka, Michel. "La production institutionnelle du racisme." *Hommes et Migrations*, no. 1211 (January-February 1998): 5-15.

Winock, Michel. "La Guerre d'Algérie." *Libération*, 26 June 1984, 22-24.

———."L'intégration fonctionne-t-elle encore?" *L'Histoire* (February 1999): 58-61.

Yerushalmi, Yosef H. "Réflexions sur l'oubli." Pp.7-21 in *Usages de l'oubli*, Yosef H. Yerushalmi, Nicole Loraux et al. Paris: Le Seuil, 1988.

Novels

Boukhedenna, Sakinna. *Journal."Nationalité: immigré(e)."* Paris: Mercure de France, 1983.

Bouzid, *La Marche*. Paris: Sindbad, 1984.

Charef, Mehdi. *Le harki de Meriem*. Paris: Mercure de France, 1989.

Daeninckx, Didier. *Meurtres pour mémoire*. Paris: Gallimard, 1984.

Imache, Tassadit. *Une fille sans histoire*. Paris: Calmann-Lévy, 1989.

———.*Le Rouge à lèvres*. Paris: Syros, 1988.

Kelouaz, Ahmed. *Celui qui regarde le soleil en face*. Algiers: Laphomic, 1987.

Kemoum, Hadjila. *Mohand le harki*. Paris: Anne Carrière, 2003.

Kenzi, Mohamed. *La Menthe sauvage*. Lutry, Switzerland: J.M. Bouclain, 1984.

Kerchouche, Dalila. *Mon père ce harki*. Paris: Seuil, 2003.

Kettane, Nacer. *Le sourire de Brahim*. Paris: Denoël, 1985.

Lallaoui, Mehdi. *La Colline aux oliviers*. Paris: Alternatives, 1998.

Nini, Soraya. *Ils disent que je suis une beurette*. Paris: Fixot, 1993.

Nozière, Jean-Paul. *Un Eté algérien*. Paris: Gallimard, 1990.

Rahmani, Zahia. *Moze*. Paris: Sabine Wespieser, 2003.

Sebbar, Leila. *Le chinois vert d'Afrique*. Paris: Stock, 1984.

Smaïl, Paul. *Vivre me tue*. Paris: Balland, 1997.

Zemouri, Kamel. *Le jardin de l'intrus*. Algiers: Enal, 1986.

Textbooks and Annales du baccalauréat

Annabac sujets Histoire-Géographie. In print form those published by Vuibert, Paris, 1996; Hatier, Paris, 1996 and 1999; Nathan 1997. In electronic form a CD-ROM, distributed by Hatier, 1998 and 1999.

Baylac, Marie-Hélène., ed. *Histoire Terminale*. Paris: Bordas, 1998.

Bernard, Henri, and François Sirel., eds. *Histoire Terminales*. Paris: Magnard, 1998.

Frank, Robert., ed. *Histoire Terminales L, E, S*. Paris: Belin, 1995.

Gauthier, André., ed. *Histoire Terminales*. Rosny-sous-Bois: Bréal, 1995.

Gracia Dorel-Ferré, ed. *Histoire Classes de Terminales L, ES, S*. Rosny-sous-Bois: Bréal, 1998.

Lambin Jean-Michel., ed. *Histoire Terminales*. Hachette,1995.

———.*Histoire Terminales*. Paris: Hachette, 1998.

Le Pellec, Jacqueline., ed. *Histoire Terminale*. Paris: Bertrand-Lacoste, 1998.

Marseille, Jacques., ed. *Histoire Terminales*. Paris: Nathan, 1995.
————.*Histoire Terminales*. Paris: Nathan, 1998.
Milza, Pierre, and Serge Berstein., eds. *De 1939 à nos jours*. Paris: Hatier, 1983/84.
————.*Histoire Terminales*. Paris: Hatier, 1995.
————.*Histoire Terminales*. Paris: Hatier, 1998.
Quétel, Claude., ed. *Histoire Terminales*. Paris: Bordas, 1989.
Zanghellini, Valéry., ed., *Histoires Terminales L, ES, S*. Paris: Belin, 1998.

Films/Documentaries

Benigni, Roberto. *La Vie est belle*, 1999.
Guerdjou, Bourlem. *Vivre au paradis*, 1999.
Lakhdar, Hamina. *Chronique des années de braise*, 1975.
Laloui, Mehdi, and Agnès Denis. *Le Silence du Fleuve*, 1991.
Pontecorvo, Gillo. *La Bataille d'Alger*, 1965.
Spielberg, Steven. *Il faut sauver le soldat Ryan*, 1998.
Stora, Benjamin. *Les Années algériennes*, 1991.
Tavernier, Bertrand, and Patrick Rotman. *La Guerre sans nom*, 1991.

Index

About the Author

Jo McCormack is a lecturer in French Studies at the Institute for International Studies at the University of Technology, Sydney, Australia. He was awarded his PhD for a thesis on "The Algerian War in the French Education System: A Case Study of the Transmission of Memory" from the University of Loughborough, UK. His research focuses on French collective memories of the Algerian War and on exile and social change. Dr McCormack is the co-editor of a special issue of *Portal: Journal of Multidisciplinary International Studies* on "Exile and Social Transformation." He is also the author of several articles and book chapters on French collective memories of the Algerian War.